MURDER AT
ROARINGWATER

MURDER AT
ROARINGWATER

The inside story of the death of
Sophie Toscan du Plantier

NICK FOSTER

MIRROR BOOKS

Nick Foster was born in Liverpool in 1966 and educated at University College London. He is a journalist and former diplomat. Foster has written for the New York Times, the Financial Times, The Times and the Daily Telegraph, among other media outlets. His first true crime book, The Jolly Roger Social Club: A True Story of a Killer in Paradise, was published in 2016. Foster lives in Brussels, Belgium, with his wife and two sons.

For Adam and Eric

The moon's an arrant thief,
And her pale fire she snatches from the sun.

William Shakespeare, *Timon of Athens*

Come, Mother, come!
For terror is thy name,
Death is in thy breath,
And every shaking step
Destroys a world forever…

Kali the Mother, Swami Vivekananda

m
B

MIRROR BOOKS

First published by Mirror Books in 2021

Mirror Books is part of Reach plc
10 Lower Thames Street
London EC3R 6EN

www.mirrorbooks.co.uk

© Nick Foster

ISBN: 978-1-913406-56-1
eBook ISBN: 978-1-913406-57-8

Edited by Jo Sollis and Chris Brereton

Production by Simon Monk and Michael McGuinness

Printed and bound in Great Britain by
CPI Group (UK) Ltd, Croydon, CR0 4YY

A CIP catalogue record for this book is available from the British Library.

Every effort has been made to fulfil requirements with regard to
reproducing copyright material. The author and publisher will be
glad to rectify any omissions at the earliest opportunity.

Cover images: Provision Photography
Maps copyright: Jack O'Driscoll

CONTENTS

A NOTE FROM THE AUTHOR

This is a true story. No scenes have been invented, nor have any names been changed. As a general rule, items of text in italics are taken from witness statements, court transcripts or newspaper stories, or are italicised for emphasis. Translations from source material in French are my own. Some passages from police notes and transcripts have been corrected for spelling and grammar. Any errors in this book are, of course, my responsibility.

INTRODUCTION

I first heard about the murder of Sophie Toscan du Plantier in early 1997. At the time, I was 30 years old, living and working in Belgium. My life was almost entirely carefree, with few responsibilities. Most evenings I would watch the French TV news to find out what was going on in the world.

In early February of that year, an unusual crime story in an isolated corner of the south of Ireland dominated the French news agenda. An Englishman – tall and broad-shouldered, with collar-length, dark hair – had been arrested for the murder of a young Frenchwoman at her remote Irish holiday home. The woman had been subject to a vicious and frenzied attack, her body struck around 50 times with a stone slab. Her assailant finally dropped a concrete cavity block on her skull before fleeing the scene. The attack happened just yards from her whitewashed house, under the cover of darkness. There were no witnesses. At the gate to his Irish smallholding, having been released by the Irish police without charge, the Englishman told reporters that he had absolutely nothing to do with the crime.

The Englishman lived on his tiny farm and wrote poetry, which seemed a nice match for his Byronesque appearance. He also filed occasional stories to local newspapers and did gardening work.

The French victim, meanwhile, looked beautiful in photos, with delicate wisps of reddish blond hair framing a light-skinned, freckled face. Sophie was 39 at the time of her murder and had a son in his mid-teens. I understood from the French TV news that she had married a man who stalked the corridors of power in Paris, and this man had money and influence in equal measure. Sophie's face betrayed a marked sensitivity, and it was no surprise when the journalists covering the case informed viewers that she had a life-long interest in literature and the arts.

Years have gone by and Sophie – a woman I never met – exists to me, and no doubt to many others, in first name only. As for the English poet, I have got to know him personally, eaten at his kitchen table, run errands with him, gone on drives in the Irish countryside, and have even passed him the occasional €50 note to keep him talking. We are both from north-west England. We have both pitched stories to newspapers as stringers. We bonded – sort of. Still, to me he is always "Bailey", referred to by his surname, although of course he has a first name, which is Ian.

French viewers of the TV news bulletin back in 1997 would likely have assumed from the strength of the report, and with a suspect publicly identified, that the wheels of justice would turn and, before too long, the dashing English poet living on his Irish plot of land would be tried in an Irish courthouse and end up behind bars.

I probably assumed the same, until I read a piece in *The New Yorker* by Irish-American poet John Montague. By that time, four years had passed since Sophie's murder. I was surprised to learn that the Irish police investigation had stalled. Ian Bailey had been arrested twice, and detectives had come calling at his home on many occasions, but he had never formally been charged with the murder of the beautiful Frenchwoman. Montague had employed Bailey casually as a gardener and painted a picture of the Englishman that was hardly complimentary: he was violent, narcissistic and unpredictable. For good measure, Montague was also critical about Bailey's gardening and the bunch of poems Bailey had subjected to Montague's expert opinion.

My interest was piqued, so I delved more into the story. Several things stood out: Bailey had an alibi that was almost comical in its uselessness; there was no DNA evidence to speak of; and Sophie's mother was on record as saying that she believed Bailey had killed her daughter. For his part, Bailey had repeatedly insisted that he had never known Sophie Toscan du Plantier.

As for the victim, it seemed the more she had played down her beauty, the more men had found her attractive. Her backstory was enigmatic, but troubling, too.

I was intrigued by the unsolved murder on the Irish moors, but it dropped off my radar. What intervened was my life – marriage, two sons, earning a living, moving house a couple of times, eventually relocating back to Belgium. Then one day in November 2014, I got a call from an Irish friend who knew I had an interest in the Sophie case. He said: "Bailey is suing the Irish state. He's about to appear in court in Dublin."

Within a couple of hours, I had bought a plane ticket to Ireland. I wanted to meet Ian Bailey; I wanted him to tell me his story. This was an excellent opportunity, and I had to strike while the iron was hot, if that is an appropriate expression for introducing myself to the long-term suspect in a cold case. The basic thrust of Bailey's date in court was in every Irish newspaper: Bailey claimed that the Irish police had engineered a massive stitch-up, and he had been fitted up for a crime he had not committed.

Like I say, when a good mystery gets under your skin, it has a strength all of its own, even if it lies dormant for years.

I write these words in lockdown in May 2020. My manuscript – the book you are reading – is nearing completion. For many of us, the onslaught of the coronavirus pandemic has turned our gaze inwards.

Where did we go right in our lives? Where did we go wrong?

When life returns to something approaching normality, what will we change? What, finally, have we learned?

Over dinner one night, the last shafts of pale, late-spring light bouncing off the cobbles in the square in front of our apartment, I ask my sons a question. It is partly to relieve the monotony of weeks cooped up indoors, partly because I am interested to hear what they think.

"Is it right to pretend to be somebody you're not, let's say when something important is at stake? What I mean is, should you ever be a bit false to somebody to find out a bigger truth?"

The boys understandably give me a blank look.

"I'll give you a specific example, okay? Say you could make someone feel better and, maybe – just maybe – take away some of the pain they have felt for a very long time, but you need to pretend to be someone else for a while if you're going to succeed."

My sons are 13 and 10. The younger one shoots back:

"You're talking about Bailey, aren't you?"

I do not deny it. Papers on the Sophie Toscan du Plantier murder case – police statements, press cuttings, scribbled notes – are strewn around our home. My sons, and my wife too, can see that I have been living the story, inhabiting the puzzle.

The boys think for a moment. No, they say, they don't see how that would work. You should always be totally straight with people. You should always be the person you are.

This, I tell my sons, is the general rule.

But sometimes you are compelled to make exceptions.

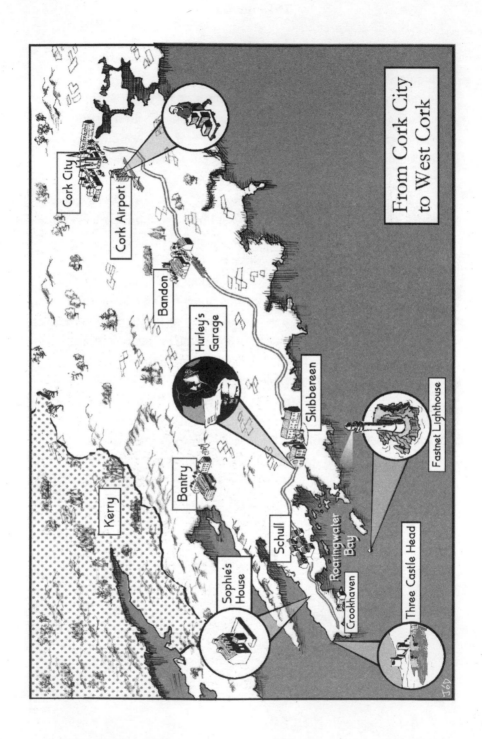

From Cork City to West Cork

Cork City
Cork Airport
Bandon
Hurley's Garage
Skibbereen
Fastnet Lighthouse
Bantry
Kerry
Schull
Roaringwater Bay
Sophie's House
Crookhaven
Three Castle Head

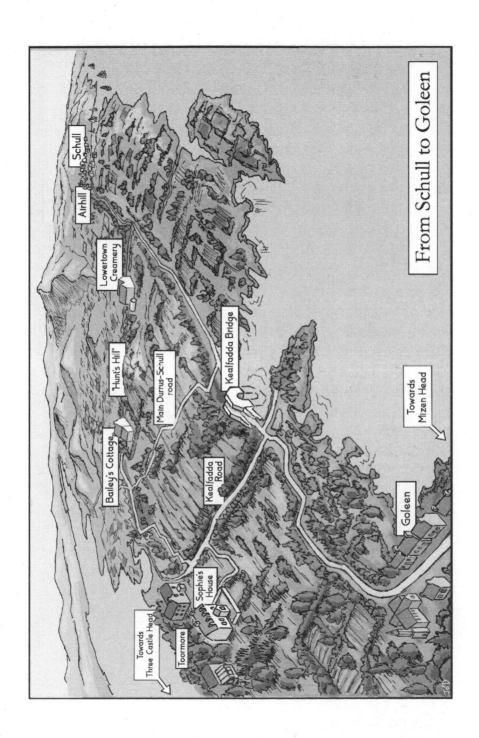

From Schull to Goleen

VII

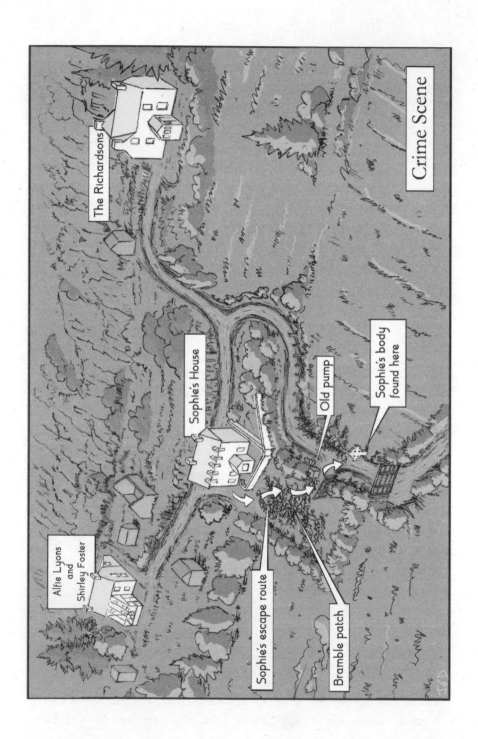

Chapter 1

A BODY ON THE TRACK

The Atlantic Ocean, so often surging and disturbed, was still that night. A full moon lit up the cloudless sky. It was three days before Christmas, 1996.

The great Irish diaspora was returning to its roots from every corner of the globe. Leaving from places where people spoke differently and thought differently, thronging public houses and crowding the pews of churches across the island. In the village of Schull on the Mizen Peninsula in County Cork, things were no different. On the night of 22nd December, locals and expat Irish raised their glasses to toast the season in Schull's half-dozen bars and pubs, doors shut hard against the freezing air.

Meanwhile Shirley Foster and Alfie Lyons, a couple in their sixties living in a house in the isolated settlement of Toormore, ate an early dinner and watched a film – the courtroom drama *A Few Good Men* – on Lyons' video cassette player, which they found very agreeable.

Foster was a retired teacher originally from Kent in England, Lyons had operated a number of restaurants in Ireland and the United States. They were hardly a couple attracted to Schull's boozy nightlife: by 10pm, they were in bed with the lights switched off. Shortly before she went to sleep, Foster noticed the light under the eaves of the neighbouring whitewashed house, used as a holiday home, 80 yards away. That was normal – her French neighbour, Sophie, usually kept the light on by the back entrance to the house when she was visiting. And Foster knew that Sophie was at home, because a woman who grazed her horses in a field adjacent to the couple's house had told her so. The woman with the horses had heard, in turn, from Sophie's housekeeper that Sophie was coming to stay in the run-up to Christmas. Sophie's housekeeper was a woman named Josephine Hellen, whose husband, Finbarr, kept cattle and sheep at Toormore.

At 10am the following morning, not long after a feeble dawn had arrived from the east, and with a mist now clinging to the green fields and rough moors, Shirley Foster left Lyons' house and got into her car, a Peugeot estate. She had to take the rubbish to the dump, and buy some provisions for Christmas in Schull, just under eight miles away.

She drove her vehicle down the lane that led to the main road. A few yards after she passed the Frenchwoman's house, Foster drew close to a grassy verge near an old water pumping station. That was when Foster saw what she initially thought was some kind of broken, oversized doll. Her eyes took in a flash of light-coloured clothing. But Foster soon realised this was no doll – it was a body – though she did not immediately recognise who it was. Terrified, Foster jammed her hand on the horn of her car. There was only one person in the shallow valley to hear it. Then she got out of her vehicle and ran, screaming, back home.

Foster's partner Alfie Lyons grabbed his house phone and called the emergency services. An Garda Síochána – the Irish police force – dispatched a patrol car. It was 10:15 when Sergeant Gerard Prendiville and Garda William Byrne received a radio call in their car alerting them to the grim discovery. Garda Martin Malone phoned Lyons from Schull Garda station, instructing him not to touch the body. He also asked Lyons for precise directions to the scene. When Malone told Lyons that Sergeant Prendiville would be taking immediate charge, Lyons said: "Gerry, I know him well". The two uniformed officers took the narrow Kealfadda Road and from there drove up the lane that led to Toormore at precisely 10:38.

Lyons hurried down the track to check quickly for himself and saw the shape of a body from a distance of about 20 yards. Remembering that his French neighbour was visiting – he had noticed a hire car outside her property over the last couple of days – Lyons went up to Sophie's house and banged on her kitchen window, calling out her name. Lyons wanted to warn Sophie about the body. There was no answer. The back door, which was the door closest to Lyons' house, was shut, and Lyons banged on that, too, but again there was no answer. To his horror, Lyons saw that there appeared to be smears of blood on the door and on the doorknob.

Subsequently, Shirley Foster realised that the light under the eaves of Sophie's house that had been on the previous evening was now off. Foster told this to the Guards, and they included it in a statement she signed.

There was a third house in the Toormore settlement, with the three houses forming a tiny hamlet. These were the only dwellings in the shallow valley. The lane leading to Toormore on the east side was the only way in and out, if you were driving. It was basically a cul-de-sac, with the lane petering out into a rough track where you came to the small group of houses. As you approached, Sophie's house was the first on the left, with Lyons' place beyond and a little above it. To the right of Sophie's house – and like Lyons' house, on slightly higher terrain – stood a holiday home owned by the Richardsons, a family from London. Lyons knew this third house was empty at present and so he did not need to knock on the Richardsons' door to warn them about the body on the track.

When Sergeant Prendiville and Garda Byrne arrived at the crime scene, they saw Foster's Peugeot at the side of the lane. Nearby was the corpse of a woman, her body pale and bloody, lying on her back and slightly on her left side. The woman's head looked mangled, with deep gashes in her face – she had clearly died in violent circumstances. Later, the embalmers would struggle to restore any semblance of order to the woman's crushed and battered face and skull.

Sergeant Prendiville instructed Garda Byrne to seal off the immediate area. Byrne kept well clear of the corpse, later noting: *I did not touch the body or go beyond the centre grass margin on the middle of the laneway.* Meanwhile, Prendiville took a closer look at the dead woman. He made a report of what he saw:

I observed that the body was scratched and cut and that the lower part of a tracksuit [actually, leggings] *white in colour was caught on a barbed wire fence, which had actually ripped part of the pants off the body. Her clothing was pushed upwards but not to the point which would reveal her breasts. Her hair was covered with blood, as was her face. However, I observed that the area around the nostrils appeared wet as distinct from dried blood.*

Prendiville saw a blood-splattered concrete cavity block and a flattish, bloodied stone close to the woman's head. She was wearing a nightshirt, and had boots on, but no socks. Some of the woman's fingers were broken and there were lacerations covering her hands and arms.

It was abundantly clear that the Guards in County Cork had a murder investigation on their hands. In the fields next to the murder scene, cows and sheep grazed peacefully. There was a faint chorus of birdsong.

Prendiville instructed Byrne to stay by the body while he interviewed Lyons and Foster. The couple were distressed, Prendiville noted: *Alfie asked me, was it a woman and was she dead? I replied, "Yes". Alfie put his hands up to his face and turned his face upwards.* By now, Lyons and Foster had realised that it was the dead body of their French neighbour on the track. They told the Guards they heard nothing – no sounds or any commotion, nor the engine of a car – during that long December night. They had had no callers. There were, unsurprisingly, no video cameras installed at Toormore

4

or on any approaches to the settlement. It looked practically certain that nobody had witnessed the Frenchwoman's murder.

The Guards had a protocol to follow. A local doctor named Larry O'Connor arrived and pronounced the woman dead, leaving the scene immediately. Father Denis Cashman, the local priest from the church at Goleen, a village down on the shore of Roaringwater Bay, was called to administer the last rites. Told by the Guards that the death was suspicious, the priest did not anoint the body or touch it. He said a prayer, he wrote later, *unaware whether the deceased was Catholic or not.*

Father Cashman later made a brief statement that entered in the police file and would later become significant: *I left the scene at 12 midday and came back to my house arriving at approximately 12:15pm. I was at home for a short while when the phone rang and it was Eddie Cassidy of the* Examiner [a Cork City-based newspaper]. *He wanted to know if I could tell him where the scene was and I said I did not want to make any comment, and that he had a mobile phone and he could contact the Gardaí* [the Guards, plural, in the Irish language] *by himself.*

Lyons and Foster told the Guards what they knew about Sophie. The woman's name was Sophie Bouniol (she rarely if ever used her married name, Toscan du Plantier, in Ireland). Sophie lived in Paris and worked as a documentary film producer. She had owned the house for about four years. The couple recalled meeting Sophie's husband on one occasion, a distinguished-looking man who appeared somewhat older than she was. However, Sophie visited her house more frequently with another male companion – a man named Bruno, who was approximately the same age as Sophie. Lyons remembered that Bruno had introduced himself as a painter. In 1993, while Foster was away working in England, Lyons had a couple of dinners with Sophie and Bruno, but in spite of their social contact in the early days, they were primarily neighbours and nothing more. "We never became too friendly," Lyons told Prendiville.

Shirley Foster also recalled Bruno from a subsequent visit,

describing him as "a fairish man, not very tall". Sophie's parents had also stayed in the house, and her son, as well, who was in his early teens. He came during the school holidays, on at least one occasion with another boy of a similar age. Sometimes Sophie's friends or family would use the house without her. Sophie was polite, but distant, said Foster. One of the statements Foster made to the Guards read: *She was not curious about us. We certainly weren't soul mates.*

Later on 23rd December, Lyons and Foster walked down to Sophie's house. Lyons pointed out to his partner the stains that appeared to be blood on the back door and the doorknob. Foster spotted something else unusual: the dustbin that was beside the back door was neat and intact, which seemed odd. Anyone rushing out of the back door would almost certainly have knocked it over, or disturbed it.

After Father Cashman left, Sophie's housekeeper Josephine Hellen arrived at the crime scene. As Hellen's husband Finbarr was due to come to Toormore to work shortly afterwards, as he did every day, the decision was taken to ask Finbarr Hellen to formally identify the body, to save his wife from this distressing task.

A tearful Josephine Hellen told the Guards that she had met Sophie for the first time after the Frenchwoman had been chatting with Finbarr while he was working in the fields at Toormore. The two women quickly came to an arrangement: Josephine Hellen would keep the house clean and wash and iron the bedsheets after each visit, taking them to her own home to do so. She would also arrange any odd jobs that needed doing at the property. Sophie would phone Hellen about a week in advance of travelling, and Hellen would do some shopping for her and – except in the summer months – light a fire so the house, with its thick stone walls, was warm when Sophie got there.

This winter visit was little different in that respect, except that it was made with less notice: Sophie called Josephine Hellen on Tuesday, 17th December to say that she would be arriving on the

Friday of the same week, 20th December, and that this time she would be travelling alone. Subsequently Hellen mentioned to about half a dozen neighbours and family and a man due to do some work at the house that the Frenchwoman would be coming in the days before Christmas.

The routine for preparing the bedrooms in Sophie's house was slightly different in the winter, compared to the summer. There were three bedrooms; Sophie's own room at the far, eastern end of the house, a room with bunk beds in the middle, and another bedroom over the kitchen, with a double bed. Hellen made sure that this bedroom – directly over the kitchen and next to the rear entrance of the house – was ready for Sophie because it was the warmest place to sleep. She also decorated the living room with sprigs of holly to make it look cheerful and festive.

Hellen did not see Sophie on her final visit, but they had a quick phone conversation on the early evening of the Friday, after she arrived, to check that all was in order. Sophie called the Hellen household on the Sunday evening at about 7:30pm, and again shortly after 9pm, but Josephine was out. The housekeeper returned Sophie's call at 10pm, when the Frenchwoman told her that she would be returning to France on Christmas Eve. "Everything appeared to be okay on the phone," said Hellen. "I got the impression there was no one in the house when I rang her."

On the other hand, when Finbarr Hellen and the couple's son, John, made their daily trek out to Toormore on Saturday 21st December, Finbarr had noticed Sophie's hire car outside the house, but Sophie did not come out to greet him and John. He felt this was sufficiently unusual to inform the Guards: *On Saturday at approximately 12 noon to 1 o'clock, I was with my son John. I saw Sophie's car* [and] *I had a notion to go to the house and talk to her, but I didn't. I thought she would come out, and she didn't, which I thought was unusual as it was the only time I never met her since she started coming around.* At about 2:30pm the same day, Finbarr and John passed by Sophie's house once again, this time with some heifers. Josephine said Finbarr told her that he thought he saw Sophie's shadow by her porch. Josephine remarked: "I think there was something wrong that she did not talk to them, as she always came out to talk."

The two women concluded the call late on the Sunday evening by agreeing that Hellen would pass by the Toormore house the following day at about 12 noon. That way, Hellen would get her pay, £4.00 an hour, and refunds for purchases made, including the coal for the fire. Usually Sophie would have a small gift ready for Hellen's children.

The only person locally on the Mizen with a set of keys to Sophie's house was Josephine Hellen.

Some time after buying her property at Toormore, Sophie had told Josephine Hellen that she was disappointed about one aspect of the purchase. It had turned out, to her surprise, that a storehouse between her house and Alfie Lyons' house belonged to her neighbour, despite being closer to her own property. Sophie felt she had been misled about the storehouse by the estate agent managing the sale. There had also been a dispute with Lyons about drainage, but these were minor problems, and they were quickly sorted out.

Meanwhile, Sophie allowed Finbarr Hellen to use her fields for grazing his cattle. Sophie had some 10 acres that went with her house. In a written statement, the Guards asked Josephine Hellen: *How much is Finbarr or yourself paying Sophie for the use and grazing of her lands?* She replied: *We are paying her nothing. She never wanted the land from day one, only to walk it. Sure, it's all mixed up* [i.e. the fields belonging to Sophie, Alfie Lyons and Finbarr Hellen himself], *you would be better off to discuss this with Finbarr. I don't know where the fields are, only that they are away over the hills there in front of you...*

It is a bane of country life that land is often not properly fenced off. Disagreements over land boundaries were not – and still are not – uncommon in this part of Ireland. She added: *All I know is that there was never a cross word over land. Sophie would come up from her grave and tell you that.*

A BODY ON THE TRACK

Josephine Hellen returned with the Guards to Sophie's Toormore property several days after the murder. The Guards knew Hellen was the person best placed to see if there was anything untoward inside the house, maybe spot a clue they had missed. Hellen knew from her husband, who had identified the body, that Sophie had her boots on, which meant that *I knew Sophie in all probability was up on Sunday night because Sophie never went upstairs with her boots on... I think Sophie was sitting by the open fire, as she loved the open fire. Maybe she thought it was me* [turning up to pay her a visit late at night] *but we had an agreement for Monday morning...* Josephine was left with a profound regret that she did not call by Sophie's house on the Sunday night. Had she done so, Hellen wondered if things might have turned out differently.

The door with the smear of blood was on the western end of the house. It was the back door by the kitchen. From the kitchen window you could look out and see who was there if someone knocked. The door had not been forced by an intruder, and there was no indication of anything missing from the house, other than one thing. Where was the little axe?

It was usually in or near a box with nails and screws and suchlike in it. The axe had a red handle and was the kind you would use to chop firewood or cut up kindling. Josephine Hellen was reasonably sure that she had seen the axe when she left the house in advance of Sophie's arrival on the Friday, since Hellen always used the rear door to go in and out. That was where there was a small covered porch, with the back door at the end of the porch. The porch opened up onto the kitchen. The axe had been in the porch.

Later, Josephine said to the Guards that *if it's missing, and if you think it was used, and if you haven't found it, I bet you it's been thrown in at Kealfadda Bridge, but it would be washed away out by now.* When the Guards asked her why she had drawn that conclusion, Hellen replied that this was merely one of the stories circulating locally at the time.

One odd thing was that there did not seem to be any presents for Hellen's children in the house. Sophie was particularly fond of Josephine Hellen's daughter Siobhán. She usually brought her a present – pens for school, that kind of thing. With it being just before Christmas, all the more reason to expect to find some gifts for the Hellens that Sophie would have given to Josephine when she passed by on the Monday. The Guards had a good look, but apart from some sweets, they found nothing. That was not like Sophie.

Josephine had one possible lead for the Guards, which was formalised in a subsequent statement. It concerned Bruno, the painter who had come to Toormore several times with Sophie. After the murder, Hellen had read something in a newspaper about someone being violent to Sophie. The person responsible for the act of violence described in the newspaper appeared to be Bruno, whose full name had been given in the press as Bruno Carbonnet. *And I said straightaway it was him, and I think he killed her.*

Josephine recalled that, after she had seen Bruno and Sophie together at the house a couple of times, Sophie made no more mention of him to her. So Hellen asked Sophie: "How is Bruno?"

She said: *"He has gone off to the South of France and good riddance to him,"* or words to that effect.

***

The Guards could make some early conclusions from looking at the crime scene.

Firstly, since the killer had not broken into his victim's home, the Guards' first hypothesis was that Sophie knew her assailant well enough to open the door to him. Nothing appeared missing from inside Sophie's house, such as cash (there was a pile of £20 notes she had taken out of an ATM in Schull on the Saturday), credit cards or the victim's passport, so robbery could rapidly be discounted as a motive. Indeed, the only item not immediately accounted for was the small axe reported by Josephine Hellen. There were also no footprints on the floors of the property. It appeared clear to the

Guards that the person who had murdered Sophie had not set foot inside.

Outside the house stood the hire car that Sophie had picked up at Cork Airport. It was a silver Ford Fiesta. It would have to be returned to the rental company, Avis, at some point. A Guard noticed that the passenger seat had been pushed right back, as if to accommodate a particularly tall person. That was not how hire car companies routinely left their vehicles for the next customer.

That the assailant was physically strong was undeniable, as the cavity block the killer had dropped on his victim weighed around 25 kilos (around 55 pounds). The Guards saw that Sophie had put up a desperate fight – there were strands of hair under her nails. The State pathologist, Professor John Harbison, responsible for covering the whole of the Republic of Ireland, and with a wealth of experience behind him (he was close to retirement age), would also surely provide helpful evidence.

In any case, when Sophie had realised it was an unequal battle, she had tried to run away. She had only got as far as a gate below her house on the edge of her property, next to the old pumping station, where there were a number of loose concrete cavity blocks like the one the killer had used on his victim. Strangely, the escape route Sophie took was in the opposite direction to Alfie Lyons' house. To escape her attacker, Sophie appeared to have run downhill through a wide clump of brambles. Perhaps the killer had blocked Sophie's way to Lyons' property? The Frenchwoman would no doubt have realised her neighbours were there, even though the lights in their house were by now switched off.

The copious amount of blood at the scene, the hair under the Frenchwoman's fingernails, all of this could potentially supply vital DNA. Most of the Guards working on the Sophie Toscan du Plantier case had started their careers long before scientific advances meant that DNA was routinely used to aid serious crime investigations. Still, in the hours and days after the murder, the hope was that forensics would point towards the killer.

Chapter 2

SUSPICIONS

The weather turned on the evening of 23rd December. The wind picked up, and clouds darkened the sky. Rain fell. By dawn on the 24th , the air had lost its crispness. A murder case on Christmas Eve was the last thing the Detective would have expected. There had not been a killing in this western section of County Cork in over 70 years – not since Michael Collins was shot dead in the Civil War. The Mizen was a place where you could leave your car unlocked. You could leave your house unlocked, if you nipped out, for that matter. This was not Cork City.

By now, the crime scene had been cordoned off with blue and white police tape. A Garda patrol vehicle blocked the laneway 150 yards from the whitewashed house on the hillside at Toormore. The arrival and departure times of all the Guards at the scene were logged. The Richardsons were away and were not expected to return to their house soon. Alfie Lyons and Shirley Foster could come and go – they lived there, after all – but that was it. Nobody else was supposed to go near Sophie's house.

The Detective had come down from Cork City. He drove right up to the house, up to where Sophie Toscan du Plantier was murdered. The Detective was the ranking officer and his arrival had been expected. The body of the woman was still there, where she had fallen, lying under a blue plastic sheet.

The Detective saw for himself how violent the attack must have been, with the woman's skull and hair covered with blood. There were scratches on her hands and arms. Next to the woman's body was the big concrete block. That had blood on it, too. The Detective looked at the concrete block. He later said: *That's what he used to batter her with. That's what he killed her with.* He had not planned to use the block, thought the Detective, but it was close by. So he picked it up, and did her in with that. The murderer started his attack with the stone slab, and finished with the concrete block.

This was an outrage, pure and simple. Who would commit such a crime?

The Detective said: *She was a human being. You wouldn't do that to a dog.*

The Detective stared at the woman's bloodied, crushed face.

Whoever did this is a fucking headcase. She was only small, petite. If someone wanted to kill her, why all that violence? It shows the fella lost control, he lost the plot completely. Something blew up in his mind and he completely lost it. A psycho, end of fucking story.

It was a puzzle: *If some fella wanted to kill her, he could put his hands around her throat and hold them there for three minutes, and she would drop down dead.*

What could explain all of this? *He went for sex,* said the Detective. *He went and possibly made an advance to her. He was refused. So she ran.*

A brown-coated horse was grazing, oblivious, in the field next to the house. A couple of years after the event, a local man would make a video suggesting that this very horse could have broken free and caused a disturbance prompting the petite woman to come out of her house in the middle of the night and engage in a spectacularly one-sided tussle with the animal. The video might have been amusing if this had not so clearly been a murder, and it had not been so vicious.

13

Near the body there were briars. *Old, heavy briars, strong briars.*

The Detective could not absolutely rule out that this was a crime committed by a woman. At this stage, nothing could be ruled in or out. But the Detective – and, for that matter, all the uniformed Guards who had been searching the site for clues, keeping the body safe for the arrival of the State pathologist through the long dark night – instinctively thought in terms of *the guy*, *the fella*. This was the action of a *fucking headcase*, and it had to be a *he* and not a *she*. Surely only a man could be big and strong enough to pick up the concrete block?

There was something else immediately apparent to the Detective. It was to do with the location of the house. The Detective had never been up this valley before. It was truly off the beaten track. It would be very difficult for an outsider to find it. It was off the main roads and it was even off the side roads. It was not signposted. *You ask the Guards in Bantry to go there, they wouldn't find it.* And Bantry wasn't far away – it was just over the hill at the rear of the house and a little way east along the bay. So the Detective knew: *the fella who did this was local.* The Detective knew it from the word go: the murderer was a local or someone with very good local knowledge.

What's more, the people who lived here would recognise a stranger a mile off. That would not happen in the summer, right enough, when people from Dublin came down, and folk from England and Europe and all over. In the winter, you just do not get the tourists. People came home for Christmas, but they were family, and that was different. People knew who they were.

Common sense told the Detective that no foreigner, nobody from Paris or from anywhere else in France, would find their way here unaided. The Detective could not dislodge the thought from his mind: *People here would recognise a stranger a mile off.* That made the murder a kind of locked-room mystery, with the locked room in this instance being the Mizen Peninsula. In purely theoretical terms, anyone on the island of Ireland could have sauntered over to the whitewashed house and killed the occupant. For that matter, someone could have come over on the ferry from Wales or England or flown in from abroad and done the same. But that was just in the realms of theory. Random killings of that type were – thankfully – vanishingly rare. The Detective knew that a massive door-to-door operation in the local area would be needed, and fast. The focus of the hunt for the Frenchwoman's killer would be the Mizen.

That Christmas Eve morning, the Guards were still waiting for the State pathologist, Professor Harbison, to arrive and examine Sophie Toscan du Plantier's lifeless body. Ultimately, the coroner would be requiring his findings. There was another issue: the Guards had no clue as to even an approximate time of Sophie's murder, but a trained and experienced pathologist could be expected to narrow the period she died to a window of two or three hours.

In the meantime, the Guards gathered evidence, combed the land around the whitewashed house for clues, cut up the coarse brown briars. That was their job. Soon they would set up an incident room, take statements, do their house-to-house enquiries. Ask people where they were and who they were with at the time of the murder. Then you cross check and that way you can eliminate people. Alerting Interpol, since this was a foreign national. Press conferences, of course. That would all be coming up. The Detective knew this.

You build up a file against a suspect or suspects, plural. There would be an arrest or arrests. To do that, the Guards needed people to be cooperative, which was what happened, for the most part, although the Detective knew that in some cases *we have to go to a witness ten times before they tell us the truth*. Ultimately, though, the Guards did not decide who would be tried in court, and who would not be – that was the task of the people who worked at the Office of the Director of Public Prosecutions, the DPP. By the time the Garda file was sent off to the DPP in Dublin, it was out of the hands of the Guards who had done the investigation, put in the footwork. Some of the Guards called them *the fucking DPP*. Others talked about *the Dublin mafia*.

This wild and windy place was the Detective's patch, and it was a long, long way from Dublin.

The Detective knew that policing could be both straightforward and complex: *There would be common sense attached to some of it, and then there's humanity and there's a whole lot of issues.* You might well cut some corners. And then there were cases that you just could not shake off, even after you were long retired from the Guards. For the Detective, this would prove to be one such case.

At the end of the day, you could count on one thing: there would always be pressure in a murder investigation. Schull was a tight-knit community, and this ramped up the pressure even more. A murder always causes a lot of concern and a lot of fear. The Detective knew this well. If there is a murder, it is important that you solve it. Thinking back, years later, the Detective would remember that some men on the Mizen became desperate for an arrest to be made. Their wives were afraid to be home alone with a murderer on the loose. After the petite Frenchwoman was killed, just about everyone kept their doors locked and bolted. Some men said: *Will you get somebody for this as soon as you can, because we can't go out for a pint on the weekend. The women won't let us out.*

As the Detective drove out of the valley at Toormore that overcast 24th December 1996, Sophie Toscan du Plantier's grieving parents, brother and aunt had embarked on their journey from Paris to Ireland. Meanwhile, Sophie's husband Daniel stayed at home at his country house near Toulouse. He did not travel to Ireland to sit at the side of his wife's body one final time, and meet with the Irish authorities. That sad job would fall to somebody else. He later remarked that he had not wanted to see his wife's delicate facial features bashed in, her beauty destroyed. He wanted to preserve a pristine, intact memory of Sophie's beautiful face. Some people both in Ireland and in France found Daniel's decision extremely perplexing.

***

The media interest that the Detective knew was inevitable had started in the early afternoon of 23rd December, the same day Sophie Toscan du Plantier's battered body was discovered. The first journalist who arrived on the scene, logged by the Guards at 2:20pm, was Ian Bailey, who announced he was working on a story for the *Examiner*. Bailey spoke with Garda Martin Malone, who was standing at the checkpoint 150 yards from the crime scene. Malone retired from the Guards in 2002, but he was relatively new to the Mizen: he had arrived at Schull in 1995 after 20 years posted to a Garda station in a town in inland County Cork.

Garda Malone later admitted that he got a bit of a shock when he saw Ian Bailey rushing up the valley of Toormore in his white Ford Fiesta. Malone had dealt with Bailey and his partner, Jules Thomas, the previous May. The circumstances were not fortuitous: Thomas had come to Schull Garda station accompanied by Bailey to withdraw a complaint of serious assault against him. The Guards working out of Schull Garda station, like Garda Malone, could hardly fail to have heard about the incident, so severe was Ian Bailey's attack on Thomas.

On 6th May 1996, Jules Thomas presented herself at Schull Garda station in what one officer on duty described as "a very bad state". She had two lumps of hair missing, "one at the top of her head that measured between two and three inches in diameter" which had left a patch that was "totally bald". She had another bald patch of similar size where Bailey had yanked out her hair from behind one of her ears. Her left eye was "swollen, closed, and black and blue in colour". Her cheek was also swollen and badly bruised. Furthermore, Thomas had needed stitches sewn into her lip. When the Guards found out about the attack, Thomas had been entirely clear that Bailey had done it. Still, she refused to press charges, and the Guards' involvement in Bailey's assault on Jules Thomas ended there.

At Toormore, Garda Malone told Ian Bailey what he could see for himself – the area was sealed off, and Bailey could go no further.

What struck Malone as odd was that Bailey did not ask him about who had been murdered or any other relevant questions.

If he was a journalist, why wasn't he trying to prise information out of the Guards? Something similar had happened with Shirley Foster. At about 2:20pm, Bailey and Thomas had driven into the lane to Toormore at the same time as Shirley Foster was driving out of it: *I got the distinct impression that he was not going to stop, the way he was driving, so I flagged him down and let down the window.* Bailey told Foster he was there on official business and mentioned the *Examiner* newspaper. Foster went on to tell the Guards: *Had I not flagged down Ian I felt he was going to drive past me. Ian never asked me any question such as had I seen or heard anything. Jules did not ask me any question either... The impression I got when I told him that there was a police barrier was that he knew it was there.*

Garda Malone noticed that Bailey was dressed very smartly in a long, dark coat. He recalled having seen Bailey working as a freelance reporter one time previously, when the story concerned an elderly man falling off a cliff. Bailey was dressed casually on that earlier occasion, when he behaved *normally*, according to a memo that Malone penned after observing Ian Bailey at Toormore. But now, *it appeared to me as if he* [Ian Bailey] *was acting at the scene of Sophie's murder.* Malone noted elsewhere, referring to Bailey: *has long hair.*

Later, Garda Malone was quizzed on precisely what he meant when he wrote 'acting' in respect of Ian Bailey's behaviour on the afternoon of 23rd December. Malone clarified: *Acting the part, he was acting the part of a reporter.*

Ian Bailey, an Englishman, who was 39 – the same age as Sophie Toscan du Plantier – was living with Jules Thomas, a Welsh artist, in a cottage on a smallholding in Lissacaha, a townland the Guards on duty at Toormore estimated as being some four kilometres, or about two and a half miles, as the crow flies, from Sophie's house. Locally, this section of Lissacaha was known as the Prairie. Bailey and Sophie were thus practically neighbours, at least in Mizen terms.

Four days later, something else came to Garda Malone's attention. On 27th December, when the security cordon was still in place, Ian Bailey and Jules Thomas had managed to pay a visit to Alfie Lyons at his house in Toormore. Bailey had apparently accessed the secure area by telling officers he had to deliver some kindling to Lyons. Malone thought this was highly suspicious – it brought Ian Bailey within several yards of where the Frenchwoman had been murdered. In fact, Malone later said that he was "astonished" and "furious" that Bailey had got so close to the crime scene. Of course, you could also see Bailey's actions that day and arrive at a different, and perfectly rational, conclusion: Bailey was a reporter chasing a story and, in that context, it was natural for him to try to ask questions of Lyons, who owned the property next to Sophie's house, and Shirley Foster, who had discovered Sophie's body on the track.

Based on Ian Bailey's history of violence towards Jules Thomas, the fact he lived relatively nearby, and what Garda Malone perceived as being his suspicious behaviour in not asking questions when he approached on 23rd December – and subsequently succeeding in accessing the secure area at Toormore on the 27th – Garda Malone promptly filed a memo. It nominated Ian Bailey as a suspect in the murder of Sophie Toscan du Plantier. The memo was short and sweet, taking up less than a page. The key sentence was: *I nominate Bailey as a good suspect from what I know about him.*

By early January 1997, there would be as many as 54 'persons of interest' in the Sophie murder case. But this figure would quickly be whittled down, until a single suspect remained.

***

Perhaps the strangest discovery inside Sophie's holiday house on the Mizen was an anthology of poetry found in the kitchen. It had been left open at a piece of verse by W.B. Yeats titled *A Dream of Death*, a poem in which Yeats imagines a loved one dying a solitary death in a foreign land. When I started reading about the murder of Sophie

19

Toscan du Plantier in the early 2000s, an image formed in my mind of that book of poetry. It was difficult to dislodge. Many years later, I saw for myself the kitchen where the book was found – left open by the victim at a poem which was eerily prescient of what was about to happen to her – and drank in the damp air at that gloomy country house.

In *A Dream of Death*, Yeats does not describe a murder but, in the retelling of a dream, a beautiful woman dies alone 'near no accustomed hand', the setting is rural (Yeats writes of the 'peasants' who have to dispose of her corpse), and the night is clear and starry (the 'indifferent stars above'). Initially it crossed my mind that the presence of the book of poetry open at this piece of verse might be a kind of local rumour that people had ended up believing as fact. However, it was easy to check provenance: it was Sophie's family who, delving numbly into the cold rooms of the whitewashed house, had found the book, and reported it.

A Dream of Death is not even one of Yeats' most celebrated poems. Yeats produced many better-known pieces of verse. This is also worth saying.

So, could the murderer have entered the house, located the book – or chanced upon it – and marked the poem as a macabre calling card? The lack of footprints in the property strongly suggested that this was not the case. Otherwise, was the verse some kind of message from Sophie to her family and friends? If so, and for the message to have any point, the victim would have known she was about to be attacked. At the very least, she must have known she was in harm's way. No, this was simply not possible. If Sophie had known she was in mortal danger, she would have run a mile, run a hundred miles. I quickly concluded that the subject matter of the poem was a remarkable, troubling coincidence, and nothing more.

Chapter 3

SOPHIE AND DANIEL

Paris, evening of 23rd December: As soon as Marguerite Bouniol heard about the Frenchwoman found dead in southern Ireland on the 8pm news bulletin on the TF1 channel, she knew in her heart that it was her beloved daughter Sophie. There was a doubt about the precise day Sophie was going to fly back to France for Christmas, but it was either going to be on the 23rd December or on Christmas Eve. Either way, her family had had no word from her, and she was not picking up the phone at her whitewashed holiday house.

Marguerite's English was not fluent, so it fell to Sophie's cousin, Alexandra, to call Josephine Hellen to try to find out what had happened. Hellen's profound distress at the other end of the phone line was confirmation enough. Meanwhile, Daniel Toscan du Plantier – Sophie's husband and thus her next of kin – received personal notification of his wife's death in a phone call from the French Foreign Minister. That meant that someone had to tell Pierre-Louis, Sophie's son – a boy of 15 with tousled chestnut-coloured hair and Sophie's freckles, tall for his age.

Pierre-Louis was staying in the countryside outside Paris with his father, Pierre, Sophie's first husband. Pierre broke the news to Pierre-Louis. The boy had already gone to bed. "Your mum is dead," Pierre told Pierre-Louis. The man held his son tight for the whole of that long night. Later, in the absence of his doting father, Pierre-Louis hugged a pillow. His long nightmare had begun.

Marguerite and her husband Georges – Sophie's father – flew to Ireland the next day, Christmas Eve 1996, with Bertrand, the elder of Sophie's two brothers, and Marie-Madeleine, who was Marguerite's sister and Alexandra's mother. She was Sophie's favourite aunt. In France, the family of a murder victim could request the status of *partie civile*, or 'private party' to an investigation. This meant – among other things – that the authorities had to inform them about progress in the case, and they could petition the authorities in return. The Bouniols expected that a similar arrangement would exist in Ireland. To their surprise and dismay, there was no such privilege in Irish law. The Guards pulled Marie-Madeleine and Bertrand aside to quiz them individually about Sophie's personality and habits. It looked like the detectives in Ireland thought the grieving family might have something to hide. To the Bouniols, this did not seem right at all.

The remains of Sophie Toscan du Plantier, *née* Bouniol, were laid out on a slab in the mortuary in Cork City. Two days had passed. It was the bleakest of St Stephen's Days, as 26th December is known in Ireland.

Bertrand entered to spend some moments with what was left of his sister. Sophie's face was smashed, her body crushed and broken, all life extinguished. Such hatred, such violence! How was it even possible?

Harbison, the pathologist, started drafting a post-mortem report directly at Toormore. He recorded that *I was able to look at the ground when the body had been moved to note that there was a slight depression with blood on it where the head had lain… This indicated to me that the body had been in this position when the blows were struck.* The assailant's force had been so powerful it had even indented the stony ground at Toormore. Harbison gave as the cause of Sophie's death: *Laceration and swelling of the brain, fracture of the skull, and multiple blunt head injuries.*

There had been no rape, or attempt at rape, or any sexual assault. Unfortunately, Harbison had arrived too late to be able to assess any residual heat in the corpse and thus give an estimate of the time the murder was committed. The reason for Harbison's delay when the gravity of the crime had been immediately clear was not explained, and is still not known. Harbison recorded the time of Sophie's death as being during the night of the Sunday to the morning of the Monday – clearly a major setback to the Guards, who would surely have been better equipped in their investigations with a narrower timeframe for the murder.

Bertrand Bouniol tried to dissuade his parents and his aunt from seeing Sophie's dead body, certain the pain would be too great. They went in anyway. Marguerite later wrote: *Until that moment, my life had been pleasant, comfortable. It had been simple and peaceful. I had not known hatred until the thought of my daughter's murderer entered my head... Sophie's last moment was full of terror and suffering, the last thing she saw was a man crushing her face with a concrete block... I was ashamed to feel such hatred, I was not used to it, and it was contrary to how I had been brought up.*

In the midst of her anguish, two incidents preyed on Marguerite's mind. The first of these happened one particularly warm and bright autumn day, a couple of months before her daughter's last journey to Ireland. Sophie, Marguerite and Marie-Madeleine had been examining the lines on the palms of their hands, making comparisons, hardly taking it seriously. It was a moment of fun, light-hearted, meaning nothing. Sophie picked out the narrow crease of her lifeline. Marguerite recalled Sophie saying that she had a short lifeline, and would die young.

The other strange thing was a day or two before she flew to Ireland. Sophie had said goodbye to Marguerite not with the standard *à bientôt* ('see you soon') or the slightly more formal *au revoir* ('goodbye', but literally, 'until we see each other again') but with the word *adieu*, meaning 'farewell' (literally, 'to God'), which to the French ear sounds not only old-fashioned, but also has a marked finality. If you know you will see the person you are speaking with again soon, or even again full stop, you would not normally choose to say *adieu*. So why did Sophie use that word? Later, speaking on the phone, Sophie said to her mother that she loved her "very much", with the emphasis on "very much", which Marguerite found unusual, and gave her a bad feeling, although she never imagined that her daughter would be in harm's way. Looking back, Marie-Madeleine said that "it really appeared like she was going off to her fate". Marie-Madeleine thought that it was strange that in the month or so before she was murdered, Sophie paid social calls on a large number of her relatives.

Back in France, Pierre-Louis emptied a waste-paper basket of its contents. Little squares of paper fluttered down to the floor. It had been a sheet of paper torn up without a second thought. The boy put it back together, piece by piece. From wherever in the world she was, Sophie had the habit of faxing Pierre-Louis handwritten messages. This was the very last fax message his mother would send him.

***

Georges Bouniol and Marguerite Gazeau fell for each other at a meeting of an association of Parisians with roots in the Lozère, a sparsely populated upland region in south-central France. It was an event where people identifying with *la France profonde* – the beating, rural heart of the country, conservative and Catholic – might find a suitable partner. Their courtship in the early 1950s had as its background the start of *les Trente Glorieuses*, the three decades following the end of the Second World War in which France – particularly its expanding urban areas – grew exponentially in prosperity. Georges and Marguerite were of modest stature, but his strikingly handsome features marked him out, as did her boundless energy. The Bouniols' first child, a daughter, was born in the summer of 1957 and baptised Sophie Andrée Jacqueline. Two sons followed, Bertrand and Stéphane. Sophie was confirmed in the Catholic faith at the Cathedral of Notre-Dame in Paris wearing a cream-coloured dress coat, with a large wooden crucifix hanging from her neck and resting on her chest.

Georges was a dentist and set up his chair and his drills in an annex of the family apartment on the Rue Tiquetonne in the second arrondissement. Marguerite got a job as a civil servant at the local town hall. A row of shops on the street below sold pots, pans, knives and other implements for the restaurant trade. A stone's throw away, the hulk of Les Halles – the market dubbed 'the Belly of Paris' – filled each morning with fruit and vegetables and meat and fish. Loudmouthed barrow boys worked the Rue Tiquetonne. It was not long before you recognised the voices and the faces. Porters loaded with provisions scurried off in all directions. This was the vibrant, earthy heart of Paris.

Nothing stays the same forever. Civic unrest shook Paris in the spring of 1968. Students occupied university campuses and, later, workers seized control of factories. Society and morality were on the cusp of change. Many young people were intoxicated with new-found freedoms within their grasp. *It is forbidden to forbid*, read one piece of iconic graffiti. Another read: *Enjoy without hindrance*, but there was a play on words here since the French verb for 'enjoy' was *jouir*, which also signifies sexual pleasure.

The twin figureheads of the 'Events of May 1968', as this period became known in France, were Daniel Cohn-Bendit, a flame-haired and voluble Franco-German student anarchist who later settled into a comfortable existence as a Member of the European Parliament, and the French existentialist philosopher Jean-Paul Sartre. It was Sartre, a diminutive middle-aged man, the target of bullies as a child, who gave the sit-ins and the strikes their intellectual foundation. Sartre claimed there was no fixed design for how a human being should be and no God to give us a purpose.

He outraged traditional-minded, middle-class people like Georges and Marguerite Bouniol by admiringly describing Ernesto 'Che' Guevara, a leader of the Cuban revolution and a sometime brutal executioner, and a controversial, litmus-test figure in France, as "the most complete human being of our age". To the protagonists of May 1968, conformity was the enemy of authenticity. Morals and received wisdom – much of it founded on the teachings of the Catholic church – were getting in the way of living a full life, of being true to oneself. By the summer of the same year, the genie was out of the bottle. There was no easy way of getting it back in. This was the France in which Sophie came of age in the 1970s.

The streets around the family apartment on the Rue Tiquetonne started to gentrify once the iron-clad Les Halles market was demolished in 1971. The contemporary piece of architecture that replaced it was all sensuous curves and colours, functioning as a shopping centre and transport hub all in one. Some people, quite predictably, declared the new Les Halles an abomination. Others, equally predictably, liked it and thought the construction admirably modern and progressive.

As a teenager, Sophie travelled a couple of times to Ireland to learn English, staying a month each time with an Irish host family in Dublin. One of the families took her on a trip around the country in a caravan. They passed through ancient landscapes marked by resistance to British rule. There were poorhouses, stories of famine. A civil war in living memory, just about. Sophie discovered Irish poets, and read their verse avidly.

It was a surprise to her friends and family when Sophie enrolled in a law degree course in Paris after high school. She clearly loved the arts – novels, paintings, films and poems – and the dry discipline of law seemed like a strangely poor fit for her interests and personality. After a couple of years studying law at university, she quit. In 1980, at the age of 22, she married Pierre, a student, dark-haired and good-looking. Sophie worked at a video rental store which Pierre's father owned, and in a bookshop. The couple were now expecting a baby, who was born less than a year after the wedding. They christened their child Pierre-Louis. But within a few months of his birth, Sophie and Pierre split up. Sophie had already dropped out of college and now she was getting divorced. Her parents worried about her future; Sophie's relationship with her mother became tense, with disagreements over her daughter's moderately left-wing views. Still, Marguerite and Georges cherished having baby Pierre-Louis nearby, and Sophie was still young, and they knew she had time to get her life back on track.

Mother and son moved into a small flat with space for just one bed. Sophie tried to instil her values and worldview in her young son. For instance, she told Pierre-Louis that right there in Paris a group of people called the Jews had been rounded up during the Second World War. They were sent to camps and had perished there. Some brave people had tried to help the Jews, taking a risk as they did so. What, she asked, would Pierre-Louis have done?

In the mid-1980s, Sophie's fortunes appeared to be on the up when she got a job as a PR officer at UniFrance, the national film board – a dream job for a movie buff like Sophie. But Sophie's relationship with her line manager soured, and he wanted to fire her. Things changed when Daniel Toscan du Plantier was installed as chairman of UniFrance. He took a shine to the beautiful blonde Sophie. Instead of showing her the door, he courted her and soon proposed marriage.

Sophie's parents were well aware of Daniel's reputation as a womaniser, but ultimately gave the union their blessing. What else could they do? Sophie was a grown woman, and she was capable of deciding for herself. Of course, they knew about Daniel – who in France didn't? Daniel Toscan du Plantier, usually bespectacled, with his wavy grey hair and luxuriant moustache, was a public figure, arguably the most powerful man in French cinema. Before taking over at UniFrance he had been chairman of the Gaumont film company. Daniel was also a celebrated producer in his own right, working with film directors such as Federico Fellini, Peter Greenaway and Maurice Pialat. With two marriages to well-known actresses behind him, together with a string of high-profile relationships with other glamorous film stars, he came with no small amount of baggage. Still, Daniel had the gift of the gab. He could talk the birds down from the trees. He had that effect on practically everyone.

The couple's wedding in the spring of 1990 was a fresh start for both mother, who was 32, and her child, who was nine. Marguerite Bouniol officiated at the ceremony at the town hall, largely at Daniel's request. She later wondered if this had been a wise decision.

People's tongues wagged about the age difference between Sophie and Daniel – he was 16 years older – but few doubted this was a love match. With marriage to Daniel, Sophie entered a world of money and celebrity. Daniel had a daughter and two sons of his own, and he was kind and affectionate towards Pierre-Louis.

Daniel's mansion – *their* mansion – off the Rue des Martyrs in Paris was a place where plots and narratives and structures of movies were picked apart and reconstructed, praised and critiqued. Deals to fund new projects were thrashed out. Fashionable actors and actresses of the day came and went through the heavy oak door of the Toscan du Plantier residence, with its bronze cherub for a doorknob. Pieces of gossip were traded elegantly and deliciously. It was said that Daniel had the ear of government ministers and that even the President of the Republic would take his call.

Strangers often asked for Daniel's autograph when he was in airports or in restaurants. He would always agree with a flash of a smile. Sometimes the people requesting an autograph were only vaguely aware of what Daniel actually did. To the everyday Frenchman or Frenchwoman, he was a familiar face off the telly, a chap in an expensive suit regularly called upon to opine about the state of the film industry or pay tribute to a dead celebrity.

In the mansion off the Rue des Martyrs you could shut out most of the hum of the city and black out the beams of the long crawl of yellow headlights pointing towards the crest of the hill of Montmartre. Paris, however, was a constant presence. This delighted Daniel; he would not have had it any other way. Even before his parents had announced they were decamping from their hometown in the French Alps to start over in the French capital, the adolescent Daniel had longed to live in Paris. He was drawn to the city with the force of a river bursting its banks.

Sophie, on the other hand, often longed for absolute peace and quiet, a place to break free from the whirlwind of film festivals and society dinners and receptions that were the mainstay of her new life. Her new husband encouraged her to develop her own creative ideas, introducing her to the head of Arte, a determinedly highbrow, state-funded Franco-German television station. Sophie set up a company to produce documentary films, naming it Les Champs Blancs ('The White Fields') after the title of a favourite painting. But she needed time and space to write. Over time, a plan crystallised in her mind. She would buy a house in Ireland, a place to reflect and pen documentary films in an unspoilt environment, in a place she already knew she loved. Daniel wondered why Sophie could not find the same tranquillity and inspiration in his own country retreat, a rambling manor house with extensive grounds in the countryside south of Toulouse. Still, Daniel readily put up the cash. The Irish holiday house would be a gift from him to his young wife.

In the dawn after Sophie died, Daniel saw that the fields surrounding his manor house were all blanketed in white. A heavy snowfall in the lowlands this far south in France was a rarity. Daniel immediately thought: "Les Champs Blancs" – the name his dead wife had given to her production company.

In the trips to Ireland in her youth, Sophie had spied pubs in every village full of music and laughter and storytelling. The Irish were naturally garrulous and started conversations with outsiders unprompted, which was unthinkable in much of rural France, her own parents' beloved Lozère being a case in point. Sophie's command of English was not extremely fluent – in spite of her language courses and reading poems – but, if anything, this helped to cement her passion for Ireland. Any detailed discussions of the drawbacks of rural life in the country probably needed a more profound understanding of the English language than Sophie had to offer. For the most part, Sophie's view of Ireland was founded on Irish poetry, a dash of the island's history, and what she had seen with her own eyes.

The only question remaining was where exactly in Ireland she would buy her bolt-hole. With her cousin Alexandra, she looked around various locations in the southern counties of Cork and Kerry before settling on the Mizen. Sophie viewed two houses there, a conventionally attractive one on the shore near Goleen, just west of Schull, and another at Toormore – the whitewashed house she ended up buying – about which Alexandra claimed to have had a "sixth sense", and found sinister. Visible from Sophie's new house was the broad sweep of the beam of the lighthouse on the jagged Fastnet Rock at the edge of Roaringwater Bay. The Fastnet was the last sight of land for many Irish people sailing to new lives in America, earning it the name 'the Teardrop of Ireland'.

Towards the end of 1992, Sophie made an appointment in the office of an Irish country solicitor. She signed a set of purchase papers and got a bunch of keys in return. The house in the shallow valley of Toormore was now hers.

***

The coin of the Fastnet lighthouse had another side. It was not all sadness and heartache. It was about arrival just as much as departure. For transatlantic passengers sailing to Europe back in the day, the light on the rock was the sign that they had almost made it, that they would soon be back ashore. If the crossing was rough, tears could well up in the eye of an eastbound passenger for reason of sheer relief. Now, as then, the revolving beam of light sweeps the horizon, lighting up the sky with its cream-coloured glow every five seconds, dipping and dissolving, and then returning, *ad infinitum*.

Today's pale lighthouse was constructed at the end of the

nineteenth century from interlocking blocks of Cornish granite, dovetailing in a design that would give it maximum strength to contend with walls of water – often as high as 30ft – that battered the structure in winter storms. The Victorian master builder insisted that the stonemasons did a dummy run at the yard in Cornwall to make sure the stones interlocked perfectly. The positioning of the structure on the rock was important, too. It appeared counter-intuitive, but by placing the lighthouse relatively low down on the rock, the building would feel the force of the biggest waves before they got to peak height. At any event, the master builder could take no chances. You only have to wander out to Mizen Head at the tip of the peninsula to see the treacherous swell and the brute power of the sea as it smacks into the land.

Is there a more generous structure than a lighthouse? They exist to make the seas safer, to preserve life. They ask for nothing back. They give everyone an equal measure of protection: all nationalities, all creeds, all ages, all trades and professions, the pure of heart, the impure of heart, those who set out on their journeys full of hope, those who depart with fear in their soul.

Yet no plan is failsafe. In 1912 the *Titanic*, then the world's biggest and most opulent passenger liner, departed Southampton in England bound for New York. After docking briefly outside the French port of Cherbourg, it made its final scheduled stop in Cobh (then named Queenstown) at the entrance to Cork harbour. True to geography as well as tradition, the *Titanic* sailed past 'the Teardrop of Ireland' on its fateful journey west. Passengers gazing from the vessel's starboard deck would have seen the Fastnet lighthouse in all its benign glory.

The bedroom that Sophie chose for herself was at the end of the house closest to the lane, on the opposite side to Alfie Lyons' place. She purposely left the windows in her bedroom free of drapes so the Fastnet light, reassuring and compassionate, would flood in while she slept, and greet her on a dark winter's morning when she woke. She even put her bed on a raised platform to give the beam from the Fastnet Rock – 10 miles away as the crow flies – its fullest effect. The rock itself was out of sight, even from the bed on the platform: the stony brow of the hill facing Sophie's house to the south blocked any view of Roaringwater Bay. No matter – Sophie fixed a framed picture of the Fastnet lighthouse to her bedroom wall.

Sophie was buried on a chilly 31st December 1996 in the tiny cemetery of a village church near Daniel's country retreat outside Toulouse. Already the Bouniols were upset that nobody in Daniel's entourage had let them know when Sophie's body was due to arrive at Toulouse Airport. Consequently, they were not there to meet it.

Daniel linked arms with young Pierre-Louis as they followed Sophie's coffin into the church. The pews were thronged with Daniel's friends, meaning Parisian celebrities, politicians and people from the world of French cinema. The singer Barbara Hendricks was there, also veteran director Maurice Pialat, Daniel's former partner Isabelle Huppert, popular philosopher Bernard-Henri Lévy, Nicolas Seydoux, the media tycoon who had given Daniel his big break at Gaumont. The minister of culture of the French Republic was in attendance. The TV cameras and newspaper reporters knew to keep a respectful distance from the funeral proceedings.

Just when it appeared things could not possibly get any worse, they did. The Bouniols listened in shock at the eulogy delivered by the priest, a man named Joseph Marty, who combined the priesthood with a sideline career as a lecturer in cinema studies. "Sophie died the death of a character in a Pasolini movie," Marty declared. "She could also have appeared in a John Ford film, with his penchant for violence and aggression, with a tenderness and a desire for truth just below the surface." And so it went on. Their precious Sophie had been killed, and Marty's speech felt more like an insult – it was hardly about Sophie at all. A couple of the Bouniols were so disgusted with what they heard they later regretted not getting out of their seats and leaving the church altogether. It would have caused a scene, for sure, but it would have been justified.

For a while, Pierre-Louis continued to live at the mansion off the

Rue des Martyrs. He liked 'Toscan', as he called his stepfather, and got on well with him. However, the rift between the Bouniols and Daniel, both sides grieving in their own way, was now becoming evident. The Bouniols had never properly understood why Daniel had stayed in his manor house rather than travel to Ireland in the wake of Sophie's murder. For the living, of course, life had to go on, as wretched as things were. Sophie's killer needed to be brought to justice, whoever he was. The Bouniols would need to engage with the journalists waiting outside the church gate to keep Sophie's case in the public eye. They dreaded this. The Bouniols were determinedly private people. But securing justice for Sophie and the welfare and future of young Pierre-Louis were now their priorities. In time, the freshly turned soil over Sophie's grave would start sprouting new blades of grass. Many people leaving the church on that sad day must have thought Sophie had found her final resting place under the ground of that quiet village cemetery.

If they did, they were wrong.

***

The couple's plan had been to enjoy a quiet Christmas at Daniel's country retreat and then fly off to west Africa to see in the New Year at the residence of the French ambassador in Dakar, capital of Senegal. Daniel and Sophie's hosts were to be the ambassador and his wife, Catherine Clément, a philosopher and novelist, and one of Daniel's closest friends.

Clément had been very fond of Sophie, who she found "different", meaning different from Daniel's other women. In the wake of the murder, Clément hurried back to France and joined a tight group of friends looking after Daniel at his mansion in Paris. Actress Marie-Christine Barrault, Daniel's first wife, was there, as was his second wife, Italian film director Francesca Comencini. There were Isabelle Huppert, Isabella Rossellini; in fact, *all his women were there*, wrote Clément, *and me, the friend who he never seduced...*

Daniel Toscan du Plantier was the king of the party, but it was a party of pain… Daniel cried, told anecdotes, cried some more and *the women who had loved him, nourished him with the milk of human kindness, their embraces kept to a minimum. In that respect, the women were useless.*

In the autumn of 1997, Daniel would meet someone new. His older children encouraged him to leave the mansion off the Rue des Martyrs with its walls smothered with paintings of nude women. He got married again the following year – his new wife was 30 on her wedding day, Daniel was 57. Some might have found the wedding hasty, in the circumstances. In Clément's view, Daniel *was incapable of living alone and, in any case, time meant nothing to him.*

When Clément cast her eye over the case, she had no trouble in finding fault with the Irish criminal justice system, reserving some extremely harsh words for Professor John Harbison, the State pathologist who had not arrived promptly at the scene of the crime. The knowledge that Sophie's lifeless body had been left out for a whole long night, covered by nothing more than a rudimentary sheet of plastic, traumatised the Bouniols. Harbison, Clément wrote, had *a place in hell waiting for him.*

When I read her comments on Harbison, I thought that Clément was taking things too far. Harbison had hardly covered himself in glory with his tardy appearance, but the only person deserving a special place in hell was surely the killer – or killers – and anyone who might have aided or conspired with them. What was certain was that here was a case where people looked at the facts, looked at the information, gave weight where they felt it was due – added a dose of emotion to the mix, perhaps – and arrived at radically different conclusions. Clément's words were a warning to me, of sorts.

Chapter 4

THE BLOW-INS

On Friday, 27th December 1996, Guards Bart O'Leary and Kevin Kelleher were strolling along Main Street, Schull, in plain clothes. The pair entered Brosnan's Spar supermarket and O'Leary spotted a man acting unusually. O'Leary asked Kelleher if he knew who it was. Kelleher told his partner that it was Ian Bailey. O'Leary subsequently noted in a memo: *He seemed to me to be barging his way towards the counter. A few people moved out of his way to allow him access... Ian Bailey was unbelievably pale. He was unshaven and his hair was in disarray.* O'Leary saw Bailey ask the shop assistant for a copy of the *Irish Times*.

I noticed that the backs of both of Bailey's hands were cut. Both were totally covered in what I think were briar marks. At this stage, I could only see up as far as his wrists.

Bailey left the shop and walked along Main Street. The two Guards followed him, and O'Leary reported that *he kept looking back at us*. If the context had not been so serious, the situation might have been rather amusing: Bailey darted into a side street and Kelleher reported that after a few seconds Bailey *peeped around the corner at us*. Other people on the Mizen had noticed scratches on Bailey's hands in the days immediately after Sophie's murder. On 24th December shortly before 12 noon, Ian Bailey had paid a visit to the shop at the Lowertown Creamery. Two shop assistants working there that day noticed scratches on at least one of Bailey's hands. One of the assistants described them to the Guards as being "mainly" on his left hand. They were the kind of scratches you get when "cutting briars". The other assistant reported seeing "multiple light scratches", also on Bailey's left hand, but said that he did not recall seeing any scratches on his right hand. This second shop assistant said that Bailey looked "pale and agitated". When he had asked Bailey if he was all right, Bailey had replied: "I hope so, in a couple of hours". What was beyond doubt was that Bailey bought a litre of 'Happy Shopper' bleach before leaving, which seemed an odd purchase to make on Christmas Eve.

When Garda Kelleher filed his own memo of the sighting of Bailey in Brosnan's, his recollection also differed somewhat from that of Garda O'Leary. While O'Leary had recognised the scratches as presumably caused by briars, Kelleher noted: *I saw Bailey's left hand and I could see scratches on his wrist. I would describe the scratches as being light and extending all along his left wrist.*

The Guards working on the case knew about the dense patch of brambles and briars that formed a barrier between Sophie's house and the place of her death, further downhill on the track. They also knew that the victim had scratches on her hands and arms that indicated that she had attempted to flee from her attacker through the briars. Anyone with similar cuts would naturally be a person of interest – and Ian Bailey's violent attack on his partner, Jules Thomas, earlier in 1996, and his speedy appearance at the crime scene and his lack of questions regarding the murder, in spite of being a journalist covering the case, had already marked him out as suspicious.

Not surprisingly, the next morning O'Leary and Kelleher trekked out to the cottage at the Prairie that Bailey shared with Thomas. The purpose was to have the couple fill in a questionnaire on their movements on the night when Sophie was killed, and on the days preceding it. Bailey told the Guards that on the night of the murder he had gone to the Courtyard bar in Schull. Separately, Jules Thomas said the same thing. They then drove home and went to bed, they said. They had only differed in their arrival times at the Prairie.

When he was speaking with the Guards in the cottage, Bailey took off his jacket. He appeared to make no special effort to cover up the scratches on his forearms, which were visible to Garda O'Leary when Bailey was inside his home. Bailey explained to O'Leary that he got the scratches when he climbed up a fir tree and cut the top off for use as a Christmas tree. O'Leary was far from convinced – he thought the scratches on Bailey's forearms and on his hands were consistent with cuts from briars. The scratches had formed scabs.

There was something else that drew O'Leary's gaze: *Ian Bailey had a cut on the right hand side of his forehead. This was not a scratch, it was deep enough.* Bailey told the Guards that the cut on his forehead had been caused by the flaying talon of a turkey that he had slaughtered on the same day. He had cut down the top of the tree and slaughtered the turkeys – three in all – on the afternoon of 22nd December 1996, the eve of Sophie's murder. What Bailey's scratches were like and where, precisely, they were on his hands and forearms, would have been easy to pin down if a photo had been taken of them. The same went for the cut on Bailey's forehead. However, none of the Guards took a photo, and nobody else came forward with one. For many years, all that investigators from Ireland and France had to rely on were assorted witness statements and a couple of sketches of the scratches and of the wound on Bailey's forehead that O'Leary and Kelleher jotted down after their visit.

Meanwhile, the Guards in the incident room in Bantry were putting together Sophie's last known movements. According to her family, Sophie had never travelled to Ireland on her own before, and had asked her best friend, Agnès Thomas, and cousin, Alexandra Lewy, to accompany her. Neither was able to, since both had commitments in the period before Christmas. Sophie had already embarked on one exhausting trip in December when she accompanied Daniel on official business to a film festival in Acapulco, Mexico. Daniel recalled that Sophie had said that the boiler in the house at Toormore needed fixing. If she did not travel to Ireland it might appear to the housekeeper that she was not taking responsibility for the property. Still, it seemed like one trip too many – after all, Daniel and Sophie were due to fly out on holiday to Dakar in west Africa for New Year.

The Guards could be sure of this: Sophie left home for Charles de Gaulle Airport in Paris on the morning of 20th December 1996 after attending the UniFrance Christmas party the previous evening at Les Bains Douches, an upscale Parisian nightclub. She travelled business class on an Aer Lingus flight that arrived in Cork Airport shortly before 2:30pm after a brief stop in Dublin. CCTV cameras showed Sophie, wearing a dark woollen coat and a green scarf, exiting the baggage reclaim area with a trolley loaded with luggage – a surprising volume for a stay of under a week. She picked up the keys to a hire car, a Ford Fiesta, at the Avis counter at the airport. About an hour and a quarter later, she apparently stopped for fuel at Hurley's Garage in Skibbereen, a market town about two-thirds of the way from the airport to her house in Toormore. Sean Murray, who was manning the pumps that afternoon, called the Guards shortly after the murder because he recognised the face of the victim from the television news. Murray was certain that Sophie had not been alone in the car – there had been a man occupying the front passenger seat. Who was this man?

In the weeks and months that followed the crime, Sean Murray's testimony was largely disregarded by the Guards.

The following day, Saturday 21st, Sophie drove into Schull and took £200 out of an ATM on Main Street, and browsed Tara Fashions, a knitwear shop run by a woman named Marie Farrell. The next day, Sunday 22nd, Sophie was more active: she went for a walk at Three Castle Head, a wild stretch of coast on the north side of the Mizen peninsula named for three ruined castles. She dropped in at the home of Tomi and Yvonne Ungerer. Sophie had got to know the Ungerers by chance since the path she liked taking along the cliffs passed through the Ungerers' property. Tomi Ungerer, who was French, was a successful illustrator and cartoonist, and his wife, Yvonne, was American. *While we were chatting*, Yvonne Ungerer told the Guards, *Sophie told me that while she was up at the castles she felt this great anxiety, almost fear*. There were superstitions associated with this section of the Mizen – stories of ghosts and sea monsters and the like. *She wasn't in a cheerful mood but she wasn't really glum either. She talked about her plans for the future and we spoke about meeting up in Paris in the spring.*

Sophie left the Ungerers at around 5:45pm. She drove to Crookhaven and ordered a pot of tea at the bar owned and run by Billy and Angela O'Sullivan. Sophie drove home and, later in the evening, spoke briefly with Josephine Hellen on the phone. The last person to speak with Sophie – other than her killer – was her husband Daniel, who spoke with his wife for about an hour between 11pm and midnight Irish time. She was in good spirits, he later said to investigators. She would make it back to his country house near Toulouse in time for Christmas. Daniel thought his wife was by then already in bed.

Sophie had bought the house in Toormore to recharge her batteries. It was her refuge, a place to write and plan documentary film projects. Nothing indicated she wanted to settle into an expat existence there, or have a busy social life, and so it was hardly a surprise that she knew so few people on the Mizen. For instance, she was friendly with the Ungerers and with Bill Hogan, an American cheese-maker, and she could count on the O'Sullivans at their pub in Crookhaven for a smile and a chat. But Billy O'Sullivan said to the Guards that he did not know Sophie's surname until the murder was announced on the TV news, which told you something. This made it difficult for the Guards to establish any kind of motive at all. On the one hand, the isolated location meant they could pretty much discount the notion that a prowler was responsible; on the other, Sophie knew so few people locally, and it was unthinkable that any of them would have had a reason to kill her. Furthermore, a murder that took place at night in the winter made it relatively easy for many people to provide an alibi – for the most part, people on the Mizen were tucked up in bed with their partners. Then there was the matter of the bloodied cavity block at the scene of the crime. How many people could have picked up and carried 25 kilos of concrete?

Perhaps more than anywhere else in Ireland, the western reaches of County Cork was a place favoured by 'blow-ins' – the local name for outsiders who come to rural parts of the country and set up home there. The Mizen had communes of new-age travellers, people determined to live off-grid, and wealthy film-types and artsy people from London. Some of them were loaded, others lived on welfare and ate what they grew in their garden. Thanks to the locals, it was a place of tolerance. Everyone could find their spot, and they were blow-ins, all of them. Sophie had this in common with the English poet and gardener with the scratches on his hands that looked like briar cuts.

***

By the end of January 1997, the Guards had eliminated all but one of the local men who had been 'persons of interest' in Sophie's murder. There had been a man who had been found pinching gas canisters from empty holiday homes; there had been another known as a voyeur with a penchant for peering at women through windows; another was a German expat known to be depressive. None of them was the killer.

Then there was Ian Bailey.

It was a puzzle. The tall Englishman with the scratches on his hands and the cut on his forehead was no shrinking violet. He had gone down to Schull pier on 25th December to watch the participants in the town's traditional Christmas Day swim. True to form, he had even performed some of his own poetry there, standing in the crowd, an impromptu thing. Bailey was also reporting on the murder for a number of newspapers. He had a gig as a local fixer for Caroline Mangez, a journalist sent over to Ireland by *Paris Match* magazine, and helped other French journalists with their stories, too.

Guards asked themselves how someone who never attended Garda press conferences appeared to know so much about the physical aspect of the crime – what injuries Sophie had suffered, including the fact Sophie had not been subject to any kind of sexual assault. They wondered, too, why the English journalist was seemingly pushing a narrative that Sophie had a complicated love-life, and that solving the murder would mean exploring its "French connection".

Meanwhile, Bailey made contact with the Guards. By mid-January 1997, he had corrected the account of his movements as given to Guards O'Leary and Kelleher on 28th December 1996. His amended story was that he had spent most of the evening of the night before the murder in the Galley bar in Schull – rather than at the Courtyard bar, as he had stated earlier – leaving shortly after midnight with his partner Jules Thomas. They had taken the scenic route home to their cottage on the Prairie along the single-track road over Hunt's Hill, which offered a splendid view over the moors towards the Sheep's Head peninsula to the north-west. When the Guards came calling for a hair follicle to check his DNA against forensic evidence found at the scene, Bailey was happy to oblige. He knew he was under suspicion. He said it would clear him.

Sophie's murder was the lead item on the news in Ireland and France for days. An Garda Síochána appealed for information from the public. Somebody surely knew something about the murder and who was responsible. If the killer was not caught, he could well strike again.

For the French journalists sent to Ireland, there was a bit of explaining required for their readers. They had to set the scene, as it were. Here was a place where the pubs were as full as the churches, although never at the same time, as one wrote. Locals were so quietly-spoken you could barely hear them. There was bleak moorland lined by rutted, unmarked tracks that petered out into nothingness. An ocean that roared and foamed and a wind that howled. The wide arc of the Fastnet light hinting that somehow everything would come good.

Most of all, the system of delivering justice was different. In France, a murder case would be led by a *juge d'instruction*, an investigating magistrate, tasked with establishing the truth, imposing order on the chaos of a crime scene. He or she would pick and then lead a team of detectives. The investigating magistrate decided whom to haul in for questioning, how the questioning would be carried out – good cop, bad cop, whatever kind of cop. They decided on the charges to be brought, if any. A well-argued case made by an investigating magistrate would be difficult for the public prosecutor's office to turn down. The French investigating magistrate bossed the investigation and, in turn, journalists knew where to go to get details of a case, if the investigating magistrate agreed to talk. If they did not, footage of an important-looking man or woman brushing away a journalist on the doorstep of their office was sometimes just as revealing.

So it was no surprise that the French journalists sought out a policeman on the Mizen who looked like he was in charge of the investigation, who looked like he was giving it direction. They found one: Detective Superintendent Dermot Dwyer, who worked under Superintendent J.P. Twomey, and would soon replace him. Dwyer was in his early fifties, with short dark hair and darting, inquisitive eyes. He smoked a pipe and often wore a trench coat. He did not draw attention to himself, and appeared a polite, patient listener. Perhaps inevitably, the French correspondents on the Mizen called him 'Columbo', after the TV detective.

On 31st January 1997, Ian Bailey got a call at his house at the Prairie. It was the Guards. Would he have time to receive one of the senior men on the case? Bailey agreed; he was always cooperative with the Guards. The senior man, Dermot Dwyer, came knocking at his door.

One thing Dwyer had learned over the years was that *even the biggest liar that ever walked tells the truth sometimes.* You could have a liking for lying, or a fetish for lying, and that was one thing. Second thing, you could dig yourself into a hole and think you have to lie through your teeth to get out of the hole you had made. In both cases, you are never going to lie the whole time. Some true words will trickle out.

Dwyer's opening gambit was to ask how Bailey had wound up on the Mizen. Bailey was happy to tell the detective his story – how he had washed up in Ireland in 1991 from England after a difficult divorce, his farm labouring in the south-east of Ireland, then a trek west to Schull, a stint at the local fish factory, his poetry. Dwyer listened to Bailey's thoughts on the case. For the most part, Dwyer already knew what these were. The Guards had been following with interest what Bailey wrote in the Irish press. Unsurprisingly, Bailey insisted that there was a "French connection" to the crime. The key to solving Sophie's murder was not in western County Cork, but much further afield.

Dwyer drank Bailey's coffee and enjoyed one of his mince pies, which he found delicious (Bailey said later that the pastries "had been hanging around since Christmas"). According to Bailey, before Dwyer left the cottage, he asked the Englishman if he knew how to play poker. Bailey replied that he didn't. Dwyer suggested that he might wish to learn. (Dwyer would later deny that he said any such thing.) Bailey also said that Dwyer told him that he had someone who would place him at Kealfadda Bridge at 3am on the night of the murder. That was hugely significant: Kealfadda Bridge was the closest point to Sophie's house on the main Schull-Goleen road. (Dwyer subsequently denied he said anything to Bailey about a witness at Kealfadda Bridge. He made the point that, at the time of their meeting, he did not even know where Kealfadda Bridge was.) Bailey asked to see Dwyer again a couple of days later. The two men met at a local fishing-themed bar called Jim's Plaice. Bailey explained to the detective that things had not been good in Sophie's marriage, and that the murderer was surely French.

As things stood, Bailey was wasting his breath expounding on his theory that the killing was ordered, or masterminded, in France. That horse had already bolted. First of all, Daniel Toscan du Plantier had a perfect alibi. He had been in his country house near Toulouse on the night of his wife's murder with his elder son, David. He had spoken to Sophie on the phone from France shortly before she died. Moreover, there was nothing to suggest that he wanted to harm his wife; quite the reverse, nobody doubted that his grief was profound and genuine.

The Bouniols, too, thought it patently absurd that Daniel might have anything to do with the crime. Could a hit man have been involved? This seemed preposterous: Sophie had only decided to travel at the last minute, which would have made planning the crime extremely difficult. What's more, both Daniel and the Bouniols confirmed that Sophie had never previously travelled to Toormore on her own. With Alfie Lyons and Shirley Foster at home most of the time, how would this French person have managed to scout out such a remote location without raising suspicion? Finally, what kind of hired killer would roll up at the home of his target without a weapon and then cast his eyes on the ground to find something – a piece of slate, a concrete cavity block – that might do the job? What kind of hit man would improvise the whole thing? None of this made any sense.

This left Bruno Carbonnet, the painter who had accompanied Sophie to Toormore on several occasions and with whom, it turned out, she had had an affair while she was married to Daniel. Carbonnet was the man who Sophie had implied in a conversation to her housekeeper Josephine Hellen that she was happy to see the back of. Various members of Sophie's circle had provided the police in France – and through them, the Guards in Ireland – with information about Carbonnet, some details of which were later reported in the French press, attributed to a lover with the initial 'B'. Most alarmingly, 'B' had attempted to strangle Sophie one evening as she left her office. When Sophie broke up with him, he cut up one of his canvases into shreds and sent the pieces to her in the mail. Another time, he was said to have hammered nails into her front door. One evening, Carbonnet and Sophie were returning to her apartment together. They got out of the lift and, without saying a word, Carbonnet allegedly pulled Sophie towards him in a very rough manner and then silently let her go. Sophie confided the episode to one of her cousins, adding that Carbonnet's behaviour scared her. For his part, the cousin found Carbonnet pleasant, and an interesting man to chat with.

French police assisted their Irish counterparts by paying Bruno Carbonnet a visit at his home on the outskirts of Le Havre on 28th December 1996. Carbonnet told the investigators that he had met Sophie at a painting workshop in Paris in 1992. *Madame Toscan du Plantier and I had an intimate friendship in the years 1992 and 1993… Our affair was secret and discreet but I think Monsieur Toscan du Plantier knew about it.* The last time he went to Ireland with Sophie was in the summer of 1993; Sophie put a final stop to the affair at Christmas of the same year *without any warning* [which] *was very difficult for me.* However, Carbonnet called Sophie in early December 1996 to see if she would lend him one of his paintings, which she owned, for an exhibition the following month, January. Carbonnet said that Sophie had agreed to his request and said she would deliver the painting herself in time for the opening night. This was confirmed by an entry in Sophie's diary – 'Opening reception, B., 8th January'. Carbonnet refused to give interviews to French journalists, who were curious about a possible suspect close to home. He was more forthcoming with the French police. *Sophie was secretive*, said Carbonnet. *She was someone who was tough and fragile at the same time… Sophie was a woman of many facets.*

Bruno Carbonnet could not have been the man who came to

Sophie's whitewashed house and murdered her. His credit card receipts and an appointment with a telephone company technician proved he was in France at the time.

The Guards were becoming confident of their case against Ian Bailey. First, he had had scratches on his hands and forearms that looked like the scratches from briars that had been seen on Sophie's dead body. Second, his movements on the night of the murder were unclear. Third, he appeared to know a lot about the injuries sustained by Sophie for someone who claimed he had nothing to do with the crime. Fourth, he had a history of violence against his partner, Jules Thomas. There had been the assault in May 1996 that had come to the attention of the Guards, and Bailey had subjected his partner to another violent beating in 1993. Now there were two other factors. A witness had come forward saying she saw Bailey in a long black coat stumbling by the side of the Schull-Goleen road at some time after 3am on the night of the murder. Two other witnesses had also approached the Guards with remarkable testimonies. Ian Bailey, they said, had appeared to confess to the killing to them.

It was hardly a surprise when a Garda vehicle drew up at the Bailey-Thomas residence at the Prairie. It was 9:25am on Monday, 10th February 1997. Three Guards got out. They had some questions for Bailey about his movements on the Saturday night before the murder, December 21st, and the night of the murder itself, Sunday into Monday.

There had been another issue with Bailey's stated movements in the period before the murder. Bailey had previously told the Guards that he had slept at the cottage at the Prairie on the Saturday night, meaning the night before he cut the Christmas tree and slaughtered the turkeys. He now said that this was not the case. He had been out drinking in Schull with Thomas, who drove home without him.

How did you discover your mistake about the Saturday night?

I pieced my thoughts together and it came back to me that I had stayed in Mark Murphy's house that night.

There had been several other people in Mark Murphy's house

in Schull on the Saturday night, including his mother, Patricia, and her partner. They had been up chatting until about 2am. Bailey had slept downstairs on the sofa.

Did you leave Mark's house at any time during the night or early morning?

Bailey replied that he had not left Mark Murphy's house during the night or early morning. Murphy had given him a lift to the Prairie at about 12:30pm and the Sunday afternoon was taken up with preparations for Christmas – slaughtering the turkeys and cutting the Christmas tree. Bailey, Thomas and Thomas's daughters – Saffron, Virginia and Fenella – then had supper. Bailey recalled they ate salmon. In the evening, Saffron and Virginia, who were 24 and 21 respectively, went out for the evening. In fact, they were all out, apart from Fenella, who was 14 and went to bed early as she had a cold. Bailey said that he and Jules left the cottage at about 9pm and came home via Hunt's Hill after their night out. Saffron and Virginia were still out when Bailey and Thomas got back.

And then what did Bailey do?

I slept with Jules and did not leave the house.

Bailey said that he got up at about 9:30am and made Jules a cup of coffee. He only left the house after Eddie Cassidy called from the offices of the *Examiner*.

Why have you now got such a good recollection?

Bailey replied that *I have been thinking a lot about the whole thing.*

One of the Guards, Detective John Culligan, read Bailey his rights. The situation was getting more serious. Bailey was being arrested on suspicion of murdering Sophie Toscan du Plantier. The Guards recalled Bailey saying: "I am shocked and horrified by this". They gave him time to put on a fresh pair of boots and brush his teeth. Bailey asked if he could have a word with Jules Thomas. According to Detective Culligan, Thomas came over to the rear window of the patrol car, next to where Bailey was sitting. The car was about to speed off to the Garda station at Bandon, 50 miles away, where Bailey was to be questioned. Bailey reminded Thomas about a phone bill that needed paying that day. Jules Thomas put her hand through the open window, and grabbed Bailey's arm. Thomas said to him: "Remember they have nothing on you and I will swear to that in court, and I love you, I love you."

"Remember they have nothing."

Chapter 5

"I DID IT"

Marie Farrell, a smallish, red-haired woman in her early thirties, was the owner and operator of Tara Fashions, the shop on Main Street in Schull. Farrell, together with her husband Chris, also owned and ran an ice-cream parlour on the same stretch of Main Street, and sold clothes, some of which they sewed up at home, at a market stall in Cork City. The Farrells had five children – four boys and a girl after whom the knitwear shop was named.

Between 2pm and 3pm on Saturday, 21st December 1996, Farrell was in her shop and noticed a sallow-skinned man wearing a beret and a long black coat – neither of these common items of clothing for men in rural County Cork – on the other side of Main Street. He was short-haired, scruffy and "weird-looking". He appeared to Farrell to be loitering, and remained in approximately the same position for about 10 minutes. Farrell did not recognise the man. At about 3pm, an elegant, foreign woman entered the shop and had a look around. "If you need any help, just let me know," Farrell said to her. Farrell's first recollection was that the woman had purchased a sweater. She later checked the credit card slips and realised that someone else had bought it. However, she was certain that the elegant, foreign woman browsing in her shop was the murdered Sophie – she had seen her picture on the TV news – and she was equally sure that there had been a man loitering outside the shop at approximately the same time. Funnily enough, Farrell saw the same man the following day. She was driving into Cork on the Sunday morning, 22nd December, past a place called Airhill, on the western side of Schull, and the man in the long black coat was there. It was strange because, although he was on the other side of the road and she was driving in the opposite direction, it looked like he was trying to thumb a lift from her.

Farrell called the Guards and made a statement on 27th December 1996. Initially she thought the man she had seen was of average height – she estimated about 5 feet 8 inches – but she revised her estimate of the man's height to 5 feet 10 inches, at the suggestion of a Guard. He pointed out that, from the perspective of where she had been standing in her shop, a man on the other side of Main Street would appear slightly shorter than was in fact the case. The next time she saw the man in the long black coat was on 17th January 1997 when she spotted him in the centre of Schull. She notified the Guards straight away. When they came, they knew immediately who it was: Ian Bailey.

In early January, the Guards had used the *Crimeline* TV programme on RTÉ, the Irish state broadcaster, to appeal for information from the public. This was standard practice in a murder investigation with few concrete lines of enquiry. A phone number flashed on the screen, and the Guards said that any leads received through that channel would be treated in confidence. A woman calling herself 'Fiona' phoned the number twice to say that she had information that might be important – she claimed to have seen a man behaving suspiciously near the crime scene on the night of the murder. Both these calls were made from public payphones, which meant identifying the caller was very difficult. The third time 'Fiona' called, she made it easier for the Guards, by error or perhaps on purpose. She called from her landline at home. The Guards traced the call to the house of none other than Marie Farrell. Detective Jim Fitzgerald, Garda Jim Slattery and Garda Kevin Kelleher went to speak with Farrell on 28th January. According to their memo of the meeting, Farrell made it clear that her evidence was delicate.

She said her husband was unaware that, on the night of the murder, she had taken a ride out in the direction of Goleen with an old flame.

I practically lived with this man one time and Chris [Farrell] *and myself have had rows over him... As we were driving towards Sylvia Connell's place on the Goleen Road I saw a man with a long black coat... I now know this man to be Ian Bailey from Schull. The time was about 3am. He appeared to be stumbling forward on the road and had his hands up on top of his head... I am in an awful state since and I could not tell Chris, and the person with me is also married and he is very worried. I cannot go to Court on this, you understand yourselves my position.*

Marie Farrell's testimony was the breakthrough the Guards were looking for. Farrell went with the Guards to the precise spot where she had seen Bailey. She had been driving the vehicle and she had her headlights on full beam when the man in the long, black coat came into view. Sylvia Connell had a shop on the road by the shore, which had initially given Farrell an approximate idea of the location, but the closest feature you would see on a map was Kealfadda Bridge, a short concrete slab over the Kealfadda stream, with a low barrier on either side. This was how Kealfadda Bridge entered the topography of the Sophie Toscan du Plantier murder case. To Irish-speaking locals, An Caol Fada, the name of the stream, meant 'the long ravine' but it also evoked the expression *nuair a bheireann an caol ort* – 'to find oneself in a tight spot'.

At any event, one thing did not seem to square. Ian Bailey was 6 feet 4 inches tall. Meanwhile, Farrell estimated that the man she saw outside her shop when Sophie was around, and again at Airhill, was between 5 feet 8 inches and 5 feet 10 inches. How could the same man have grown six or more inches in under 24 hours? It seemed preposterous. In a new statement given to Garda Kelleher, Farrell reconsidered her Main Street-Airhill sightings: *He was very tall, I could not say in measurements.*

***

The significance of Kealfadda Bridge was that it was at the southern end of the Kealfadda Road that led up to Sophie's house. Looking at a map, you could think of it as a triangle. A Guard reported that it was 1.6 miles from Sophie's house to Kealfadda Bridge, and he had walked the route in 25 minutes. If you carried on walking uphill from Kealfadda Bridge to the Bailey-Thomas residence at the Prairie by the shortest route by road, it was 2.4 miles. It took the Guard – presumably a man fast on his feet – 40 minutes to walk this stretch. Meanwhile, the shortest route from the Prairie to Sophie's place was directly over the moor. There was no track and not even a rough footpath. The distance was again precisely 2.4 miles. Hiking it took a brisk 40 minutes, as well. That meant that Bailey could have walked over the moor, killed Sophie, and returned home via Kealfadda Bridge, preferring the paved route for reasons unknown, in two hours or a little more.

In the interview room at Bandon Garda station, Bailey was given a mug of tea. The Guards had some questions about Bailey's alleged oddball behaviour:

Do you recall being out late at night with nothing on you but jocks and a hat in the rain?

That did not happen.

What do you say about you being out late at night shouting and singing, and on another occasion you tried to fly?

I have a reputation for being eccentric.

The Guards had some more relevant cards up their sleeves. They told Bailey that there were witnesses saying he had already admitted the murder to them.

Bailey had received his marching orders from a gig he'd got at the *Sunday Tribune* after a phone conversation with the news editor,

Helen Callanan. Callanan, who was based in Dublin, needed a stringer to cover the breaking story about Sophie's murder. She obtained Bailey's phone number and she spoke with him for the first time on Thursday, 26th December. The pair spoke each week, on a Thursday or Friday, over the course of five weeks, to see what story on the Sophie case the *Tribune* could run the following weekend. In the course of their conversations, Bailey told Callanan that he had been questioned by the Guards *and that he had spoken to Sophie before she was murdered, that is, he had met her before.*

On Thursday, 30th January, Callanan told Bailey that she had heard rumours that he might be a suspect. Was he aware of that? Callanan told the Guards that Bailey was keen to know where the rumour was coming from. She refused to give him a name. Bailey called Callanan on Saturday, 1st February and asked her again about the source of the rumour. Again, Callanan refused to give Bailey a name *and then he said, "Yes, I did it. I killed her to resurrect my career as a journalist".*

The Guards at Bandon asked Bailey if he had told Helen Callanan that he had killed Sophie. Bailey replied: *I said to her as a joke that I was the murderer and that I did it to further my career.*

There was also an incident with a boy named Malachi Reed. Malachi went to school with Fenella, Jules Thomas's daughter, and lived with his mother close to Bailey's cottage at the Prairie. On the Mizen, it was common for parents to give their neighbours' children a lift home – everyone helped everyone else in the same way. On 4th February 1997, a Tuesday, Malachi had stayed on in Schull with some friends after school. He spotted Ian Bailey on Main Street. *I asked him for a lift home as I knew he was going my way. Ian was rough-looking but other than that there was nothing unusual about him.*

Bailey told Malachi that he had a couple of errands to run, and said that he would meet him later outside a pub. When they set off, Malachi was the only passenger. Malachi told the Guards that Bailey started the engine of his white Ford Fiesta and they started talking right away. Malachi thought Bailey looked *anxious, preoccupied with himself, holding his head and cursing to himself.* Malachi asked Bailey how his work was going. Bailey replied that it was going fine *until I went up there one night with a rock and bashed her fucking brains in.* Malachi said he got a shock when he heard Bailey say that – it was immediately clear to the boy that the reference was to the murder of the Frenchwoman, there was no doubt about it. A cold shiver ran down Malachi's spine. He thought it wise to say nothing for a few minutes, until conversation resumed in a more conventional manner. Bailey asked Malachi how things were going at school and, when Malachi said that his English classes were a bit of a problem, Bailey gave him a couple of book recommendations.

At Bandon Garda station, the Guards took turns at questioning Bailey. Detective Superintendent Dermot Dwyer – the recipient of a couple of Bailey's possibly stale mince pies – took over. Dwyer asked Bailey if he had talked to anyone about the murder, specifically on the Tuesday of the previous week – the date he had given Malachi a lift home. The record of the arrest, signed by Bailey and Dwyer reads: *He did not answer.*

Dwyer: *Did you give anyone a lift home that night?*

Bailey: *Yes, a young boy who lives up the Prairie*

Did you know Sophie?

I saw her once. I was gardening up at Alfie's last year or the year before.

What did she look like?

To my recollection, she was plain.

Did you see her on the Saturday before the murder?

No.

Weren't you in Schull that afternoon?

I was.

What were you wearing?

A long black coat, I think.

Dwyer said to Bailey that the Guards had evidence that he was involved in Sophie's murder. They had witnesses who had seen him at about 3:15am near Kealfadda Bridge. The Detective Superintendent *urged* [Bailey] *to tell the truth.*

These people are mistaken, said Bailey. *I was in bed.*

One developing issue for Ian Bailey was that, half an hour after his arrest, Jules Thomas had also been detained by the Guards on suspicion of covering up the murder of Sophie. What was striking to the Guards was that Thomas's recollection of the night of the murder was quite different to Bailey's. In another room at Bandon Garda station, Thomas had already told the Guards that her partner had got out of bed on the night of the murder and, when she saw him the following morning, he had a mark on his forehead.

The Guards let Ian Bailey know that Thomas was answering their questions at that very moment. Bailey's account of the night in question began to change: *We got home between one and two o'clock and went to bed. I had stopped on my way home at Hunt's Hill and looked at the moon.* He said that at that moment he had a *premonition that something was going to happen.* In the interview room, Bailey suddenly appeared to clam up about his premonition on that cold moonlit night: *I won't put it any further, I don't want to.*

Then came this:

Some time after going to bed, I got up. I did a bit of writing in the kitchen. I then went down to the studio, I am not sure what time it was, but it was dark.

The 'studio' was a small house that Thomas owned about 150 yards from the cottage. For a while, she had used it to paint large canvases. Bailey had spent time living there in the earlier days of the couple's relationship, before he moved into the cottage and became, in Thomas's words, "the man about the house". Bailey sometimes wrote in the studio, but it was sparsely furnished and it was unheated.

The Guards were wondering about two things. First, why would someone leave a warm home on a freezing winter night in hours of darkness to write in an equally freezing and much less comfortable space? Also, the admission that he had twice left the bed he shared with Thomas on the night of the murder – initially he went to the kitchen to write, and on the second occasion he left the cottage altogether to go to the studio – meant that Bailey's alibi was not watertight after all. In fact, it had two significant holes in it. It was even faintly absurd. From that day on, there would never be another suspect in the murder of Sophie Toscan du Plantier. When Dermot Dwyer wound up his session with Bailey, he added to Bailey's statement the words: *Denied repeatedly committing the murder.* The Guards released Bailey without bringing charges.

***

In 1997 and 1998, one-time friends, or drinking buddies, of Ian Bailey described other alleged confessions in evidence to the Guards. Bailey responded by saying he had been misunderstood, or simply claimed these accounts never happened.

In January 1998, Bailey was arrested for a second time, The Guards had gathered more witness statements by then – Marie Farrell's evidence had been fleshed out in particular – and the file had benefited from the input of a small detachment of serious crime officers from Dublin, but the Garda case remained essentially the same. Gallingly, the Guards had not managed to find any of the killer's DNA at the scene, despite the copious amounts of blood on the ground and the clear evidence of a struggle, albeit one that was likely brief. Fresh DNA tests carried out in a laboratory in the UK yielded no new clues.

At his second arrest, Bailey maintained his innocence. There was no forensic evidence against him whatsoever. It was also counter-intuitive that a suspect spotted wearing a long coat should have sustained scratches on his forearms. Had Bailey been the murderer, he surely would have needed to take off the coat before the crime was committed. For a second time, no charges were brought. Under the rules in force, if the Guards arrested Bailey a third time on suspicion of committing the same offence, they would need to charge him. The case file was submitted to the Office of the Irish Director of Public Prosecutions, the DPP, in February 1998.

However, the DPP was unconvinced by the Garda case against Ian Bailey, and refused to endorse a prosecution. An updated case file was submitted in 2001, but again the DPP rejected the Garda case against Bailey.

In 2003, Bailey tried to act on the front foot by suing eight Irish and British newspapers for libel at the Circuit Court in Cork. Bailey's argument was that, as a direct result of their reporting, he had been branded a "murderer" on the Mizen, and his life had been made a "nightmare". Bailey also claimed he had cooperated with several journalists working for those titles, only because they said they would portray him sympathetically in their stories. In any case, the two-week hearing ended catastrophically for Bailey. The judge ruled that none of the newspapers had defamed Bailey except where a couple of them had suggested that Bailey had been violent towards his ex-wife (he had thrown objects around the marital home, but had not physically assaulted her). At the beginning of the proceedings, Bailey had announced to the courtroom that, "I am here to prove my innocence", but he was left with a huge bill for costs – which he could not pay, he had no assets or savings to speak of. Then there were the words of the judge ringing in his ears: Ian Bailey was a "violent man" who "likes a certain amount of notoriety, likes to be in the limelight".

There had been developments in France. As the immediate family of the victim, the Bouniols, together with Daniel Toscan du Plantier, had secured the status of *partie civile* – the 'private party' to the investigation. This meant that the French state had to keep Daniel and the Bouniols abreast of any progress. Since France was one of very few countries claiming unlimited jurisdiction in the case of serious crimes against its citizens overseas, a criminal investigation could be set up there. In 2007, and despairing of the position of the DPP, Sophie's family and supporters set up a Justice Committee to press Ireland or France to secure a prosecution in the case. The Sophie Justice Committee was headed by Jean-Pierre Gazeau, a physics professor who was a younger brother of Marguerite

Bouniol, and a retired engineer called Jean-Antoine Bloc, a friend of the Bouniol family.

However, the DPP did not budge. It seemed that the only chance Sophie's family had of seeing Bailey in the dock was via the French criminal justice system. In fact, a French investigation into Sophie's killing was ultimately set up: in 2010, France tried to place the loosest of nooses around Bailey's neck by issuing a European Arrest Warrant. France wanted to have Bailey shipped over for questioning, French-style. The European Arrest Warrant mechanism was supposed to ensure that someone wanted for arrest in any signatory country – all of the member states of the European Union were signatories – would be delivered to the country issuing the warrant without hindrance. France's application was processed by the Irish State, and endorsed by a judge. However, Bailey appealed, and the warrant was ultimately rejected by the Irish Supreme Court, giving him a reprieve.

Ireland's Supreme Court had baulked at another country attempting to prosecute someone for a crime committed on Irish territory for which its own prosecution body had decided not to hold a trial. Some Irish commentators talked unhappily about a lingering sense of 'colonialism' on the part of the French Republic, criticising the perception that the French criminal justice system felt it was entitled to barge into the internal affairs of another nation. With Bailey's victory in the Supreme Court, it looked as if the advantage was back with him.

In 2011, a team of Paris-based detectives visited Ireland, interviewing a number of witnesses. In other countries – the United Kingdom or Germany, for example – such a development would have been difficult to imagine. At the least, it seemed odd that France, another country, could run its own parallel investigation on Irish soil and with official support and approval from the Irish authorities.

However, the upshot of the European Arrest Warrant was that Bailey could not travel outside Ireland – if he crossed the border into

Northern Ireland, for instance, or took a ferry to Britain, he risked arrest, since the warrant could still be served in the UK. The Justice Committee set up by Sophie's family had been successful in keeping the case in the public eye in France, but another piece of litigation was winding its way across the desks of the civil courts system in Ireland. Bailey had filed a complaint against the Irish police and the Irish state for wrongful arrest and conspiracy. Bailey was suing because he claimed the Guards had stitched him up for a crime he did not commit. Proceedings were due to open in November 2014, and there was a lot at stake. If Bailey were to win in Dublin, it could well be a fatal blow for French hopes of prosecuting him.

***

In February 1998, Daniel Toscan du Plantier gave the French newspaper *Le Figaro* his first interview on the subject of his wife's murder. *I haven't kept my silence out of indifference*, he said. *Sophie would have hated me speaking to the press.* This was no doubt true: in the early part of their marriage, Daniel had invited a glossy magazine into his Paris mansion to do a lavish photo feature on him and his family life. Sophie refused point-blank to participate. The nature of Sophie's death was another aspect. *A murder is not like a car accident. It's like the person died twice, there's the fact of the fatality, but on top of that, someone wanted to kill her. You know that the murderer is still out there somewhere.*

According to Daniel, the Guards told him about Ian Bailey's first arrest as soon as it happened. *"We've got him* [said the Guards], *he's in the car." I never asked for a name if they couldn't prove he did it.* Daniel thought the situation was almost incredible. *My criticism is that they* [the Guards] *gave us a name in a way that lacked all seriousness, because if there is one chance in a hundred that he's innocent, it would be shocking.* Bailey's new-found fame hurt Daniel terribly, but it also made him think. Bailey had made an explicit choice. *It's amazing but he has a new job title: 'I am not the murderer of Sophie Toscan du Plantier'. He has made an asset out of it. Nobody had ever heard of him before and now he pops up frequently in the media. Even people in Paris ask me what he's up to. It strikes me that wanting to talk so much stokes the fires of suspicion. If it had been me, and I was innocent, I would have got out of there quickly, changed my name, found a new life for myself.* Still, Daniel could not quite bring himself to say to the interviewer that Ian Bailey had murdered his wife. Bailey was only the suspect – although he was the prime suspect, and nobody else was in the frame.

Daniel's view of the motive for the killing hardly wavered over the years. The crime was not premeditated, he thought. The murderer may well have gone to her house with a view of seducing her. She turned him down, and there was a struggle. Sophie was never afraid of anything, and she tended to speak her mind. She walked around alone at night. She would take out cash from the ATM in Paris at one in the morning. She would go to bed without bothering to lower the shutters. That night, Sophie was attacked with extreme violence, the sort of violence you never imagine you would see. Her attacker wanted sex and *she must have told him exactly what she thought… he killed her to shut her up.*

In the summer of 1998, Daniel married for the fourth time. His bride, Melita Nikolic, had been a model and, later, a stewardess at the Cannes Film Festival. She subsequently joined UniFrance, where Daniel had met her, as he had met Sophie a decade earlier. The couple welcomed two children into the world, a girl and a boy.

Daniel was attending the Berlin Film Festival in February 2003, about to enter the dining room of a big hotel for a working lunch. He collapsed and an ambulance was called. He died there and then, at the age of 61.

Melita buried her husband in the Père-Lachaise cemetery in Paris. That left Sophie resting alone, so to speak, in her grave at the church near Daniel's country house in Ambax, near Toulouse, the same church where the priest had so upset the Bouniols during Sophie's funeral with his untimely discourse on cinema. The Bouniols decided to have Sophie's coffin exhumed and they buried her for a second time in the family plot in a country churchyard close to their house in Combret, in the Lozère, the austere uplands that Sophie's parents called home.

In 2008, the dark earth that covered the coffin of Sophie Toscan du Plantier was broken again. This time, there was a police cordon and the operation took place in the dead of a summer's night. The Bouniols stayed away. The French investigating magistrate in Paris in charge of Sophie's case had requested a new forensic study of her remains. The hope was that this new study would benefit from the most recent advances in DNA harvesting.

Disappointingly, it yielded no new clues at all.

Chapter 6

TO DUBLIN

On a moist, grey early morning in November 2014, I boarded a plane bound for Dublin at Brussels Airport. My trip was a punt, pure and simple. I had lost track of developments in the Sophie Toscan du Plantier murder case, but as soon as I had heard that Ian Bailey's civil action against the Guards and the Irish state was starting, I booked my flight and a hotel. Next, I scrambled to put a file together – newspaper articles, a book on the case written by an Irish journalist, published in 2002, and John Montague's first-person piece in *The New Yorker* that had initially sparked my interest.

I made a few bullet-points on a sheet of paper: *No forensic evidence incriminating Bailey, no alibi, Bailey arrested twice but never charged, French investigation ongoing, star witness out of the picture?* I underlined the words: *No motive* and *only circumstantial evidence*. I was pretty much winging it.

My plane banked and emerged through scattered clouds into bright sunlight. I thought about the angle I could take in the feature story I would try selling to a newspaper or a magazine: How Bailey had got himself into a dire mess, and how he pulled himself out of it. The Englishman abroad who offered a stiff upper lip in the face of adversity. A man who had paid for his errors and his bad temper, and had won back the woman he loved. A story about a David – but an older man with a history of violence, so the parallel was not perfect, I had to admit it – taking on a Goliath, which was the entire machinery of a western European state. As for the weighty Garda file, it was "two thousand pages of rumours," in Bailey's memorable phrase.

There was now something else in the mix. In early 1997, Marie Farrell had told the Guards she had seen Ian Bailey at Kealfadda Bridge on the night of the murder. She was a big plank – the *main* plank – of the Garda case against Bailey. But in a dramatic television interview in 2005, she had recanted. She told the interviewer that key parts of her testimony were simply not true. The man she had seen was not Ian Bailey, she claimed. Back in 1997, Farrell had also been on record saying that Bailey had tried to pressurise her into withdrawing her evidence. She had even gone to the trouble of getting a solicitor to write Bailey a letter warning him to stop intimidating her. Bailey, she now said, had done nothing of the sort, and she had been coerced by the Guards into putting Bailey in the frame for Sophie's murder. Her conscience had told her to set the record straight. She now deeply regretted the wrongs done to Ian Bailey.

Farrell had switched camps; she was going to appear in the Dublin courthouse as a witness for Bailey, the plaintiff. How would this affect the outcome of the action?

***

Tom Creed, Ian Bailey's lead barrister, had opened his client's case against An Garda Síochána, the Irish police force, and the Irish state, by listing the ways that the Guards were at fault in their investigation of Ian Bailey in the aftermath of the murder of Sophie Toscan du Plantier. "Essentially," said Creed, addressing the jury, "it is a claim for damages for conspiracy for unlawful arrest, false imprisonment, assault, battery, trespass to the person, intentional infliction of emotional and psychological harm, harassment, intimidation, terrorising and oppressive behaviour, and breach of constitutional rights".

Creed paused for effect. "That is a big mouthful."

The gist of Bailey's case was that the Guards set about blaming him for a crime he had not committed and that they had conspired to manufacture evidence against him, with a view to convincing the Director of Public Prosecutions to launch a prosecution. Creed said that over the past 18 years the Guards had "destroyed" Bailey's life, and the same "corrupt evidence", as he put it, had been used by the French to try to get Bailey sent to France under a European Arrest Warrant. Creed also read out a letter that Bailey's partner, Jules Thomas, had sent to the Director of Public Prosecutions, James Hamilton, in 2011. Thomas wrote: *I am making an appeal to you to charge Ian Bailey so that he can receive a fair trial in Ireland so that we can be put out of living in this mental torture for any longer.* The deputy director replied to Thomas saying that *It would not be appropriate for the Director to institute a prosecution for the reasons put forward by you… the Director can prosecute only where he is satisfied that there is sufficient evidence to justify a prosecution.*

This was one of the aspects of the case that made it so peculiar. Marguerite Bouniol had petitioned DPP Hamilton for precisely the same thing. Both Sophie's mother and Bailey's partner were at least in agreement on this: they both wanted a prosecution on Irish soil.

Many suspects would surely run a mile from a trial where the result could be a very long stretch in prison, but here was someone trying – *begging*, even – to get the chance to be put in the dock and forced to argue his way out of a murder charge. I had wondered how desperate Bailey must have become to ask his partner to pen such a letter. But perhaps it had nothing to do with desperation. Maybe Bailey was so confident that he could not imagine failing. Then again, he might equally well be entirely innocent of killing Sophie Toscan du Plantier and, viewed through this prism, petitioning the public prosecutor for a trial was the honourable course of action of a man apparently so comprehensively framed by the Irish cops.

As I rushed from my plane to see Bailey take the stand at Dublin's High Court, I saw the front pages of a couple of newspapers. They had prominent photos of a dapper Bailey in a pin-striped suit, his neat grey hair combed back. His partner, Jules Thomas, was by his side. She was tall and slim, lips pursed, looking straight ahead. Rarely had a civil action in Ireland made the headlines in this way. Then again, the vicious murder that lurked behind the proceedings meant this was no ordinary case.

I took a place on the crammed press bench. There was a low hum of expectation in the room. We were waiting for the day's session to begin, waiting for Ian Bailey to take the stand. Next to me was an older man whose face I recognised. My neighbour was former Chief Superintendent Dermot Dwyer, the senior Guard who had led the investigation against Ian Bailey. Dwyer was holding a rolled-up magazine. He showed it to me. "Have you read this?" Dwyer asked. I told him I had. It was a much-thumbed copy of *The New Yorker*, open at the article by John Montague that had sparked my interest in the case.

The judge, a soft-spoken, balding man named John Hedigan, had warned both sides that the purpose of the hearing was not to discuss whether Ian Bailey had killed Sophie Toscan du Plantier. The proceedings were "not about the guilt or innocence of Mr Bailey".

Right, I thought, and the Pope is not a Catholic.

The barrister for the defence was a youngish, dark-haired jurist named Luán Ó Braonáin. The previous day, Ó Braonáin had described a series of newspaper and magazine features with Bailey's byline, written while he was still working in England. These seemed intended to bring Bailey down a peg – stories with corny alliteration (*Butter Bites Back* by Ian Bailey) or terrible puns (*A Shaw Thing for Next Year's Race* about a racing driver called Shaw). Bailey answered Ó Braonáin's questions in a calm, measured tone. The two men looked well matched. Bailey was coming across as a journalist who had rarely found the big story, but he had kept plugging away at his chosen career. Many of us do the same, whatever job we have. We cannot all be super-successful. Ó Braonáin was pin-sharp, but his depiction of Bailey's journeyman career as a newspaperman cast Bailey as an underdog. I wondered how this would play out with the jury.

Ó Braonáin turned to the events of 23rd December 1996, and the call from Eddie Cassidy of the *Examiner* at 1:40pm that prompted Bailey to drive over to Sophie Toscan du Plantier's house. This phone call was a significant part of the case against Bailey, and he had already given his account of the call in court to his own barrister a couple of days earlier.

Ó Braonáin reminded Bailey that, when he was giving his own evidence, he had said the following to his barrister regarding the call from Eddie Cassidy: "I'm not absolutely sure a hundred percent that he said French but I have a recollection, a very strong recollection, that he said French."

Bailey insisted that he thought Eddie Cassidy had said that the body was of a Frenchwoman. Ó Braonáin reminded Bailey that under oath at the libel hearing in Cork in 2003 he had said that Cassidy had told him the dead woman was foreign, but that Cassidy had not mentioned her nationality.

Ó Braonáin: "You have, on some occasions, said that Mr Cassidy said one thing and you have, on other occasions, said that Mr Cassidy said something else. Isn't that right?"

Bailey: "Um, there may be a variance."

Ó Braonáin continued: "The identification of the deceased as French, as opposed to just a foreign national, she could have been Dutch, she could have been English, she could have been German, any of these things, but identifying her as French was an important piece of information. Isn't that right?"

Bailey was forced to agree, but he added that the nationality of the dead woman was given out as French on a radio news bulletin at 2pm, and Cassidy had given him a rough idea of where the incident had taken place. Bailey and his partner, Jules Thomas, appeared to have driven in the direction of Sophie's house almost immediately after hearing the breaking news about the dead body. On the way, they saw Shirley Foster – the woman who had discovered the corpse earlier that morning – driving in the opposite direction, and Foster and Bailey exchanged a brief word. Bailey knew that a Frenchwoman lived there (Alfie Lyons was on record as saying he was "ninety percent sure" he had introduced Bailey to Sophie) but Bailey told the court he was "a thousand percent sure" that he had never been introduced to the victim. The rampant inflation in Bailey's certainty rather summed up his tongue-in-cheek self-confidence.

I noted the questions and replies. What happened on the morning of 23rd December 1996 in the Bailey-Thomas household was vital – who said what, and when; and who went where, and when. There were a number of phone calls to photographers and a neighbour, too. There was a lingering suggestion that the phone call from Eddie Cassidy at 1:40pm was not the first Bailey had known about the murder. There was no getting away from it – this was a complicated story.

Shirley Foster, the woman who had discovered the body, was another case in point. Foster's recollection of her brief conversation with Bailey near the entrance of the lane leading up the valley to Toormore was very much at odds with Bailey's version of the exchange. I knew that several local witnesses had taken the stand in Cork at Bailey's libel hearing in 2003 and had disputed Bailey's recollection of events on the day of the murder in particular. I would need to get hold of the Cork transcripts for a better understanding. I would have to speak with the witnesses. This was not just a cold case, it was like one of those Russian dolls you take apart, and you find another doll inside. To make matters worse, each doll was coated with the dust of time. It was a well-worn cliché, but that was how I pictured it.

Bailey recounted how he had gone to the post office to find out the name of the dead woman.

"I'm not sure how it's pronounced," Bailey said. "I think it is

B. O. U. N. O. I. L. or something like that." My ears perked up. That seemed odd. After 18 years, could it really be true that Bailey did not know the correct spelling of Sophie's maiden name, the name she used in Ireland? He had worked as a fixer with French journalists. The name surely would have come up in conversation. They would have mentioned it. Bouniol was a name that had hardly been out of the newspapers, since that was what Sophie's parents were called, and it was the name the victim used in Ireland. The case as a whole, and the finger of suspicion pointed firmly in his direction, had ruined his life, Bailey maintained. Of all foreign names, then, this was the one Bailey should surely have known how to pronounce.

There was palpable tension in the exchanges between Ó Braonáin and Bailey. When the barrister examined Bailey's history of beating up Jules Thomas, I felt he scored a direct hit. Bailey commented that an attack on Thomas in 2001 – it earned him a suspended prison sentence – was an act of "disgraceful irresponsibility," Ó Braonáin said, quick as a flash, "No, Mr Bailey, disgraceful *violence*".

Bailey's choice of the word 'irresponsibility' should have set a warning light flashing, thinking back. Indeed, much of what Bailey said that morning seemed to be an attempt to downplay his domestic violence – other people were doing it too; it was a sort of accident ("I hit her, not intentionally"); it all happened a long time ago; or he simply couldn't remember the details of the attacks when Ó Braonáin asked him to describe them. Bailey even suggested that Jules Thomas was at fault for starting the arguments.

The judge adjourned the session for lunch. Some journalists hurried off to write their copy. The pensioners in the public gallery trooped out of the courtroom, a few of them whispering animatedly with expressions of exaggerated, pantomime horror. It appeared to me that they were having a hard time believing that Bailey's assaults on his partner were six of one and half a dozen of the other, so to speak. Not everyone appeared so caught up in the proceedings:

a couple of young women in tracksuits looked like they had been dozing.

At the other end of the press bench was a man in a t-shirt and a leather jacket fumbling for his mobile phone. I recognised him from television – it was BBC investigative reporter Donal MacIntyre. This was a man known for putting his heart and soul into his crime programmes. His most famous exploit was to infiltrate a group of football hooligans who followed Chelsea F.C. MacIntyre's *modus operandi* was to go undercover, with concealed cameras, secret microphones and the like, and he was determined. So determined in fact that to pass as a football hooligan he even got a Chelsea F.C. tattoo on his arm.

***

Ian Bailey, meanwhile, was known for being the reporter who ended up being accused of committing the crime he was covering. Bailey contributed to a range of titles in the aftermath of the murder, sometimes using the name 'Eoin' Bailey, a Gaelicised version of 'Ian', a variant of his name he sometimes used socially, as well. Whereas, in his earlier questioning about his journalism, Ó Braonáin had made Bailey seem like a hopeful battler in his chosen career, when he started to pick apart 'Eoin' Bailey's newspaper stories on the Sophie murder investigation, you sensed the barrister had the bit between his teeth.

Some of the most eye-catching stories were for the *Sunday Tribune* – the newspaper which had employed Bailey's services until its news editor Helen Callanan had the phone call with Bailey in which Bailey seemed to admit to committing the murder. Bailey's admission to Callanan – along with his comments on the crime to Malachi Reed, the schoolboy he gave a lift in his car to – had been key grounds for his first arrest.

The first *Sunday Tribune* article Ó Braonáin read out was dated 29th December 1996.

Detectives from Dublin and Cork City have been drafted to West Cork in the hunt for the brutal slayer who left the twice-married film producer battered and beaten only yards from her remote holiday retreat near Toormore, eight miles west of Schull. It has emerged that Ms du Plantier may have had a visitor late on Sunday evening – the last time she was known to be alive. There was some indication of a struggle in the house but no sign of forced entry. It is believed that Ms du Plantier fled by the back door, on which blood was found…

Ó Braonáin had already been through a number of pieces apparently penned by Bailey, specifically for the *Star*, where Bailey had suggested that his copy had been changed, or someone else had added material. Here, though, he confirmed that he had spoken with Josephine Hellen, Sophie's housekeeper, and Alfie Lyons, her neighbour, before writing the piece. It was Lyons who was first to spot the drops of blood on the back door after the killing, so that made sense.

Ó Braonáin held up a photocopy of Bailey's piece on the murder that came out in the *Tribune* on 29th December 1996. "Okay. Then it goes on to say:"

The evidence indicates that she was pursued down the rocky track from her home and killed by repeated blows to the back of the head.

"Where did that information come from?"

Bailey: "I think that was just generally what was circulating and what was being said."

"Where?"

"In various media."

Ó Braonáin moved on to the next *Sunday Tribune* piece with Bailey's byline, dated 5th January 1997. But Bailey had a problem with making out the print. It was small and without his reading glasses, he could not make it out. He said he would remedy the problem by the next day. "I must get a pair, I must get to Specsavers," he quipped, referencing a popular TV advert.

There were a few groans at Bailey's gag on the press bench. It seemed odd that he was making a joke in a case that had such huge implications for his future.

French police who have been conducting investigations on behalf of Irish Gardaí have requested further information from one French national who knew Ms du Plantier and who may have travelled to Ireland with her in the past.

Ó Braonáin: "Did you have contact with the French police to get that information?"

Bailey: "No, I didn't."

"So where did that come from?"

"I am not sure. I am sure that is not an adequate response, but I am not sure."

"Again, it seems to be pointing a finger of suspicion out of Ireland towards France, isn't that right?"

"Yes."

There are two main lines of investigation being followed – that the killer was a local who may have been known to the woman, or that he followed the dead woman from France.

Ó Braonáin: "What Guard told you about the two lines of inquiry?"

Bailey: "I don't think any Guard told me about that, I think that was…"

"Is that again just something that was obvious?"

"…a deduction from what had been out in other media."

Bailey confirmed that the Guards had held occasional press conferences on the Sophie murder investigation, but he had not attended any. He also had not contacted the Guards to find out when they were being scheduled. That seemed strange for someone reporting so extensively on the case. Ó Braonáin continued reading from his large pile of clippings.

Ms du Plantier was killed by a blow to the back of the head and then brutally battered. The cause of death was multiple fractures to the skull. Extensive searches of the area with metal detectors have so far failed to produce any sign of the weapon.

Ó Braonáin: "The information that she was killed by a blow to the back of the head and then brutally battered, how did you have that information?"

Bailey: "I am too sure [*sic*] that I did have that information, I think that was information that was just in... As I said to you, on the night of 23rd in Schull, for instance, everybody knew, don't ask me how they knew, but everybody knew she had been battered and a block or a brick had been dropped onto her head. That was common knowledge, common gossip."

The way Bailey said it sounded curious. But then, was it really surprising that the news of the specifics of the crime – physically how it was carried out – had moved swiftly across the Mizen? After all, there are plenty of events and occurrences even on our own doorsteps that we don't understand, and we accept them anyway. That was my reasoning that day.

The next Sunday, 12th January 1997, another news story penned by Ian Bailey appeared in the *Tribune*.

Daniel Toscan du Plantier is expected next week to visit the isolated cottage he bought with his wife six years ago... Gardaí have made no significant breakthrough in the hunt for her killer.

Ó Braonáin: "What was the basis for that information?"

Bailey: "The basis of that information would be self-evident, that they hadn't made any major breakthrough."

"Sorry, how was that self-evident?"

"Inasmuch as there was no new information coming out about any breakthrough. At this stage, where are we now, is it two weeks, or so, after the actual event and I am reporting that apparently there has been no significant breakthrough."

"Where is the word 'apparently' there? Did you have a Garda source who said to you: We haven't made any breakthrough?"

"No."

"So you had no factual information to the effect that there hadn't been a breakthrough, isn't that right?"

I looked around me. It was 3:50pm. Some of the journalists on the press bench with deadlines to meet had already left. They had missed the best bit, I thought. The sparring between the clean-cut Irish barrister and the older English poet and gardener was about to end for today. The word 'apparently' – the qualifier that had found its way out of Bailey's article – was stuck in my ear as I put my notebook into my briefcase.

Donal MacIntyre was a few feet away, putting away his phone.

"What do you make of it?" I asked him. We agreed it was one of the greatest mysteries, anywhere. MacIntyre had been to County Cork to dig around a bit. He had spoken with a few people. He was clearly as hooked as I was.

He asked me where I had flown in from and I told him, Brussels. That seemed to surprise him. I planned to write about the case, I explained. Firstly, I had to get my head around it, then I would see if there was a story I could tell. MacIntyre was going to do a documentary on the murder and had already started filming, but there was one tricky thing. We retired to a pub across the road from the courthouse to carry on our conversation.

The tricky thing, MacIntyre said, was getting the French family on board. Every project needed to explain who the victim was. You had to tell Sophie's story, too. That was the bit MacIntyre was missing. However, it was the bit I could do, since I spoke French. Much of the rest, of course, I was missing. I liked the sound of the arrangement that seemed to offer itself organically. I would approach the French family, the Bouniols, and see if they would agree to some interviews. In return, I would hang out on the set from time to time, and that was bound to give me insight into the story.

Deal done. We shook on it, there and then.

MacIntyre looked at his watch and realised he was needed at a shoot in a studio somewhere in town. The main thing was this: MacIntyre said he would be ramping up his Sophie Toscan du Plantier filming the following spring, so I would have to start talking with the Bouniols soon.

It was warm in the pub and MacIntyre had taken his jacket off. In a moment of banter with the bartender, I stole a look. Yes, it was still there, the Chelsea tattoo, half-covered by the arm of his t-shirt.

Chapter 7

SMOKE AND MIRRORS

The weather the next morning was foul. Justice Hedigan told the jury that they were probably better off in the courtroom than anywhere else. The jurors appeared unconvinced: for the most part, they stared blankly ahead. The public gallery was full once again. The court rose and the proceedings opened. Ian Bailey took the stand and the cross-examination continued.

Ó Braonáin paused before holding up a newspaper story I recognised. The layout and fonts looked old-fashioned, a reminder that we were discussing events that happened almost 18 years earlier. I had seen the story in a French TV documentary hosted by a roving crime journalist who kept his sunglasses glued to his face on even the murkiest Irish days. The documentary had featured an interview with Alain Spilliaert, the Bouniol family lawyer. Spilliaert had briefly pointed to a newspaper story titled *Pieced together – the final days of Sophie Toscan du Plantier*. A few paragraphs had been highlighted with a yellow marker pen. Spilliaert had remarked on camera that this piece in particular was highly suspicious.

The story had run in the *Sunday Tribune* on 19th January 1997. After this piece, Bailey would not write for the *Tribune* again. Now Ó

Braonáin was going to take the opportunity to quiz Bailey about it. "It seems to be under the byline of both yourself and Sophie Rieu?" Ó Braonáin asked.

"Yes, it is," Bailey replied. "Sophie Rieu was a freelance journalist working for the – a French speaking, a French national working for the *Sunday Tribune* and the news desk assigned her to work on the story from Dublin. She was liaising with me by telephone down in West Cork."

The story began:

Murdered French film-maker Sophie Toscan du Plantier experienced a deep sense of unexplainable dread only hours before her brutal slaying. The Frenchwoman confided in friends on the afternoon of Sunday, 22nd December that she had been engulfed in a feeling of unexplained terror. The next morning she was dead...

Bailey explained that the friends mentioned in the piece were Yvonne and Tomi Ungerer. "Yvonne Ungerer told me that Madame du Plantier had told her that while down at Three Castle Head she had experienced a deep sense of dread. Yvonne Ungerer told me that and I used that information in the story."

Ó Braonáin read out another section of the piece, referring to Sophie's arrival in Ireland on her final visit:

The Gardaí have studied video footage at Cork Airport...

"Was that information you got from the Gardaí?"

"How did I get that information? I think that was in the common domain."

"Okay. Was that information then that you think came from a press conference?"

"Did it come from a press conference? I don't know... It had definitely come out, the fact that there was video footage of her arriving at Cork Airport."

They [the Guards] *had pieced together much of the few days she spent at the house she bought with her husband in West Cork and are sure she had a guest on the night of her murder because there were two rinsed wine glasses on the draining board of her kitchen sink when her body was discovered outside.*

"Did you have information from the Gardaí that they were sure that she had had a guest that night?" Ó Braonáin asked.

Bailey: "No, and that wouldn't have been mine. I think that was Sophie Rieu's contribution and that would have been a bit of, shall we say, educated supposition."

"The presence of wine glasses on a draining board in a kitchen, who knows when they were put there?"

"Absolutely."

"So, how could one infer from that that there was a guest on the night of the murder?"

"You couldn't."

"Okay, but it was done. That certainty was attributed, yes?"

"I didn't author that paragraph, Sophie Rieu did…"

"What age was Sophie Rieu?"

"Because I never met her, I couldn't tell you."

"I want to suggest to you, Mr Bailey, that she was a relatively young and inexperienced journalist. The reason your byline was first, ahead of hers, was because you were the principal author of the piece… It would be customary for the principal author's byline to be first. Isn't that right?"

"Yes, it may be that because of what you just told me about her that I would be more senior and that would be why they put my name first."

Ó Braonáin changed tack slightly, speeding up his questions: "A great deal of this article deals with the position of Sophie Toscan du Plantier's husband, Daniel du Plantier."

Her 55 year-old husband will be formally interviewed over the weekend or early this week. He did not travel to Ireland to identify his wife's body.

A brief pause. Bailey interjected: "Yes?"

Gardaí in Bantry were hoping that he would travel to Ireland to be interviewed but he has repeatedly said that he has too many business commitments in France at the moment to allow him to travel abroad.

Bailey: "Yes, and that's quite shocking, isn't it, really. I didn't write that. That is nothing to do with me – that is all Ms Rieu."

"Why do you feel that that was shocking?"

"I think that it was shocking that the gentleman who had lost his wife... sent over his [wife's] family to identify the body. He wouldn't come to identify his wife's body... If I had a wife and she was murdered somewhere, I would travel to the scene. I think that was very strange. I think it's also very strange then he refuses to, he is too busy, too many business commitments to be able to come over and assist the Irish police. You can draw your own conclusions. I just find that very, very strange and bizarre."

Bailey had the attention of the whole court. He appeared animated; it looked like he was speaking freely, openly. I sensed every pair of eyes in the room was fixed on the Englishman. This was getting exciting.

Ó Braonáin: "Well, what conclusions *did* you draw?"

"The conclusions I drew, and if I step out of line please stop me, as a journalist, the difference between a detective and a journalist sometimes isn't very different. You know you are looking for the truth, you are looking to try to pull out the truth of the matter, and it became quite clear that one of the things you do look for when you begin a murder investigation is you look for motive. This is just common sense, you look for motive and then you maybe look at people who might have motive. Now I am not saying anything about anybody, but when you look at the information that was coming out of France and what we now know to be true, it is highly, highly suspect to say the least. If you want me to expand on that, I will, but I am not too sure I should."

Ó Braonáin: "I am sorry, I am not quite sure I understand, Mr Bailey, but the impression that I am getting is that you were suggesting that in some way Daniel du Plantier was involved in or responsible for the death. Is that what you are saying?"

Bailey appeared to backtrack: "I am not exactly using those words but..."

"No, you're not but there is smoke and mirrors?"

"You talk to me about smoke and mirrors... There was an awful lot of information that was coming out of France from the French journalists… They had split, the marriage was over. She was his third trophy wife. He had settled the divorces with the other two amicably. She had told people in West Cork she was leaving him and she was going to come and live here in West Cork, in rural Ireland, because it was wonderful and she could get everything that she wanted. Her life in France was far too complex. Then out of France come the stories about how close they were, how close they were…"

Ian Bailey's delivery was speeding up. The barrister must have thought it a wise ploy to let the man talk, not to interrupt. There was no telling what Bailey might say.

"…On the Wednesday before she came over there was a UniFrance party and this can be checked, Daniel Toscan du Plantier, who was the Managing Editor [*sic*] of UniFrance, and there was a big Christmas party on the Wednesday night before she came and at that party, this lady, Sophie Toscan du Plantier, his third wife, met Daniel Toscan du Plantier's current mistress who he went on to subsequently marry and there was a cat fight in a bar."

You could have heard a pin drop in the old courtroom.

Bailey added, pointlessly: "This is background, really."

"It's a very interesting background, isn't it, Mr Bailey?"

"It is, and it would have been very interesting if there had been a serious inquiry into it as well, which there never was of course."

"Mr Bailey, I thought that you said that this information about the husband and his attitude towards coming over and his attitude towards his business and his priorities and so on, that that didn't come from you?"

"Specifically in this article the references to that, those were written by Ms Rieu."

"I see. Because you seem to have had a very particular interest in that?"

"Um, well I'm…"

Ó Braonáin interjected: "It would be remarkable that you

wouldn't, as the principal author of the piece, have written that yourself, wouldn't it? What I am saying to you is that given your interest, which is quite evident, it is surprising to hear you say that this part of the article would not have been authored by you as the principal author of the article?"

Bailey again denied that he had authored the part of the story dealing with Sophie's allegedly troubled marriage to Daniel.

Ó Braonáin: "You were, for some time before this article was written, interested in the French angle, if I could put it that way?"

Bailey: "The French connection?"

"The French connection, indeed…"

All the court correspondents on the press bench were scribbling notes furiously by now, checking quotes with each other.

I was surprised by the pitch of Bailey's voice when he spoke about the "French connection". It seemed higher; he was also talking faster than usual. Up to that moment, he had kept his cool and his voice was level and confident. Apart from the "French connection" exchanges, Bailey had a firm handle on his story. It struck me that he almost always struck the right tone – patient, level, unruffled.

Ó Braonáin took his time with many of his questions, one foot perched on a chair, often looking at his adversary out of the corner of one eye. From time to time, Bailey carved out the chance to make the odd gag. Some were straightforward crowd-pleasers. For instance, after his first arrest, he recalled that he agreed to take part in an identity parade. In the end, it didn't happen. "There was a shortage of six feet four inch individuals in Bandon that day," Bailey deadpanned.

However, some of his humour seemed to have a more specific purpose. He mentioned that a pair of wellington boots had been taken away by the Guards and that he hadn't seen them since, "and I wouldn't mind them being returned if they are available, if anyone knows where they are". I understood it was a message to the jury: *I have little or no money. I am not a wealthy man. The damages I am seeking matter to me.*

***

In 2020, I tracked down Sophie Rieu. She had spent all of the intervening years in Ireland, some of that time designing and producing women's clothes, and writing, too.

Rieu was the perfect example of a 'blow-in' who had made Ireland her home – "and now English is practically my second language," she told me. Rieu had no idea that her name had come up in Bailey's court case in 2014. She was surprised. Why hadn't they called her? She could have answered the questions for herself. She could have taken the stand. I filled her in on the details of who said what. Rieu recalled her work with Bailey had been cordial and professional.

"What about the information that Sophie had a guest on the night of the murder?"

"No, that didn't come from me, not at all."

"And the two rinsed glasses on the draining board of her kitchen sink?"

"No, I don't think that came from me. But there was a lot of information being shared between journalists at the time, and there were a lot of rumours about the case." This backed up what Bailey said in the courtroom in Dublin. Rieu said that in the month or so after the murder, *Paris Match* had also been a significant source of background details on the case.

A day later Sophie Rieu sent me a follow-up email. She wrote: *Ian Bailey really pushed the French angle during our phone conversations and wanted me to uncover something controversial about Daniel Toscan du Plantier.*

The piece Bailey and Rieu co-wrote mentioned that Daniel's production company had run into financial trouble and there were rumours of a divorce, too. *He* [Ian Bailey] *was fanning the flames, so to speak, on those rumours.*

***

On my third day attending proceedings, I worked out a way of approaching Ian Bailey. At lunchtime the previous day, I had seen him walk across a yard in the court compound in the direction of a cafeteria mainly frequented by young barristers. I noticed he was on his own and he knew where he was going. That might become a routine. Jules Thomas, meanwhile, was nowhere to be seen.

"Mr Bailey," I called out, as he exited the courtroom in the direction of the yard, "I wonder if you would have time for a quick word?" I explained that I was interested in the case and in his story and wanted to write about it.

"Where are you from?"

I told him, Liverpool.

"A Scouser!"

That seemed to seal it. Bailey was from Manchester, after all. In spite of our cities' great rivalry, he would let me buy him a cup of tea. Looking back, had my hometown been Penzance or Aberdeen, I don't think the outcome would have been any different. Some people love talking about themselves. It's in their nature and it's unstoppable. And it's not a bad thing, don't get me wrong. Bailey was – still is – one of those people.

In the cafeteria, Bailey greeted the lady behind the old bar as if she was a long-lost friend. I noticed the eyes of the customers settled on my tall, elegantly-suited companion. Bailey said he was "grand" a couple of times, but otherwise his vocabulary and diction were entirely English. We only had a couple of minutes to drink our tea – Bailey wanted to go to a newsagents to get a pack of ciggies. Would I go with him?

The newsagents was a couple of blocks away along the north quays of the River Liffey. It wasn't easy to talk at lunchtime, Bailey said to me. Better to plan to see each other one evening. Jules would come too. I was returning to Dublin the following week. I now had his phone number so we could be in touch, we could arrange something.

Again, I noticed how the eyes of many of the pedestrians who walked by stared at Bailey. In the newsagents, we joined a small queue. A middle-aged woman in front of us was holding a tiny dog in a basket. Bailey stroked the dog's neck in the manner of a provincial politician canvassing for votes. The woman looked up at him and looked away. No reaction, no recognition. When she came to pay, she said something to the woman behind the counter in an eastern European language, maybe Polish. When it was our turn, Bailey asked for his box of smokes and the woman behind the counter gave him the briefest of glances, too. For a moment, Bailey had returned to anonymity.

***

Bailey's diary entries were bound to make an appearance at some point. These were the colourful musings that Bailey had described as "abstract" at the Cork libel hearing and that, back in 2003, had filled the nation's newspaper pages for a week. Many Irish people had been gripped by the self-penned revelations, not least because it was as obvious as the nose on your face that they were pretty much the opposite of "abstract".

"I think that when one looks at your writings, Mr Bailey," said Ó Braonáin, "what becomes apparent is that there was... an absence of a 'joie de vivre' during the course of the period up to 1996, that life was not always happy... I have to suggest to you, Mr Bailey, for instance one of the things that you found difficult was that there was a terrible absence of money. Isn't that right?"

In 1991, Bailey took a break from his farm work and went up to Dublin. He was now *in the city of Joyce and Yeats and many besides*. He found himself on the south side of the centre of Dublin, wealthy Georgian townhouses all around, people out shopping, filling fancy restaurants and well-kept pubs.

"Then you talk about sitting in St Stephen's Green feeling alone?"

"Yes."

"Feeling angry mixed with a feeling of depression?"

"Yes."

Anger at having so often and so repeatedly thrown away opportunities… I have always been an outsider.

There is an atmosphere of sedate style and comfortable living. The problem that I have is no home or base. At the same time, I have no money.

Bailey countered that later, in Schull, they did have enough money, despite the fish factory job only lasting a single season. In his diaries, he had written about making some leather holders for cigarette lighters to raise some cash. He was living on £100 a week.

"I think at the time your consideration was that that was the only thing that you could make money out of?"

"Well, no, I mean, I was gardening. I had been doing some landscape gardening for people, for Mr Lyons and I did some for John Montague. I came to the conclusion that I was actually better off using my intellectual energies than my physical energies."

Bailey hoped he could carve out a career as a poet, and make money from writing poems. This was a big theme in his diaries in the early 1990s: *It's a great pity I could not get to a word processor for a day. I would produce a saleable collection. I have a great imagination, how can I ever exploit that? I need an adviser.*

Elsewhere Ian Bailey had written: *It's a bummer when you are as unknown and as unpublished as myself. I always seem to fuck up. There is nothing that I have touched in my life which I haven't ruined or hasn't fallen apart, even here in Ireland I have fucked up more than anybody would be expected.*

The words seemed to hang in the close courtroom air:

I always seem to fuck up… I have fucked up more than anybody would be expected.

Ó Braonáin told Bailey that he took no pleasure from reading out these diary entries. But the court had to hear them since, earlier in the case, Bailey had painted a picture of a satisfying outdoors lifestyle that had been blighted by the actions of the Guards in the aftermath of the murder of Sophie Toscan du Plantier.

This picture was not accurate, said the barrister.

Ó Braonáin said that he would need to explore other themes in the plaintiff's diaries. Bailey was outraged: It was an "absolute intrusion of my personal, private thoughts". The diaries had been taken from him illegally by the Guards, Bailey said, and now the young barrister facing him was exposing his jottings and writings "like a magician bringing a rabbit out of a hat". Ó Braonáin carried on regardless.

In 1989, while still in England, Ian Bailey wrote: *I will not be able to rest easy until all is done to free me of the shackles of material and consumer society.* He was then filing stories to newspapers, commuting between Cheltenham and London, his marriage over. *I am so disgusted with how I have let things slip on all levels. I feel self-loathing, a hatred for myself. I must expunge these feelings.*

Later, in Schull, in 1992: *I object to fools and arrogant idiots… I feel my energies have waned slightly after a high between the 21st and 30th December. The moon is filling quickly and we are heading into Aquarius, the zone of rebirth…*

Turning the page, Ó Braonáin found a section with what appeared to be a series of calculations. Bailey explained: "Just at the bottom there it says '20,000 words, 8,000 words a month, 2,000 words a week'. I was actually working out how many words, you know, if you needed to produce a book how many words you would have to write and reckoned that if I could write about 8,000 words a month, I might be able to pull something together."

There were a lot of papers and photocopies on Ó Braonáin's table, and Bailey referred to a fragment of a poem he had in mind, or a musing, or something, and the barrister could not immediately find it in the pile of material. Leaning conspiratorially into his microphone, Bailey said to Ó Braonáin that he was sorry and that "I didn't mean to drop you in it". There were a couple of men on the press bench I recognised as retired Guards, and even they laughed at this one.

Bailey suddenly spotted a fragment of poetry on the page. His

84

tone perked up in an instant. "I mean this is quite good. You've done a strange thing for me in a way because you've reminded me of the things that I've actually forgotten that I've written and I am seeing stuff that I haven't actually seen for, probably since I wrote it. I am talking about the garden growing full... What I am doing actually is I am writing about the garden growing full and I am likening it to a girl child entering maidenhood, her body filling with the fruits of nature. And this..."

Justice Hedigan interjected: "You would be much better off to just answer the questions... At this stage, heaven knows what you will find."

I was sorry the judge had stopped him.

Bailey wrote about his *rainy-day J's* [joints], that hash gave him *enhanced powers of visualisation.* Also: *I think I have been drinking too much for the past 20 years... I often drink myself to sickness even though I know it's unwise... Just felt my annoyance rising, slept in late lazily... Just wondering what and why, feeling listless and nothing but grump, stop it, stop it...*

Why should someone of undoubted intelligence behave in such a foolish and self-destructive fashion?

New Year's Eve, 1993: *I was contemplating the trait of denial and fantasy. In our minds, we create fantasies to somehow convince ourselves we are on the right track. What I am thinking is how we convince ourselves we are right when we know we are wrong. Everybody does it at some time, and when we do, we can convince ourselves black is white.*

Bailey went into Schull that night, 31ˢᵗ December 1993. *At New Year's Eve at the witching hour, I swung a blow at a boy who was bothering me. It was witnessed and remarked on.*

Bailey: "I can tell you what that was. I was in the Courtyard bar and some 'eejit' [idiot], for want of a better word, came up and started bothering me and I sort of shooed him away."

Ó Braonáin: "Can I say, Mr Bailey, it says it was a boy, not a man?"

"I don't know, a young man, a young man."

"It doesn't say a young man, it says a boy."

"Okay."

I was just trying to remember how old I am. I thought I might have been 38 for a moment, but then I realised I am still only 37. I know the core of me wants to shine…

I need to bring about great change. I can see I am in great moral danger. I need to somehow wipe out much of the old and bring about a rebirth.

It was another mention of a "rebirth". However, another couple of years would pass without any significant reinvention. Bailey spent most of the following year, 1996, unemployed, some of the time merely kicking his heels. In the spring of that year, he gave Jules Thomas a severe beating, the one that came to the attention of the Guards in Schull. So much for a "rebirth". Still, that day, sitting on the hard press bench in the courtroom, I was transfixed. The drama of the occasion – the wigs, the gowns, the formality, the stilted court jargon – can have that effect on you. Here was a man baring his soul in his writings, trying to find the right words. On the one hand, it was pleasantly mundane (*I grew some prize-winning onions… the mangetout should be a good cash crop this year*); on the other, it was troubling (*I sacrificed my life to debauchery*). This was navel-gazing with a wide audience, thanks to the assembled media, but who was to say that it was not sincere?

***

Ian Bailey and I had agreed to meet at a bar on the north side of the River Liffey. It was seven in the evening. I arrived 10 minutes early and was surprised to find him and Jules Thomas were already there waiting for me. Bailey was wearing a yellow rugby shirt and a dark orange scarf. Thomas looked elegant in a light-coloured raincoat, but her face looked pinched and drawn. I had written down their ages on a sheet with some questions I had – Bailey was 57 and Thomas was 65.

"How about a quick pint first?" Bailey said.

I nipped into the bar with Bailey and got a couple of beers – his a Guinness, mine a lager – and a white wine for Thomas, which she promptly sent back, as there had been a mix-up – she had asked for a Chardonnay and got a Riesling, or vice-versa. It was crowded inside so we perched on stools assembled around one of several tiny tables on the pavement. Most of the other customers were youngish office workers.

An older, evidently drunk man approached us, his eyes on Thomas, who ignored him. He was just a random passer-by.

"Now she's a lovely lady," the man said. He turned to shake Bailey's hand, smiled and walked away.

We did not discuss the case there and then outside the pub. I tried to think of some small talk. With Bailey, it was easy – he was hugely relaxed and engaging. I asked them where they were staying. Immediately I sensed some strange secrecy about their lodgings. Thomas replied by saying something like, "It's just around the corner, it's just a place…" until Bailey interrupted her saying, with heavy emphasis on each word, and not bothering to hide his irritation with his partner: "Remember, we're not talking about that."

I thought, 'They cannot even coordinate a simple decision like whether or not to speak about their digs'. That stayed with me – and Bailey's flash of temper when he corrected Thomas.

Our conversation turned to money. Bailey wanted to know how much I was paying for my hotel. He appeared to want a specific figure. I tried to oblige. He asked the same for the going rate for newspaper stories these days. I gave him a few figures, pitching my numbers as low as possible. He wanted to know how I got a start writing for newspapers. There had been quite a bit of talk on the press bench in the courthouse about how much Bailey was likely to get for damages if he won his case. The consensus seemed to be a couple of million euros.

I sensed that Bailey was quietly confident about the proceedings so far: *Feels he's approaching the end of "18 years of hell"*, I wrote in my notebook. Bailey thought that he was getting the better of 'Luán', as he referred to Ó Braonáin, the barrister. Bailey said, in as many words, that he viewed him as a kindred spirit.

"He looks at me," Jules said in a matter-of-fact way.

We made our way to an Italian restaurant nearby. It would make a nice change, said Thomas, since they had been living off Chinese takeaways. As we entered, a couple of diners looked up, recognising Bailey or, otherwise, their eyes drawn to the very tall, distinguished – and vaguely patrician-looking – man. I faced Bailey and Thomas at our table, moving my place setting so it was midway between them, a tacit but hardly conscious recognition that they both were interesting, that the story was about them jointly, and not just about Ian Bailey, full stop.

Thomas was missing her smallholding. It sounded like paradise, the way she described it: fresh food on your doorstep, fresh air, plenty of space. They had a big, old-fashioned oven, which turned out delicious pizzas and Danish pastries. Food was clearly their shared passion. Thomas had a camera with her and she showed me photos of the cottage and its luxuriant, well-tended garden, tussocky fields all around.

When we came to one photo, with a moor looming in the distance, Thomas said: "The Frenchwoman lived somewhere over there."

Thomas picked at a salad. Bailey ate his pasta dish heartily. "It was a stitch-up," said Bailey. "I was the long English bollox. Their whole case was built on a stinking, rotten lie."

Bailey mentioned some suspects who he said were never properly investigated. And then there was a petrol station owner who had mentioned something to the Guards and it had been overlooked. This petrol station chap had apparently seen something important to the case.

I told Bailey I had been speaking with Dermot Dwyer. Dwyer had warned me not to be taken in by Bailey, but this advice I kept to myself. Bailey quizzed me on what Dwyer had been saying. I gave

him the vaguest reply I could get away with. In fact, Dwyer had
said very little to the journalists on the press bench as far as I could
tell, apart from passing around John Montague's article in *The New
Yorker*. Thomas said that Montague's feature was a "nasty piece",
adding that Bailey had toiled for a day in the man's garden and
asked for £30, but Montague had ended up paying him less.

Over dessert, Bailey recited a poem, his voice raised by a few
decibels. Several people on neighbouring tables cast a glance in our
direction. I was getting used to the attention my dining companion
was attracting. I couldn't tell you what the poem was about. My eyes
were on Thomas. She, in turn, was looking intently at Bailey, lapping
up her partner's piece of verse. This was the man, I thought, who
had beaten her so hard she had ended up in hospital. The medics
had done reconstructive surgery to her face. She had needed to get a
barring order for fear he would do more harm to her. And yet, here
she was, looking at him adoringly as he recited his poetry.

By the end of the meal, I got an invitation to visit Bailey and
Thomas at their cottage on the Mizen. I chalked this up as the ideal
result: it was what I needed to continue delving into the Sophie
story. Bailey listed a few things we had in common – we were both
from north-west England, we both had freelanced for newspapers.
I sensed I had passed some kind of test at that Italian restaurant
in Dublin. I asked for the bill while Bailey folded up some uneaten
ciabatta in a paper napkin. I thought I heard Bailey say to Thomas,
"for breakfast", or something similar.

We made our separate ways in the Irish night. Bailey said to me
that he was happy to have met me. He was happy to have a new
"supporter". Not for the last time, I felt both uncomfortable and
intrigued.

Chapter 8

RUSSIAN DOLLS

Eleven days into the hearing, Jules Thomas took the witness stand. She was dressed head to toe in black. Even when Thomas was answering softball questions from her own barrister, she looked like she wanted nothing more than for a hole to open in the floor of the courtroom to swallow her up.

The court quickly learned the basics of her life – psychiatrist father, artist mother, boarding school in Devon, an enduring love of painting. In London in the early 1970s, Thomas had met a man called Michael Oliver and they went to south-west Ireland. The rent in London had been £100 a week. Around the Mizen, the countryside and the seascapes were lovely. Rent was two pounds a week. What's more, you could buy your own house outright for a few thousand pounds, Thomas said.

One day Thomas and Oliver were driving across the Prairie when they ran out of petrol. They saw a cottage set back from the road, a ramshackle two-storey construction that looked low to the ground, as if it were sinking into the peaty moor. The cottage appeared empty. A farmer came to give them a hand, offered to take them into Schull to get fuel for their car. The farmer mentioned that he knew the owner of the cottage, and that it might be available. It is on such a chance encounter that the course of a life is sometimes set. Thomas and Oliver moved into the ramshackle cottage and set about doing it up. They had two daughters, Saffron and Virginia. The couple split, and Thomas later married Chris Thomas, the father of her third daughter, Fenella. (Chris took Jules's surname – the idea was that it would be easier for the girls if they all had the same surname.) After her relationship with Chris ended, Jules Thomas stayed in the same house at the Prairie, building her career as an artist. The cottage on the moor and her paintings were the two constants in Thomas's life.

Thomas said that Ian Bailey's violence to her was "kind of unforgivable, but I do believe that there is good in everyone". I looked at the women on the jury when Thomas was describing Bailey's attacks on her. They had their eyes fixed on Thomas, and were hanging on every sad word. Meanwhile in the public gallery, the expressions were inscrutable. I spotted a middle-aged woman with a face turned orange from some kind of self-tanning product, and somebody wearing a t-shirt with the words *BAH HUMBUG!* printed across it. No longer taking the stand, no longer under cross-examination, Bailey yawned from time to time.

Thomas described her arrest on 10th February 1997 on suspicion of covering up for the murder of Sophie Toscan du Plantier. What Thomas had told the Guards at Bandon police station, where she was questioned, had been an important part of the Garda's case against Ian Bailey, in particular her account of their journey home from the Galley pub via Hunt's Hill, and Bailey's physical appearance and demeanour on the morning after the murder. During her arrest, Thomas's replies to the various questions posed by the detectives had been written down by a Guard on sheets of paper. These statements were the formal record of the questioning, and Thomas had signed those sheets of paper. No audio recording was made of the questioning, but that was normal procedure in Ireland at that time.

Thomas claimed that the Guards had doctored her signed statements: "There were additions, there were omissions, there were inventions," Jules Thomas told the court. "Oh, it was just dreadful."

Dreadful they may have been, but the State's barrister, a slim, grey-haired man named Paul O'Higgins, wanted to go into them in detail.

Thomas had recounted the afternoon of 22nd December 1996. Bailey and Saffron Thomas had gone to cut a Christmas tree near the studio. The idea had been to saw the top off a fir tree and put it in the sitting room of the cottage. The three turkeys had already been slaughtered at this point. O'Higgins read from Thomas's statement:

Following the cutting of the tree, his forearms were scratched, but there was no scratch on his forehead.

The significance of the statement would not have been lost on the Guards, because a number of witnesses – including Gardaí – had seen Bailey with a cut or wound on his forehead in the days after the murder.

Thomas: "No, there was no scratch on his forehead."

O'Higgins asked Thomas where there had been a scratch, if anywhere.

"There was a nick, it was tiny, on his hairline..."

It seemed curious that in her signed statement Thomas had not mentioned the "nick" on the hairline to the Guards at the time, rather than say to them that, in her recollection, there had been no scratch on Bailey's forehead.

Incredulous, O'Higgins asked Thomas if the Guard was "miswriting 'nick on the hairline'" when he wrote down that there was no scratch on Bailey's forehead.

"I don't know," Thomas replied.

The "nick" on Bailey's hairline, Thomas claimed, had been caused by the talon of a flapping turkey, and was "so small you could barely say it was a scratch. It wasn't even an open wound, it was like an abrasion, really".

The older barrister was not going to let this one go. The

atmosphere in the courtroom was flatter, and slightly more relaxed, than when Bailey was under cross-examination. Still, I sensed that this exchange went to the heart of the mystery.

O'Higgins asked Thomas if she had actually mentioned the "nick on the hairline" to the Guards during her arrest.

Thomas: "Yes."

O'Higgins: "You did?"

"Yeah."

"They didn't write it down?"

"I believe it is not there."

O'Higgins remarked that in 2006, Thomas had made a series of complaints about her arrest, and she had spoken about it in Bailey's 2003 libel action. On neither of these occasions had there been mention of Thomas saying Bailey had a "nick on the hairline" after killing the turkeys. So why was Thomas only bringing up this information now?

O'Higgins: "Has that ever been said before?"

Thomas: "I don't know what you want, I am sorry."

O'Higgins turned to Thomas's account to the Guards about the journey home from the Galley pub on the moonlit night of 22nd December. Close to Lowertown Creamery, Bailey, who was driving, took the turning up Hunt's Hill.

I stayed in the car and Ian got out for a few minutes... He asked me to get out and I refused as it was too cold.

O'Higgins: "That is correct, is that so?"

Thomas: "It was freezing, yeah."

Ian got back in and said he had a bad feeling about something going to happen.

Thomas: "No. He didn't say he had a bad feeling about anything about to happen."

O'Higgins: "That is an invention by the Gardaí?"

"I believe so."

When we were looking across the terrain Ian remarked, "Is that Alfie's house across the way?" and said, "There is a light on there".

Thomas: "Absolute invention."

O'Higgins: "What were you doing when he wrote all those things? Did you ever say, 'What are you writing now?'"

Thomas replied that at that stage of the questioning her brain was "beginning to feel a bit fried to be honest... it is very hard to describe, it is not a nice experience at all".

There was more: *The two of us then went home and very little was said except some words to the effect that he was going over later or sometime, if I wanted to go, and I said I was too tired. I got the impression that he was going over to Alfie's but I wasn't sure if it was that night or not.*

"This is pure invention."

O'Higgins' tone approached sarcasm: "That whole passage was presumably written out in front of you and presumably it means you would have had to have said something, something completely different would need to have been written and you watched that being written, is that correct, or was there just silence as he wrote?"

Thomas's statement went on to say Bailey left his clothes on a cane chair outside the bedroom door before getting into bed. Thomas had taken painkillers for period pain, and she said she fell asleep almost straight away.

I was in a sleep and Ian was tossing and turning. He then got up from bed and I would estimate that he got up about an hour later.

Thomas said she did not say to the Guards that Bailey was tossing and turning and did not remember Bailey getting out of bed.

Bailey brought a cup of coffee to Thomas in bed. It was now about nine o'clock.

I saw a scratch on his forehead. I am sure and I have no recollection of seeing this scratch on his forehead on the Sunday. The scratch was raw and I asked him what happened as it was fresh and a bit bloodied and he said he got it from a stick.

"This is an invention."

I did notice the scratches on his hands.

Thomas said: "He had a small scratch on his hand, the likes of something that you would get from a bramble, I suppose, I think. I can't remember."

This seemed odd to me. Wasn't the issue with the scratches that Bailey had insisted they had come from cutting the Christmas tree? Anyway, O'Higgins moved on.

Apart from being tired and drawn, he was otherwise normal.

"Did you say that or not?"

"I don't remember saying he was tired and drawn at all, he looked fine."

I recall Eddie Cassidy ringing my house and Ian answering the phone. When Ian was finished talking to Eddie Cassidy on the phone he said to me, "You won't believe this, but there's been a murder near us somewhere between Dunmanus Castle and Toormore". He said that Eddie Cassidy wanted him to find out what's going on.

At that time, you can call me green but I never associated the comments made by Ian on Hunt's Hill the night before when we were looking up at Alfie's house and him getting a bad feeling about something going to happen there, and the murder subsequently happening and the fact that he was missing the night before.

Thomas: "I didn't say it."

O'Higgins: "Invention?"

"Yes, I didn't say it."

Again, O'Higgins wondered what Thomas was doing when the Guards were writing down these quite lengthy passages. I sensed that if Bailey was going to get a big payout from the State, the jury would need to be convinced that the Guards had acted corruptly in this questioning of Thomas under arrest. Bailey was the plaintiff, but I was surprised that his direct experience of Garda wrongdoing was so paltry. He had claimed to have been poked in the ribs by one Guard in the squad car that took him away on his first arrest, and that another Garda drew his crotch near to Bailey's face when they arrived at the station. That was pretty much it.

At the same time, the detail of what Thomas denied she said to the Guards under questioning was rather suspicious when you looked at its wider implications: Ian Bailey looked out from Hunt's Hill across in the direction of Toormore and said to Thomas he wanted to go over to Alfie's. Bailey got up about an hour after they went to bed, therefore at about 2:30am, since it was undisputed that the couple went to bed at about 1:30am. Then there was the noticeable "fresh" and "bloodied" scratch on Bailey's forehead by 9am the next morning. If the Guards had fabricated only half of what Thomas had claimed, this would have been a stitch-up.

O'Higgins read out another passage from Thomas's statement to the court.

He [Bailey] *said that he had seen her* [Sophie] *at Brosnan's supermarket in Schull on that weekend. He did not elaborate on whether she was on her own or otherwise, only that it was the weekend she was murdered.*

Jules Thomas said that no, she had never said that to the Guards.

He was in Schull on Saturday afternoon during shopping time and was not there on Friday and Sunday.

"Was he in Schull on Saturday afternoon?"

"I couldn't remember."

We were approaching the end of the day's session. I was looking at the poised, thin woman in the witness stand, her partner observing her from his seat in the old courtroom, and I had something else on my mind.

Jules Thomas had accused the Guards of inventing much of what she said at Bandon Garda Station on 10th February 1997. But Thomas's accusations of fabrications did not end there, and specifically they did not end with the agents of An Garda Síochána. I looked over my notes. In the Dublin courtroom, Thomas had accused several other people of lying or of recalling incidents incorrectly, among them Michael McSweeney, Pádraig Beirne, Caroline Leftwick and James Camier. I had read something about all of them. McSweeney and Beirne, who were involved in press photography, and Leftwick, who was a woman with a market garden known to Bailey and Thomas, had given the Guards evidence about phone calls involving Ian Bailey on the morning and early afternoon of 23ʳᵈ December. I thought of the Russian dolls again, one smiling wooden doll concealing another, peeling back the layers.

James Camier was important, but in a different way. He had said he had seen Jules Thomas at his fruit and vegetable stall in Goleen, a village west of Schull on the Mizen peninsula, on the morning of 23ʳᵈ December 1996. According to Camier, Thomas had told him about the murder there and then, a couple of hours before Bailey had said he had found out about it from Eddie Cassidy of the *Examiner*.

Meanwhile, a gardener called Bill Fuller – a man who Bailey had done gardening jobs with – claimed to have seen Thomas driving in the direction of Goleen, close to Kealfadda Bridge on the morning of 23ʳᵈ December in the couple's white Ford Fiesta. And yet Bailey and Thomas had insisted under oath that they were at home at the Prairie for all of the morning and early afternoon of 23ʳᵈ December 1996 until they left the cottage to drive in the direction of Toormore shortly after 2pm.

The following morning in court, O'Higgins turned to what the Guards had written down as replies that Jules Thomas had made to their questions about her movements on 23ʳᵈ December. O'Higgins started reading out loud to the courtroom:

On the Monday of the murder, Ian was busy getting an article ready for the press.

Thomas: "Yes."

I drove down past the scene at about 11am, and on to the causeway [meaning, the strip of coast close to Kealfadda Bridge].

Thomas: "No, I never said that… It is ridiculous, I didn't go out that morning."

O'Higgins: "I am putting it to you that you did in fact say you went down that morning."

Thomas: "That is an absolute fabrication because it did not happen."

If Fenella said I brought home some vegetables it must have been on the Monday I was in Goleen.

Thomas: "That doesn't make sense at all."

O'Higgins told the court that Fenella Thomas, Jules Thomas's youngest daughter, had made a statement to the Guards: "One of the things she [Fenella] said… is that yourself and Ian had gone out for I think two hours on the Monday morning."

Thomas: "She wasn't out of bed even, she couldn't have said that… I suggest she got the wrong day."

O'Higgins: "Can I suggest to you that you have recently sought to pressurise her to change her statement to the Gardaí that you had been out for about two hours on the Monday morning, but she has not done so?"

Jules Thomas repeated that her daughter Fenella had been in bed the whole time, so Fenella would not have known if she, Jules, had gone out. O'Higgins said that Thomas had called Fenella to "pressurise her to change her statement". He gave a date: 12th May 2014, around six months before the court hearing I was observing. This would have been when the evidence for Bailey's case against the Guards and the Irish state was being prepared. However, Thomas denied that she had put her daughter under any pressure. "I can't lie," said Thomas, "I can't make things up."

As O'Higgins had said, Fenella Thomas had refused to budge. She was still on record as saying that her mother and Ian Bailey went out of the cottage for around two hours on the morning of the murder of Sophie Toscan du Plantier. O'Higgins reminded Thomas that Bill Fuller was on record as having seen Thomas driving her car near Kealfadda Bridge on the morning after the murder. Thomas said she was aware of Fuller's testimony.

O'Higgins: "You say that is just wrong?"

Thomas: "Absolutely. We have a witness who says that he was selling Christmas trees in Schull High Street that morning, so it is quite impossible for him to have seen me there [driving near Kealfadda Bridge], and I wasn't there anyway."

"Who is that witness?"

"Marie Farrell."

Chapter 9

THE SIDE OF THE GOOD

The Sophie Toscan du Plantier murder case plucked Marie Farrell, the Schull shopkeeper and mother-of-five, from obscurity and placed her centre stage. Or, to put it slightly differently, a Schull shopkeeper and mother-of-five had placed herself centre stage in the mystery, and had been dealing with the fallout ever since. Farrell steadfastly denied that she had ever revelled in the attention the Sophie case had brought her.

Farrell had once been the State's star witness, on the back of her anonymous call to the Guards saying that she had seen a man wearing a long, black coat in the vicinity of Kealfadda Bridge at around 3am on the night Sophie was killed. Farrell had identified this man as Ian Bailey. She had seen the same man on Schull's Main Street on the Saturday before the murder at the same time that Sophie was there shopping, and early on the morning of the Sunday, thumbing a lift on the outskirts of Schull.

On top of that, Farrell had said under oath at the libel case in Cork in 2003 that Bailey had repeatedly attempted to intimidate her with a view to her withdrawing her testimony about seeing him at Kealfadda Bridge. Bailey had made "cut-throat" gestures at her, and she had been "terrified" of him. Bailey had also said to her that he had found out Farrell was in trouble with the UK's Department of Social Security and had received subsidies to which she was not entitled during a period she was living in London. On a visit to her shop around six months after the murder, Bailey had revealed he knew Farrell's old London address and was prepared to denounce her to the UK authorities. "There are people being extradited for less," Farrell had claimed Bailey had said to her. "I think it was at that stage he said, 'Well, you scratch my back and I will scratch yours'. He said at one point, 'I didn't kill Sophie but I know you saw me at the bridge'." Bailey's intimidation was so bad it amounted to Bailey "torturing me".

Following her Damascene conversion, Farrell's story had changed. Now she said that the comments about mutual back-scratching and Bailey knowing that Farrell had seen him at the bridge never happened. It never felt like Bailey was torturing her, she insisted. Only the bit about Bailey saying he had not killed Sophie was true.

Since 2005, Farrell's story was, in essence, that the Guards had coerced her to stitch up Ian Bailey. What was already in the public domain regarding her new testimony was already a potent cocktail. It was about to get properly explosive.

I saw Marie Farrell standing to my left, ready to enter the courtroom. She was about 15 minutes late, and the judge was visibly irritated, poking his finger in the direction of Bailey's barristers. Farrell was wearing black leggings and a black blouse under an overcoat. I recognised her immediately from her short hair, dyed a russet red, and plumpish face. Now in her early fifties, Farrell looked nervous and appeared to be biting her lip.

Bailey's barrister, Tom Creed, asked Farrell if she had taken an oath when she gave evidence at Bailey's libel case in 2003.

Farrell: "That's correct."

"Did you tell the truth, the whole truth and nothing but the truth at that libel action?"

THE SIDE OF THE GOOD

"No, I didn't."

Tom Creed read out a statement Farrell signed on 14th February 1997, subsequent to her call to the Guards as 'Fiona', informing them that she had seen a man acting suspiciously on the night of the murder in the vicinity of Kealfadda Bridge:

On Sunday, 22nd December 1996, I left my home at about 10pm... In Schull I went to the car park outside the East End Hotel. I had agreed to meet someone there who I do not wish to name in this statement. That person was in the car park and I then left Schull on my own and travelled to Goleen. The person I agreed to meet followed me in his own car.

The statement records Farrell as saying that she got in the other person's car and they drove around a bit together, stopping to chat a couple of times, including at Barleycove Beach, a wild stretch of sand on the way to Mizen Head.

We had a conversation in the car at the Main Street in Goleen. While we were on this journey, I saw no one on the road. We may have met a few cars. We then left Goleen village again and travelled to Toormore. When we were approaching Sylvia Connell's shop [i.e. Kealfadda Bridge] *I could see a man walking on the road, the time was approximately 3am, he was walking towards Goleen and on his right-hand side. As I got near this man, I could see he was stumbling forward. He had his two hands to the side of his face, but I could see his face... I immediately recognised this man as the same man as I had seen at Main Street, Schull on Saturday, 21st December 1996, and at Airhill, Schull, on Sunday, 22nd December 1996, and which I referred to in my previous statement. I now know this man to be Ian Bailey... I arrived home at 4:10am on 23rd December 1996. I took note of the time when I got home.*

Farrell had signed that statement and the previous one, detailing the sightings of Bailey on the Saturday and the Sunday, and had initialled each sheet separately. Now Farrell claimed that she had signed blank sheets of paper on the understanding the Guards would fill them in as appropriate. Although most observers expected that Farrell would say something along these lines, it had the effect of someone lobbing a hand grenade at the Garda case. Farrell said

101

bits of the statement were true, and other bits were not. For instance, she did meet a man in Schull that night, but the drive was shorter, since they did not stop at Barleycove Beach. She said she did see a man in a long black coat near to Kealfadda Bridge, stumbling with his hands holding his face, but it was not Ian Bailey. Farrell said she thought the sighting of the man happened "before 2am".

Farrell had no comment to make about the time she arrived home. In the chronology of the night with her male friend, she only changed the time of the sighting of the man who had been stumbling around, and who had appeared to Farrell as being "slightly intoxicated". The other timings stayed the same. I noted down "approximately 3am" and an arrow and "before 2am", and then a question mark. It just seemed odd. Why had she changed that detail?

The Guard who was Farrell's main point of contact was Detective Jim Fitzgerald. Garda Fitzgerald had the reputation of being a problem-solver (his colleagues apparently had the habit of saying "Jim'll fix it"). In early 1997, Fitzgerald gave Farrell a Garda mobile phone – something of a novelty on the Mizen at the time – to keep in touch. Some fines for minor motoring offences committed by Marie Farrell and her husband appeared to have been brushed under the carpet by several of the Guards during this period.

An apparently easy and fluid relationship developed between Farrell and Fitzgerald. According to Farrell, Fitzgerald had said that her statement identifying Bailey at Kealfadda Bridge was going to be a great help. Bailey was very dangerous, but he was also a very odd character: "Not only did they tell me that he killed this woman, but that he was into all sorts of weird things, that he would sit outside and howl at the moon. When there was a full moon, he would sit on the beach in Barleycove naked in a rocking chair and that 10 lesbians would dance round him reciting poetry. You know, just the strangest things, but I believed them."

Some of the people in the public gallery were shaking their heads in disbelief. Bailey and Thomas looked impassive.

In fact, Farrell had only just got started.

Farrell said that, a couple of years after the murder, she closed her ice cream parlour and got a job doing front of house at the restaurant at a golf club outside Schull. One night, one of the Guards working on the case came to the club for dinner with his wife. They joined Farrell and her husband and the two couples had a few drinks together. Farrell said it was also her job to clean the toilets, and at the end of the evening, she went into the Ladies only to turn round to find the Guard in question standing behind her. Farrell told the court: "He was fairly well intoxicated but he got me up against the wall [and] started trying to open my clothes... He opened his own trousers. He exposed himself and he said something along the lines of, you know: 'What would you like to do with that?' Isn't it a real turn on fitting up 'that long English bollox', or 'that black bollox' or 'long black bollox', whatever they used to call Ian Bailey."

Farrell added: "He was trying to kiss me as well."

Farrell also claimed that another Guard had sneaked into a holiday home Farrell was cleaning, and which was otherwise empty, and had stripped off in a downstairs bedroom, and requested sex from her.

Farrell's evidence was excruciating in its detail, but it was also easy for the State's barrister to swipe away. The exposure in the Ladies toilets at the golf club happened with the door open, so anyone could have walked past and looked in. How likely was that? What's more, Farrell appeared to slip up on the layout of the Ladies toilet – where the row of washbasins were, and so on – when the Guard allegedly whipped out his penis. It emerged that Farrell did not even have the job of cleaning the toilets, anyway.

Meanwhile, Farrell backed up her story about the amorous Guard lurking in the holiday home by referring to a growth in his groin that she said she had spotted. It turned out that the Guard had told her about the growth in a coffee shop, with other people present, when blood became apparent on his trousers. By way of explanation, the Guard had said that he needed to have it tested, as he was worried it might be cancerous. For good measure, Farrell could not remember the year the naked cop event happened, and for some reason had kept quiet about both incidents for many years.

"Did you think I was never propositioned by a man when I was young and a lot thinner and maybe a bit better looking?" asked Farrell. "Do you think I want to be sitting here and another headline in the paper about Marie Farrell and what was going on?"

I was sitting next to Dermot Dwyer and I could see he was livid. Farrell had mentioned both Guards' names, subsequently widely reported in the Irish press. "Those are family men," I heard Dwyer say under his breath, barely containing his anger.

Some individual Guards had also made an audio appearance in the courtroom on tapes of some of their phone conversations with Farrell. It transpired that the tapes had been made without the participants' knowledge, which did not surprise me given their content. Justice Hedigan said he had ordered the sections with names and details of people not relevant to the case to be redacted with beeps, which was amusing in itself, as you don't generally try to cover up the harmless bits. What was left was a dense smorgasbord of cursing, with a side portion of self-pity. "Jesus Christ! Fucking hell!" An angry male voice, identified as a Guard, saying Marie this, Marie the other, "sure, it's fucking eating into me". "Why, why, why the fuck?" and "You think I've no fucking headache and all the fucking worry?" It felt to me like some level of pressure was being exerted on Marie Farrell, but it also looked like Farrell was capable of standing up for herself. She summed up her unusual position on the tape: "It's like having three fucking husbands." At one point, Farrell said to a Guard, not unkindly, "You are a pervert". He replied, "I fucking am not... if I am, I'm talking to another one." Far off, in the big city outside, an Angelus bell chimed.

Then came the biggest firework of them all.

When O'Higgins asked Marie Farrell to tell the court the name of the man who was with her when she sighted Ian Bailey at

Kealfadda Bridge, and the judge told her she had to comply, Marie Farrell grabbed her handbag and her coat and stormed out of the courtroom. Bailey's legal team looked shocked. This was clearly a million miles away from what they had expected. From where I was sitting on the press bench, Farrell's departure felt like rubbernecking a car crash. I was only a couple of yards from her as she exited. It was difficult to read the expression on Farrell's face – nose raised, frowning, it was part anger, part disgust, I thought. Whatever her intention, she had effectively ensured her image would displace that of Ian Bailey on the front page of the Dublin newspapers the next morning. From that moment, I really started to wonder about Marie Farrell. Frankly, I have been wondering ever since.

Farrell returned several hours later and was warned by Justice Hedigan that she was under oath. Lying in court had serious consequences, he said. Also, he would not tolerate any more disappearances.

Back in 1997, Garda Fitzgerald had asked Farrell a few questions about the man she was with on the night of Sophie's murder, made some enquiries, and figured that Farrell had been with a former acquaintance named Jan Bartells. However, Bartells was soon eliminated from the Guards' enquiries: he had not seen Farrell in years and, in any case, had a firm alibi for the night of 22nd December 1996. Subsequently, Farrell had produced the name of Oliver Croghan, a musician who had died in the meantime.

Now, on the witness stand in Dublin, Farrell gave a new name: John Reilly, a man who, according to her, had also died in the interim. For the State's barrister, Paul O'Higgins, this seemed too much of a coincidence. When he questioned Farrell about Reilly, she was unable to say where he was from, what he did for a living or what he did in his spare time, where they had met, hardly anything about what he looked like. I was looking straight at Farrell from the press bench, and it felt like staring at another particularly bloody traffic accident. If you were a reporter, where would you begin? There was so much colourful material. But there were also some exchanges that made me think hard about the Sophie case. For example, Marie Farrell's revelation about the silver buttons.

Until Bailey's hearing in Dublin, Farrell's description of the man she spotted in the night at Kealfadda Bridge and twice elsewhere had changed in at least two significant ways. In her initial account, the man she had seen on the opposite side of the road to her shop in Schull on the afternoon of Saturday 21st December 1996 had been of average height – between 5 feet 8 inches and 5 feet 10 inches. The man at Kealfadda Bridge on the night of the murder was the same man as she had seen in Schull, she claimed, and the same man she had seen thumbing a lift at Airhill early on the Sunday morning. Farrell's statement to the Guards in February 1997 that all three sightings were of the same man, meant that the man of average stature on Schull Main Street had to be at least six inches taller than Farrell had recalled, since Ian Bailey was 6 feet 4 inches. This was the first implicit change. But when Farrell withdrew her statements in 2005, her bombshell was that this man, sighted at three different places, was not Ian Bailey after all – a second change. Now Farrell's account was to change for the third time.

Farrell had told the Dublin court that the man at Kealfadda Bridge had been wearing a long black coat with "silver buttons". This was a remarkable piece of detail. In his cross-examination, O'Higgins wanted to know why Farrell had never mentioned this in her earlier statements. Farrell had been running a clothes shop – she must have known that men's overcoats with silver buttons are very rare, except for military dress coats.

Ian Bailey did indeed own and wear a long, black coat as described by Marie Farrell in her previous statements. But if Farrell's new claim were to be taken at face value, Bailey could plausibly argue that it could not have been him stumbling on the side of the road in the darkness at Kealfadda Bridge, for the simple reason that the black coat he had been wearing in 1996 did not have silver buttons.

Why had Marie Farrell brought up this detail now?

It was the 23rd day of the hearing, two days after Farrell's sudden exit from the proceedings. It was almost 4pm. The press bench had been emptying out, as it usually did at this time. The journalists had their stories to file for the next day's newspapers. Marie Farrell's cross-examination felt like it was finally winding up. I glanced at the public gallery. It was still full. There was another piece of clothing there with a message on it. A man in the front row was wearing a t-shirt printed with the words *THE TURKEY DID IT*.

Paul O'Higgins asked Farrell if she knew Bill Fuller, and if she recalled seeing him on 23rd December 1996.

Farrell: "Yes... He was outside the shop selling Christmas trees."

"When did you first remember that?"

"I have always known that."

"You have always known that?"

"Yes."

"When did you first tell anyone that?"

"I don't know, I don't think it was ever an issue."

"Do you not? Well, can I suggest to you that in all of your statements before 2006, there was never a word about Billy [Bill] Fuller outside your shop on the 23rd December 1996?"

"But nothing had happened outside the shop on 23rd December."

"So, in that case why would you remember Billy Fuller having been outside or not outside?"

"I remember him being there."

O'Higgins clearly thought he was on to something. It was somehow similar to how she had suddenly remembered the silver buttons. Why had Farrell remembered seeing Bill Fuller outside her shop many years after the event?

Farrell: "I remember him being there because he came that morning and he started putting all the trees outside the shop and I went out to him and I asked him what he was doing..."

O'Higgins asked her again, very sternly this time: why had Farrell only included the recollection of Bill Fuller and his Christmas trees on Schull Main Street in her testimony after 2006?

Farrell: "Because it was [previously] never an issue."

"Can I put it to you then another way, if nothing had happened and it didn't seem to be of any relevance, why did you include it in the statement you made 10 years later in 2006?"

"Um, I really don't know."

"It was completely irrelevant, on the face of it, whether Billy Fuller was or wasn't there because no-one saw anyone there or saw anything there on the 23rd December 1996. Isn't that right? So, why then do you suddenly remember that Billy Fuller was there?"

"Well, he was there at 10 and he was there all morning."

"You clearly remember that, although you never said it to anyone?"

O'Higgins suggested to Farrell that by the time she made her statement in 2006, she knew that the testimony of Bill Fuller was an important issue. He said the reason Farrell had made the comment about Fuller selling his Christmas trees outside her shop was because she knew that on the morning of the 23rd December 1996 – that same morning that Farrell now said he had been outside her shop – Bill Fuller claimed he had seen Jules Thomas in her white Ford Fiesta near Kealfadda Bridge at around eleven o'clock.

I knew 2006 was a year after Marie Farrell, in Bailey's memorable phrase to the court a couple of weeks earlier, "came over to the side of the good".

Farrell had effectively turned into what might be a significant plank in Bailey's effort to secure damages for conspiracy and wrongful arrest. Implicitly, she was a significant plank, too, in Bailey's longstanding quest to clear his name for Sophie's murder. The two things were related.

But was Bailey's project unravelling before his eyes?

O'Higgins stared hard at Marie Farrell. Farrell looked uncomfortable but, then again, she had looked uncomfortable pretty much since her cross-examination had begun three days previously. Metaphorically, the barrister swooped in for the kill:

"You had discovered that Jules Thomas needed someone to

put Billy Fuller somewhere away from Kealfadda Bridge so that he couldn't have seen Jules Thomas."

***

On the 55th day of the case, 6th March 2015, a woman named Geraldine O'Brien took the stand in the High Court as a witness for the defence. In 1997, when she was 17, O'Brien had a part-time job helping Marie Farrell out in the ice-cream parlour for the summer season. O'Brien moved to Cork when she was 18, but kept in loose contact with Farrell in subsequent years, principally because O'Brien spent her summers on the Mizen. The two women had an occasional coffee together, and Farrell would give O'Brien news about her children, the eldest of whom were approximately the same age as O'Brien.

At some point over the Christmas period in 2013, or a few weeks before it – O'Brien was not sure about the date – the two women bumped into each other out shopping in Cork. O'Brien told Farrell that she was about to open a new business venture, a private further education college. Farrell was immediately interested in enrolling her daughter and the girlfriend of one of her sons. She enquired about grants, and O'Brien replied that you could get a subsidy of about €500, but the course fees were between €2,500 and €5,000, and the participants were expected to find the rest of the money themselves. Farrell continued to quiz O'Brien about where she would need to go to apply for a subsidy – she appeared very interested in the course for her daughter and her son's girlfriend. The next part of the exchange, as recalled by O'Brien, Farrell maintained did not take place. O'Brien, who like everyone else appearing in court was doing so under oath, said that Farrell subsequently said to her that *there was a case coming up that Mr Bailey was involved in and that she was going to be a witness. She had been told that he would receive substantial amounts of money.*

O'Higgins: *Did she estimate any kind of amount?*

O'Brien: *She said a couple of million.*
O'Higgins: *Yes?*
O'Brien: *Then she said she would probably get something from that, too.*

***

I had arranged to meet Bailey and Thomas again on the evening of one of the first couple of days when Marie Farrell was giving evidence, before her pyrotechnics really started. It was early December 2014 and we were now into the third week of the High Court proceedings. I wondered how they thought things were going. Bailey told me he wanted a resolution by the time of his birthday on 27th January 2015. He seemed upbeat.

We walked over the Ha'penny Bridge, the dark liquid crawl of the Liffey beneath us. It was chilly and breezy but the narrow bridge was thronged. Someone called out, "Murderer!" My two new friends did not react. I turned round but saw only couples linking arms, their scarves floating in the wind, and groups of young people with bright eyes and ruddy cheeks. I asked Bailey: "Ian, does that happen often, someone shouting 'murderer?'" He replied: "Oh, about every week or so".

We strolled into Temple Bar and found a pub, Gogarty's, with a corner booth. After a few rounds of drinks, I started to feel at ease. The Georgian streets outside, with their sash windows and columns, reminded me of my hometown on the other side of the Irish Sea. Bailey talked about his love of good food, his Saturday job as a boy on the fish market, the cuts of meat his father, a butcher, brought home.

Bailey told me that the progressive – to some, hopelessly anarchic – boarding school in Devon that Jules Thomas had attended had garnered a reputation for scandal. Also, as a baby his partner had been cradled in the arms of Welsh poet Dylan Thomas, who was apparently no relation. Thomas did not say much that night – Bailey basically spoke for the two of them. At some point, Thin Lizzy's version of *Whiskey in the Jar* came on the pub's sound system and Bailey sang along lustily here and there. Since then, every time I've heard that song, I've thought of that night, and maybe it was the mention of Dylan Thomas, a poet Bailey much admired, that got us talking about poems and poetry in general. Bailey mentioned a recent piece of verse by Carol Ann Duffy that he had particularly liked, which he said I might want to check out. It was called *Last Post* and Bailey said it was about "insignificance". At the time I thought he meant how insignificant and little and minute each of us was set against everything in the wide world outside the confines of that Dublin pub. I don't recall exactly, but I probably countered Bailey's poetry tip with one of my own, most likely the title of a favourite poem by Philip Larkin. I imagine I was talking about Larkin for a while, and consequently I'm going to say I have Larkin to blame for putting *Last Post* to the back of my mind. It was many months before I noticed the name of Duffy's poem in my notebook with the word *insignificance* written down next to it. I was curious, and looked up the poem.

Of course, I understand we can read a poem or a book or hear a song and say, it's about this, or it's about that, and in a sense we can all be right, but in my view *Last Post* is about time going in the reverse direction, backwards not forwards. It is about re-writing history in a different, better, way. The poem speaks of lives cut short, and then thrillingly, blissfully, restored. In her poem, Duffy imagines the First World War happening and then *not* happening, as if in a piece of film, spooling backwards, spilled blood pouring back into the corpses, the dead on the battlefield coming back to life, the atrocity and waste gone forever. The mistakes of the past wiped clean. Young lives about to start again on a fresh canvas.

Chapter 10

LIKE PUPPETS ON STRINGS

On 30th March 2015, Ian Bailey's civil action against the Irish police force and the Irish state ended catastrophically for him. After a marathon 64 days of evidence, the jury took just two hours to reach their verdict (on a reduced volume of evidence, since late in the process the judge ruled favourably on an application by the State to apply the Statute of Limitations, which struck out many of Bailey's claims, including those for wrongful arrest). The jury found that the Guards had not conspired to implicate Bailey in the murder of Sophie Toscan du Plantier. Instead of a massive pay-out, Bailey was on course to be saddled with costs in the millions of euros.

This was money that he would surely never pay, since the cottage at the Prairie was owned in Thomas's name, and he had no or very few meaningful assets. It was a deflated but calm Ian Bailey who faced the television cameras and newspaper reporters outside the Dublin courthouse with Jules Thomas at his side. Financially speaking, suing An Garda Síochána had been a risk-free venture for the Englishman. In the bigger scheme of things, Bailey's loss gave fresh momentum to the French investigation of Sophie's murder. Six months before the civil action had opened, Bailey's solicitor had written to the Irish Minister for Justice demanding the suspension of all relevant mutual assistance arrangements with France. These were the agreements that allowed the French investigating magistrate to conduct interviews on Irish soil, and were a key step towards building up an indictment against Bailey. Those agreements were up and running. In September 2015, investigating magistrate Patrick Gachon sent a team of detectives from Paris to County Cork. Surely Bailey's defeat at the High Court gave the Bouniols a glimmer of hope? I would soon have the chance to ask Sophie's son directly.

First, though, I was headed to Ireland myself, to see Bailey on home territory. I was travelling in roughly the same direction as Gachon's French cops, and at roughly the same time. After landing at Cork Airport, I got the correct exit from the roundabout outside the terminal at the second attempt, found the fastest setting for my windscreen wipers, and headed west. Bailey had given me directions to his cottage – stay on the Goleen road after Schull, then take a right onto the Bantry road. The entrance to the cottage was gated, with a hand-made signpost that read: *Artist's Studio & Gallery*. I recognised it immediately from the impromptu interviews that a younger Ian Bailey – woollen sweater, long strands of dark hair framing a pale face – had given to French and Irish television reporters in January and February 1997.

Bailey and Jules Thomas greeted me warmly. I offloaded a box of Belgian chocolates and a couple of bottles of Bordeaux. We had a short while to talk before Donal MacIntyre and his camera team were due to arrive. Bailey said we would all be able to have a proper catch-up over an early dinner. Thomas offered me a cup of coffee and left me alone with Bailey. We were at the rear of the cottage in the kitchen, which doubled as a dining room with its heavy wooden table. 'A lovely country kitchen' was my first thought. There was a line of plant pots on a long windowsill. On the table, a bowl of giant, rose-red apples, an old, dusty tape recorder, a laptop and a pile of papers. Outside I saw the outlines of a couple of greenhouses and a barn through the condensation on the window. I could hear some fowl squawking. I sipped my coffee. I thought of the turkeys – the three he had slaughtered on the day before Sophie was murdered.

Bailey had been cooking when I arrived. He had a rack of lamb dripping beads of fat in the oven, with a tray of roast potatoes browning nicely. There would be butter beans to go with it, and some greens that came from their garden. It was a brilliantly old-school menu, as if someone had turned the clock back to the 1970s.

Bailey said that he had some news. The gist was that a film director called Jim Sheridan had approached him. Sheridan was movie-world royalty in Ireland, forever jetting off to Hollywood or wherever. He had directed *My Left Foot* and *In the Name of the Father*. The latter was a film about the Guildford Four, a drama about a miscarriage of justice.

The Guildford Four scandal was one of the very lowest points in the history of criminal justice in England. A group of Irish men had been fitted up by the police for a pub bombing which they had nothing to do with. The bombing had happened at the height of the Troubles in Northern Ireland. The evidence against the Irishmen had been entirely suspect, but in 1975 a jury had convicted them. With the help of campaigning journalists and documentary-makers, the men had managed to clear their names and were awarded financial compensation. However much money these men were given, it would have been scant recompense for over a decade wasted in a prison cell.

"Anyway," said Bailey, "I met Jim and then I thought, I have to introduce him to Donal. That way, they can join forces." Bailey appeared delighted about the outcome, all on his initiative.

There had been other people wanting to come here, no doubt hoping to sit at this very table with their own cup of coffee, and film Bailey and make a story, but Bailey said he had gelled with Sheridan the first time he had met him, so that was that.

I asked Bailey if he was writing himself. He said he wasn't. Didn't he miss it? After all, he had looked like he was getting back into journalism, in the late autumn of 1996, a few first, tentative steps to get back into the trade, and then Sophie was murdered and the whole thing fell apart. After his arrest, he found himself effectively unemployable as a journalist.

My question had been about writing in general, journalism in the broadest sense, but Bailey replied saying that no, he couldn't write about the affair – that's how he called it, the *affair* – himself.

"Now," said Bailey, "I can work the journalists like puppets on strings."

I did not know what to say. I wrote his response in my notebook: *He can't write about the affair himself but "now I can work the journalists like puppets on strings".*

Bailey's strange comment was on my mind for the rest of the evening. MacIntyre arrived, and he explained to Bailey how the filming the next day might go. Bailey had plenty of ideas for content. For instance, there was a job he had to do at a nearby quarry, and we were welcome to go with him. We discussed the arrival of the French detectives. Bailey said that a couple of days earlier, he had seen some people hanging around at the end of his drive. It might well have been the French cops. When he approached, they walked away to a parked car.

Jules Thomas joined us for dinner. When talk turned to the enquiry in France and the far-off possibility of a trial there, of Bailey being prosecuted, Thomas shook her head sadly and frowned. It was terrible, she said, they had been carrying the burden of this false accusation for nearly 19 years. At the beginning, it had been worse. People had clapped when Bailey left a pub. They crossed the street to avoid passing him on the same pavement. One time, at a party, a woman had started chanting: "Ian is a murderer." I had heard about that one. Bailey had apparently said nothing to the woman and he had calmly left the room. Those darkest of dark days were behind them.

There had been happy times, too, of course. Thomas arrived on the Mizen as a young woman, much of her life ahead of her. Rural Ireland 40 years ago lacked some creature comforts, but if you were a blow-in, you could live the life you pleased. "We were the hippies," she said.

Thomas was quite easy to like, more so than Bailey. When the time came to leave the Prairie and drive back to Schull, Thomas said goodbye in the farmyard. It was a clear night. To the south of the cottage, a pale arc lit up the sky, and disappeared. "You can't see the Fastnet from here, just the gleam of light," said Thomas. "Everyone is fond of lighthouses, aren't they?" she added.

***

The next day, true to his word, Bailey took us to the quarry. I drove to the Prairie in my hire car while MacIntyre, the cameraman and the sound guy arrived in another car. I reversed into Bailey's narrow drive slowly, not to say inch-by-inch. I hadn't purchased extra insurance from the car hire company, so if I damaged the vehicle, I was aware I'd have a massive bill to pay. At one point, I got the reversing wrong and I had to go forward to set my course straight. It took me at least a minute to get to the cottage. The engine of the unfamiliar car might have done a bit of noisy revving, too, if I'm honest. When I got out, Bailey and MacIntyre and the team were having a good laugh at my driving.

"Mr Bean!" exclaimed Bailey, "it's like watching Mr Bean!"

Bailey went into his house to fetch his wallet. MacIntyre said quietly: "Mr Bean? Let him think that. It might be useful for you." Bailey drove ahead to the quarry and MacIntyre, the film crew and I followed in my car, with me driving. There was a bit more parking awkwardness at the quarry as I was worried about slipping into a ditch.

"Mr Bean!" said Bailey again, grinning.

We started filming. The quarry was just a pile of stones in a muddy patch of land off a country lane. Bailey explained that he needed some of the stones for his dry stone wall, which marked the perimeter of his property at the Prairie. Bailey took a hammer and a chisel and a rough piece of cloth out of his car. He looked around at the stones in the quarry, appearing to size them up. Then he put down the cloth and knelt on it. He selected a piece of dark grey rock and held it so the narrow side was facing up. From where I was standing, I saw Bailey trace a line on the rock; then he gave the chisel a couple of soft blows with the hammer. Then a single hard blow. The dark grey rock split in two. "There," said Bailey getting up. "The face of that stone hasn't seen the light of day in millions of years." He repeated the operation on a few more pieces of rock. Even when they were cut up, they were heavy, maybe 10 or 15 kilos each. Bailey carried each one effortlessly back to his vehicle.

The reveal of the inside of the stone was indeed something to think about. The other thing I was thinking about was that on the night of the murder, Sophie's killer used a piece of slate to attack her skull. "Unbelievable," said MacIntyre when we were in the car, tailing Bailey. This place, of all places. Why had he wanted to bring us here? Why did he crack open those slabs of slate? Why did he feel like showing us he could still carry heavy rocks around?

Later that day, MacIntyre and the crew and I took the Bantry road as far as the Schull-Goleen junction and turned right in the direction of Kealfadda Bridge. From there we drove inland along the narrow Kealfadda Road and made a left turn into the Toormore valley along an unsignposted track. This was where Shirley Foster had seen Bailey and Thomas speeding to the murder scene at about 2:20pm on 23rd December 1996. Foster said that Bailey and Thomas had already turned onto the track leading to Sophie's house – meaning that they knew where they were going – but Bailey maintained that he saw Foster and *then* turned.

When we entered the valley, not more than 30 seconds later, we noticed a saloon car driving very fast towards us. I pulled off the track into a verge to make way. The car was being driven by a woman and there were three male passengers, who at first sight appeared to be formally dressed. I caught sight of one of them quite well: a broad-shouldered man with short dark hair, stern-looking.

We were pretty sure of it – these were the French investigators in an unmarked Garda car. Were these the same people who Bailey had said had been checking out the cottage at the Prairie from a distance? It seemed likely.

Sophie's house still had its solid, comfortable aspect – it even looked rather imposing. If you didn't know differently, you might think it belonged to someone with a position of status in the local community – a doctor, say, or a solicitor. In the meantime, all the briars – the *old, heavy briars, strong briars* that the detective saw on 24th December 1996 – had been removed. A granite Celtic-type cross lay at the place Sophie fell, where her killer had dropped a concrete cavity block on her slender frame. The inscription read simply *SOPHIE*. The old pumping station, where the concrete block came from, was still there. I imagined Shirley Foster jamming the palm of her hand on her car horn when she saw the appalling sight of the corpse lying half in the ditch. I thought of the blue plastic sheet covering the body. The fluttering police tape. The Guards in their patrol car watching over that place all through the night, waiting for the delayed State pathologist. The horses at pasture, oblivious to it all.

I had long wondered why Sophie had not run towards her neighbours. I stood with my back to the rear door of Sophie's house, the door the killer perhaps rapped with his fists to make his presence known. Alfie Lyons and Shirley Foster lived uphill. The murderer could also have known that they were very likely to be in – even if their lights had been out for some hours – and he might have blocked Sophie's escape route uphill for that reason. What Sophie knew, he could have known, too. The wet paving stones outside the house glimmered, catching an unexpected ray of sunshine. A pair of gulls circled above.

It was time to pay a visit to Alfie Lyons.

Lyons opened his door about a foot. I saw a pile of old *Guardian* newspapers on a chair. I could hear a radio talk show in the background. Lyons was wearing a sweatshirt and sweatpants. No, he didn't want to talk. He had taken the decision long ago not to speak to journalists any more. He frowned at the mention of Ian Bailey. He said that Sophie's son Pierre-Louis had swapped him a portion of his fields for the storehouse, the one Sophie had been disappointed to find out didn't belong to her. Downhill, where Lyons' property abutted Sophie's, there were sacks of building materials and bits of machinery. Someone was getting some work done.

Lyons kindly gave me permission to walk around his land. At Easter 1995, he had the idea of revamping his garden as a present to Shirley Foster, who was retiring from her job as a teacher in England and coming to live with him. Bailey was one of the men doing the landscape gardening during that period. About 40 yards from Lyons' door, his garden dips a little, and there I had it: a perfect view of the back of Sophie's house, an unobstructed line of vision into Sophie's kitchen. Anyone in the kitchen looking out at the fields in front of the whitewashed house, to keep an eye on a couple of teenage boys larking about, for example, would have been nicely in profile, viewed from here. However, if you were in Sophie's kitchen and you were curious enough to want to look up to the far end of Lyons' garden, you would need to turn your head. My guess was that you could look into Sophie's kitchen from that precise spot in Alfie Lyons' garden for quite some time before anyone in the kitchen noticed you.

My first visit to the Mizen was coming to an end. Later, we returned to the Prairie. MacIntyre wanted to set up some sequences of Bailey and Thomas strolling around their garden, examining some of the vegetables growing in the neat plots. I looked at the front of the house, and peered into the room where Thomas did her painting. The signpost with *Artist's Studio & Gallery* on it had not had much impact, Bailey had told me. One day a young Israeli couple had walked down the drive and introduced themselves. Was the Gallery open? It turned out that the Israelis were more interested in discussing the pros and cons of moving to the Mizen than buying one of Thomas's seascapes. They were pretty much the only people who called. The location might also have played a role, I thought. It wasn't as remote as Sophie's place but, still, the cottage was basically in the middle of nowhere.

I spotted an easel in the centre of the room, next to a table loaded with tins and tubes of paint. There were boxes full of what looked like old magazines. A dozen canvases hung on the wall, in varying states of completion. It was as if Thomas had started painting them, and then paused and thought, 'Okay, where do I go from here'?

Before I left, while MacIntyre and the crew were packing away their equipment, Bailey called me into the kitchen. He opened his laptop, and asked me if I had a memory stick. What he had in mind would only take a minute or two. What I could see on the screen was the police file. He scrolled through what appeared to be a vast number of statements, labelled individually in Word files, encouraging me to look. In fact, I have been reading them ever since. Most were titled *Affidavit* followed by the name of the person giving their testimony to the Guards. Bailey downloaded the whole thing for me, plus the transcript of the failed Dublin action, and the transcript of his 2003 court case against the newspapers. There was also the DPP paper there that explained why Bailey was never put on trial in Ireland – a text that Bailey a couple of times had already said "exonerated" him.

Bailey mentioned once again something about me being a "supporter". I did not catch all of what he said as I was thinking about the precious memory stick. Before I left, I handed him a €100 note. "For petrol," I said. Bailey thanked me and shook my hand warmly. As I slowly drove away, I heard him crack another 'Mr Bean' joke, and saw the two of them in my rear-view mirror and – maybe because I had been thinking of art and artists generally – the couple in the *American Gothic* painting by Grant Wood came to mind. Bailey and Thomas were standing in front of their rural home, like Wood's couple. Bailey, like the man in *American Gothic*, but minus the pitchfork, was looking ahead; Thomas, like the woman in the painting, was glancing to one side, her expression suddenly melancholy.

I wondered if something was starting right there and then with this story – a real story with a beginning, a middle and an end. If I was going to commit to writing it, then I would have to gather my ideas together and start soon, and heaven knew how long the thing would take.

***

It was the autumn of 1989. Sophie was 32 and had recently met Daniel. There was excitement in her life: with Daniel's encouragement, Sophie was in the throes of setting up her own film production company with the intention of making documentaries, telling true stories in her own way. Her venture was named for the title of her favourite painting, *Les Champs Blancs* – a large, abstract canvas of near-whites and light greys and watery blues – the gift of an artist friend that today hangs in the apartment on the Rue Tiquetonne in Paris that is still the home of Georges and Marguerite Bouniol.

In November of that year, Sophie and Daniel took a trip to India. Sophie kept a record of the journey in a notebook. After her death, the notebook was stored away in a filing cabinet in her parents' apartment in Paris, along with many other of her jottings, travelogues and short stories. For the most part, Sophie's writings lay undisturbed. If there was something especially significant about this notebook or its contents, it was not apparent to those tasked with investigating Sophie's murder. Indeed, it's likely they never read it.

At that time, Daniel's great friend Catherine Clément was living in New Delhi, where her husband was French ambassador. For Sophie, there was no better introduction to the religions and culture of India than Clément, who was writing about this quite prolifically, explaining the country's profound exoticism to the French-speaking public.

First, the couple visited Bombay. Sophie's view out to the ocean from her hotel room was like her precious painting, mist hanging over the blue-grey sea, the sky and water mixing, hardly distinguishable. The only fixed points were a few ships far out in the horizon, and a tiny rocky island closer to shore. Sophie breathed in. The seawater was dirty, it stank. She wrote in her diary: *And yet, in the heat, the sea is a false friend, tempting me to throw myself in.* Behind her, a row of tower blocks; gaudy, ostentatious, housing for the wealthy. They made Sophie imagine the rich part of Bombay as a woman wearing too much make-up, crossing the line into vulgarity, but proud of the spectacle she was giving those observing her, and proud of the spectacle she was giving herself. Set against this, what was there? The poor quarters, at nightfall lit up by thousands upon thousands of naked bulbs, as if in celebration of something, but there they had nothing to celebrate, she wrote, *they have scored no victories and offered no resistanc*e.

On to Calcutta: at first sight, an English-style city after an aerial bombardment, rubble for buildings, run-down, roads full of holes. And yet, what vitality! She summed it up thus: *All life is there and there is all life.* With death so near, too. Say you take two fingers and place them together. Well, death here is that close, like those two fingers. Life and death have found a balance, thought Sophie, under the plastic sheets for roofs and among the dirt and the garbage.

In the heat, Sophie saw the Indians bathing. Then they let the rays of the sun fall on their skin to burn away the glistening droplets of water. Meanwhile, flowers passed from one human hand to the next, given as gifts. The joy of it all! *It's a joy that lasts until the very last breath of life*, Sophie thought, or it almost did, *before death buries the final screams and vomiting.*

Reaching deep into her imagination, Sophie conjured up a woman in a white robe. She wrote: *It is difficult to accept, to die dressed in white under a ton of petals.* This, to Sophie, was precisely the contradiction: life in Calcutta was about survival, you could see this all around you. But life was also a preparation for dying, an apprenticeship if you will, played out on the stage that was this teeming Indian city. Kali, the goddess of Calcutta, was also the goddess of death, wasn't she?

Down at the riverbank, once a year, Kali is sent bobbing away into the inky night. On the one hand, she's there in effigies on altars in every street; on the other, you have this: the spectacle of the people of Calcutta pushing their papier-mâché figures of Kali out onto the water. It takes time – the figures don't get caught by the current quickly – but the water is warm and it seeps into the papier-mâché. So the figures ultimately sink, and the people of Calcutta watch them sink. They see their goddess of death Kali drown in their river.

Sophie thought: but what if? What if you took one of those figures in the river by her hand? In her diary Sophie wrote: *What if you got carried away by the current with her, and drowned with her?*

That's surely not the thought uppermost in the minds of the multitudes on the riverbank. Once a year they take their revenge on their goddess. Inside they are angry, they are aggressive and they are violent. It is cathartic.

The people see Kali drown, wrote Sophie.

And they take pleasure from it.

Chapter 11

THE FILE

My memory stick contained the items of the discovery that An Garda Síochána and the Irish state had made available to Bailey's legal team in advance of his civil action in 2014-2015. In all, there were over 700 witness statements. I now also had the transcript of Bailey's earlier libel action in 2003, as well as the transcript of the lengthy civil case in Dublin.

There was a raft of correspondence from Bailey and Thomas to the Taoiseach (Irish prime minister) and other ministers, complaining about the behaviour of the Guards. I also had a copy of the controversial position paper from the Office of the Director of Public Prosecutions. That was the first item I read, double-clicking with the enthusiasm of a hungry child ripping open a bag of sweets.

I had been looking over Bailey's shoulder when he transferred the files and he seemed to copy over all of the Garda statements. I had to expect some gaps since I already knew that the DPP had criticised the Guards for leaving out some witness statements when they submitted their file proposing Bailey's prosecution. The Guards had, quite simply, lost a number of other statements. It was almost impossible to know if I had the complete police file, minus those gaps. I could hardly knock on the door of Schull Garda station, show them the long list of statements, and ask them what they thought – but my sense was that this was the real deal.

When he put the files onto my memory stick, Bailey had said words to the effect that there was a bunch of documents that I wouldn't need, that weren't important. Here, I thought he was referring to items of correspondence with his lawyers, something like that. If that was the case, he was right – I didn't need them. As for the court transcripts, checking they were all there was as simple as counting the number of daily sessions and seeing I had the same number of individual PDFs.

Driving back towards Cork in the gathering darkness, I wondered about Bailey's motivation. I had decided against a magazine feature, since it would not do the case justice. I had told him my plan was to write a book. On that first visit to the Mizen, Bailey offered to help me with it. I had thanked him for his kindness. Now, I smiled to myself. What had one of the French journalists written, back in the day? It was a freighted comment: *When he* [Bailey] *was arrested, the Irish press lost its best-informed journalist.*

Without the police file, in particular, researching a book on the Sophie case would be an uphill struggle. I was sure Bailey knew that. Both sets of barristers, in both of Bailey's civil actions, had quoted from Garda statements and memos. However, I wanted to get to the source, so the original signed testimonies from witnesses were crucial.

My theory was that if I approached the mystery without too many preconceptions, rewinding the story right back to the beginning, and giving every piece of evidence an equal chance, so to speak, I might get somewhere. Sometimes a degree of distance is a good thing when you're trying to solve a thorny problem. Isn't that why businesses sometimes bring in outside consultants – to give them fresh ideas? Then again, I might get nowhere. I had to accept that risk. A cold case, by its very nature, means that years will have passed, memories will have faded, and witnesses died. The best friend of a long-ago murderer hoping to avoid detection is the passage of time.

At the libel trial, the lawyers for the newspapers had prioritised an all-out attack on Bailey's assertion that he had been at home with Thomas on the morning of the discovery of Sophie's corpse on the track. They also had picked away at Bailey's claim that he only found out about the discovery of the dead body from *Examiner* news editor Eddie Cassidy at around 1:40pm that day, and learned that it was a French national involved thanks to the headline of a 2pm radio bulletin. What could I learn from the file?

It was clear from Bailey's own account of the night of the murder that he had not been in bed with Thomas the whole time. He said to the Guards at his first arrest that he got up in the night to write – on a sheet of paper – a feature about the internet arriving in rural County Cork, sitting at his kitchen table. Later, at about 9am, or shortly afterwards, he left the cottage altogether to type up the feature in the unheated 'studio' building, some 150 yards from the cottage. He had no watch, so the timings of both events were sketchy, but he estimated that he was in the studio until about 10:30am that morning; he subsequently got through to the office of the *Sunday Tribune* in Dublin by telephone and found out he could dictate the story over the phone the following day.

What was significant was that both Bailey and Thomas claimed that they stayed in the cottage for the rest of the morning, indeed until hearing the news on the radio at 2pm, following which they left in haste in the direction of Toormore. However, Thomas's daughter Fenella, who was confined to the cottage with a cold on the night of the crime, told the Guards that her mother and Ian Bailey left home for a couple of hours that Monday morning. At the courthouse in Dublin, I remembered Thomas conceding that she had asked Fenella to change her statement – she denied that she had attempted to "pressurise" her – but Fenella had refused to do so.

If Thomas had not left the cottage, it would have been impossible for Bill Fuller, then a gardener who sometimes worked and drank with Bailey, to have seen her on the morning of the murder. Fuller told the court in Cork in 2003, when Bailey was suing the newspapers, that on 23rd December 1996 he had been driving around the local area trying to sell a few remaining Christmas trees. It was not going as well as Fuller had hoped, so in the late morning he changed plan. He decided to visit an elderly client in Lowertown, near Schull, to work on his garden for a while, which in any case was a regular appointment on Mondays. Fuller took the Kealfadda road south in the direction of Schull. It was about 11:20am.

In the courthouse in Cork, the barrister for the newspapers asked Fuller: *Did you see another car on the road?*

I did, yes, Bill Fuller replied. *It was Jules's car.*

Jules Thomas?

Yes, and she was driving.

In what direction was she driving?

She was driving down towards the Kealfadda Bridge from the area of Sophie du Plantier's house, down the hill.

Fuller said that at one point as she went over a bump in the road, he saw Thomas put her arm out, ostensibly to stop something on the passenger seat from falling off. Fuller said that Thomas was driving on her own, and when she reached Kealfadda Bridge, she turned in the direction of Goleen. Fuller drove off in the opposite direction – towards Lowertown and Schull.

James Camier, an organic vegetable seller with a stall on the main road in Goleen, also took the stand in Cork. Camier knew Ian Bailey quite well, as Bailey had worked for him on a casual basis several times. He confirmed in the courtroom a statement he had given to the Guards. On Monday, 23rd December 1996, Camier had been working on the stall in Goleen with his wife, Geraldine. *Between 11am and 11:30am, Jules Thomas, whom I know well, approached the stall... I was struck by the fact that she was very distressed. There was a distraught, strange complexion about her. She looked very worried. There was casual talk about the vegetables.* Camier enquired about Ian Bailey. *Out of the blue,* said Camier, Thomas told him that Bailey "...*is gone to Drinane* [Toormore] *to report on the murder".* I may have asked her, "What murder?" She replied, "A Frenchwoman". She hung her head [and said], "it's sad, but that's his job, to report on these things", or something like that. I was shocked. It was the first I heard that there was a murder.

At the courtroom in Cork, Bailey's barrister put it to Camier that he could have got the days mixed up, that Thomas agreed she had spoken with him at his stall, but that she had done so on the Tuesday, Christmas Eve, rather than on the Monday, 23rd December. But Camier was adamant. Turning to the judge, he said: *Your worship, how do I remember it quite clearly is for the simple reason Christmas Day was on a Wednesday and there was a lapse of a day between that* [day] *and Christmas.* Camier recalled that on what he had termed the "spare day" between finding out about the murder from Thomas and Christmas Day – on Christmas Eve, in other words – there had been *a lot of speculation and a lot of talk.* He remembered, too, that it was only at about 2:45pm on the day of the murder, 23rd December, that another customer mentioned that he had heard about the gruesome discovery of a dead body.

What I found interesting was that Camier had approached the Guards a long time after the crime, following a conversation with Bill Fuller. He had not realised up to that point the significance of the precise timing of Thomas's comments about the murder of the Frenchwoman. *I will stress*, said Camier to the court in Cork, *the statement I made I made it by my own mind, my own heart, my own thinking. No-one influenced it, no way in the world.*

Bailey's barrister countered by repeating that Jules Thomas was not at Camier's stall on the Monday at all. Moreover, the barrister said: *She says that she went there on Christmas Eve and that Jimmy Camier said to her that "it was an awful thing about the Frenchwoman".* Bailey's legal team was suggesting that not only was Camier mixed up with the days, he was confused about who said what, and to whom.

Camier: [to the judge] *How could I say that, your worship, when I knew nothing whatsoever about it until she said it to me?*

Bailey's barrister: *I am putting it to you that you are mistaken.*

Camier: [again, to the judge] *No, your worship, no.*

Jules Thomas maintained that both Bill Fuller and James Camier were mistaken about seeing her – and in Camier's case, talking to her – on the morning of Monday, 23rd December 1996, insisting it had happened in the late morning of Christmas Eve. However, one thing struck me as curious. Bailey and Thomas had one car between them at that time. I knew Bailey had paid a visit to the Lowertown Creamery at about 12 noon on 24th December, and had exchanged words with one of the shop assistants, a conversation that stuck in the assistant's head, and Bailey had bought a bottle of 'Happy Shopper' bleach there. So how could Jules Thomas have been in Goleen at almost exactly the same time?

It was about six miles from the Prairie to Goleen, and about five miles via the main road (slightly less via Hunt's Hill) from the Prairie to Lowertown. These were journeys that Bailey and Thomas habitually made by car. And I knew that Bailey had taken the car with him to Lowertown on the late morning of Christmas Eve, as he had given a lift to two friends of Saffron and Virginia – this was a matter of record, the two people concerned had given statements to this effect. (In one of the statements, one of the friends also made an explicit reference to Jules Thomas being at home in the cottage at the Prairie before they got the lift from Bailey.) Since Ian Bailey was at Lowertown Creamery at approximately 12 noon on Christmas Eve, and was using the Ford Fiesta, Jules Thomas could presumably not have been shopping for organic produce at James Camier's stall in Goleen on the same day, at close to the same time, without the use of a vehicle.

Later, I came across an interesting piece of research undertaken by the Guards that gave some context for the question of how much Bailey knew about the crime, and when. Toormore was split up into a number of sub-districts. The section of the valley where Sophie, Alfie Lyons and Shirley Foster, and the Richardsons had their properties was commonly referred to as Drinane. One of the Guards put it quite clearly in a memo: *Due to my local knowledge and enquiries I am aware that there are 41 non-nationals* [foreigners] *living in the Toormore area of Schull. The Toormore area would comprise of 13 different townlands. By this, I mean that these 13 townlands would incorporate the name Toormore in their postal address.* That meant that if you said you had a foreign friend living in Toormore at the end of 1996, it could have been any one of these 41 people.

Eddie Cassidy called Ian Bailey at 1:40pm on the day of the murder. Cassidy told Bailey a body had been found in the area of Toormore. Bailey had been in contact with Cassidy about a month earlier, expressing a desire to write pieces for the *Examiner*, as he was kick-starting his career as a journalist, so Bailey's name came to Cassidy's mind that day. Cassidy told the court in Cork in 2003 that he didn't know the nationality of the dead woman at the time he called Ian Bailey, only that she was foreign. Cassidy also said that he had no inkling that it was even a murder – he imagined that it was a traffic accident, perhaps some kind of hit-and-run, or a fatality among the large community of new-age travellers that lived on the Mizen. Bailey, for his part, told the Guards that he drove towards Sophie's house on account of "local knowledge" and only had his hunch confirmed when he saw Shirley Foster at the end of the lane leading up the valley – a version of the incident, of course, disputed by Foster.

Let's stick with events in the Bailey-Thomas residence on 23rd December 1996.

A woman living on the Mizen peninsula told the court in Cork that Ian Bailey had phoned her at about 12 noon. The woman, named Caroline Leftwick, originally from Devon, England, said that Bailey *said he would be unable to keep his appointment with us that day. The appointment was to collect some garlic we had been saving for him.*

The barrister for the newspapers asked Leftwick if Bailey had explained to her the reason he was unable to keep the appointment.

Leftwick: *Because there had been a murder... There had been a murder in the locality, in his locality, and he had the story, the job to cover the story. He sounded kind of excited about it... I was shocked, obviously. And so I asked him if he knew who the victim was, because I was concerned it might be someone known to me.*

According to Leftwick, Bailey had replied that it was a Frenchwoman, someone who had been on holiday, and not someone Leftwick would have known. Bailey's barrister put it to Leftwick that Bailey *denies saying that to you, because he says he was unaware of that himself at the time. Are you certain about this?* Leftwick replied: *I am certain about this.*

In May 1997, a Guard paid a visit to the offices of the *Irish Independent* newspaper in Dublin, and took a statement from Pádraig Beirne, who was the newspaper's long standing photographic editor. *On December 23rd 1996*, Beirne declared, *I recall receiving a telephone call at about 1.55pm… A man introduced himself as Bailey, a photographer from Schull. To the best of my recollection, the call came via our general switch. Mr Bailey told me the body of a woman had been found dead in West Cork. He knew the woman was a French native. He said he had a picture of her and asked me was I interested in getting it for publication in the* Irish Independent. *As far as I recollect I asked him how he had the picture of her and he replied that he had taken it himself, and that she was a very good-looking woman.*

Beirne asked Bailey how he could get the picture to him. Could he wire it? Bailey said that he couldn't, so Beirne thought the best thing would be for a freelance photographer he knew, Michael McSweeney, who was based in Cork, to make contact with Bailey, collect the picture of the dead woman and wire it to the *Independent*'s offices in Dublin. *As far as I recall, Bailey offered me pictures of the scene of where the body was found, but I was not interested, as McSweeney would do that job for me.* The photo that Bailey had offered Beirne, and the one that he could have used, was a 'pick-up' picture, meaning a photo taken when a person was alive. *I gave him* [Bailey] *the mobile telephone number of freelance photographer Michael McSweeney.* Beirne said to Bailey that he would phone McSweeney to make sure the two men got in touch. *Our conversation ended there.*

Beirne told the Guard taking his statement that he then called

Michael McSweeney and let him know what Bailey had said on the phone, and encouraged McSweeney to travel from his home in Cork City to the west of the county. *My conversation with Mr Bailey lasted a matter of two to three minutes. I never heard from Mr Bailey again. I went to our daily editors' conference at 2:30. The murder was discussed, and I outlined that our freelance photographer was en route to West Cork and that we hoped to have a 'pick-up' pic of the dead woman.*

Beirne's testimony was fascinating for several reasons. First, Beirne claimed that Bailey had told him that he had a 'pick-up' photo of the dead woman, and had proceeded to inform his colleagues of Bailey's offer at an editorial meeting around half an hour later. Knowing Bailey, I could well imagine him saying to Beirne that he had a photo when he didn't have one. Bailey might have assumed that he could lay his hands on one later that day, so perhaps he took a chance. Bailey was getting back into journalism after a barren period, work-wise, so I could accept that, under pressure to benefit from the huge breaking news story, he might have promised a photo editor of a national newspaper more than he might be able to deliver. However, Beirne's recollection of Bailey's extra detail that he had taken the photo of the dead woman *himself* was entirely gratuitous. Why would Bailey say such a thing?

Another aspect was the timing of the conversation. Beirne told the Guards that Bailey's call had come through at about 1:55pm, meaning *after* Eddie Cassidy's call to Bailey at 1:40pm but *before* the news bulletin on the radio at 2pm that, in Bailey's own version of events, confirmed the nationality of the dead woman. Beirne's testimony was clear: *He knew the woman was a French native.*

Beirne's evidence interlocked with that of Michael McSweeney, the freelance photographer who also ran a photo agency. McSweeney told the Guards that at about 2:10pm – so, around 10 minutes after Beirne wound up his short phone conversation with Bailey – Beirne called him to say *he had been contacted by a Mr Bailey and he had photographs of the scene. Neither of us knew this guy Bailey but I got his phone number from Beirne. Bailey contacted me before I had a chance to telephone him, this would be around 2:15 to 2:20pm.* McSweeney was sure of the time of Bailey's call because he had just listened to the radio news at 2pm. The call, then, would have presumably been made seconds before Bailey and Thomas drove to Toormore. *Mr Bailey said he had pictures of the scene... I enquired what the pictures showed, how close they were, what sort of lens, if there were people in the picture. Bailey seemed vague and then said his girlfriend had taken them earlier that day.*

Bailey's "girlfriend" had to be a reference to Jules Thomas. Bill Fuller said that he spotted Jules Thomas driving alone at around 11:20am along the Kealfadda Road just beyond the turn-off for Sophie's house on the morning of the murder. Thomas had denied being anywhere at that time other than at home in her cottage. In any case, Shirley Foster had discovered the body at 10am and the Guards had arrived at 10:38am. Surely, after that point it would have been difficult to take photos, or simply drive down the lane from the Kealfadda Road towards Sophie's place, without being noticed?

I looked at the negatives myself and found that they were of no use editorially as they were shot through bushes and weren't very clear. "Shot through bushes" implied that the photographer was partly concealed – could that be right? *I could make out that there were Gardaí at the scene, but other than that they were of no editorial value.* The Guards in the photos of the crime scene apparently supplied by Bailey proved that they were taken after 10:38am. McSweeney told the Guards that as far as he could remember, he threw the film away, since it was of no use. What was curious was that – if the timing of his phone conversation with Bailey was correct – Bailey had mentioned the crime scene photos to McSweeney *before* they were taken. By this, I mean *before they were taken in Bailey's subsequent version of events.* To recap, Bailey had been the first journalist on the scene, noted by Garda Malone in his memo. According to Bailey, it was only after arriving at Toormore, therefore at some point after 2:20pm, that Thomas had taken her photos with her camera, an expensive piece of equipment with a long lens that, as a rule, she did not let anyone else use. As for the 'pick-up' photo that had interested Pádraig Beirne of the *Irish Independent*, McSweeney stated: *I can also confirm that Ian Bailey never offered me a photograph of the deceased at any time.*

The Cork libel case added more detail to McSweeney's statements to the Guards. I also understood from the exchanges in the courtroom why McSweeney might well have thought of using some amateur photos of the crime scene. In the courtroom in 2003, McSweeney said:

We were under pressure of falling light, so I asked [Bailey] *when the pictures were taken. It was hard to get any real, solid answer but in the end, towards the end of our conversation, he said the pictures were done that morning between 10:00 and 11:00.* The timing was important to McSweeney, because the window of opportunity for a photographer working out of doors on a late December day was short, and time was running out. It thus made sense that he would have insisted on knowing from Bailey when the photos were shot.

The barrister for the newspapers checked what Bailey had said: *They were done that morning between 10:00 and 11:00?*

McSweeney: *That's right.*

***

I had read about the testimonies of Malachi Reed and Helen Callanan – brought up by the Guards during Ian Bailey's first arrest – that suggested to them that Bailey had admitted to the crime. The police file contained a couple of roughly similar pieces of evidence that caught my interest.

One concerned the same Bill Fuller who claimed to have seen Thomas in her car on the Kealfadda Road on the morning of the murder. Fuller said that he went to Bailey's house in early February 1997 and Bailey said to him, among other things: *You fancied her, you went up there to try and see what you could get... You realised you went too far and you had to finish her off.* This was certainly a troubling piece of testimony. The use of the second person was unusual, too. Was Bailey trying to finger Fuller for the crime? Or was it a kind of rant where the person says 'you' when they really mean 'I'? But Fuller's testimony was an outlier in the sense that Bailey denied that he had said anything at all to him. According to Bailey, Fuller had invented the whole thing. I thought I would put Bill Fuller's recollection of his conversation with Bailey to one side for the moment, and concentrate on evidence which seemed to hang on how it was interpreted.

Evidence like Richard and Rosie Shelley's night out on New Year's Eve, 1998.

On 31st December 1998, so just over two years after Sophie's murder, Richard and Rosie Shelley, a couple in their thirties, were enjoying a drink in Hackett's bar in Schull. The bar is small and it was heaving; Ian Bailey and Jules Thomas were in Hackett's as well to welcome in the New Year. Everyone was consuming alcohol – Richard Shelley recalled that he had six or seven pints of Heineken that evening, his wife about half that amount. The couple were not driving that night.

During the course of the evening, Bailey invited the Shelleys back to the Prairie to continue the New Year's celebrations. Bailey told the Shelleys that another couple would be going, too. Bailey, Thomas and the Shelleys bought some cans of beer as a take-out and departed the bar for the Prairie at 12:30am. The Shelleys thought it strange that the other couple did not materialise.

At the cottage, Bailey fetched half a bottle of spirits – in Richard Shelley's recollection it was probably gin, maybe vodka. He wasn't sure if there was a mixer available. What he *was* sure about was the topic of conversation: the four of them were in the sitting room at the Prairie, and Bailey went into a neighbouring room and fetched a large number of newspaper clippings on Sophie's murder. Bailey and Thomas were both speaking about the killing – but especially Bailey. It was the only topic of conversation. Richard Shelley recalled that after a couple of hours, Thomas went upstairs to bed.

The Shelleys had been offered the chance to sleep in the living room – it was close to 3am by now, and Thomas had given them some blankets – but Rosie was adamant she wanted to go, said Richard in the courthouse in Cork, *because my wife was uneasy with the way the night was going with the cuttings*. Bailey by now had gone into a room just off the sitting room, and Richard Shelley followed him in to ask him for a phone to call his father to arrange for a lift. The room was equipped as a study and had a single bed in it. Bailey was lying down. He told Shelley the phone was in the kitchen. Shelley left the study room and called his father, who agreed to come and pick them up.

After Shelley finished the call, Bailey came towards him. He looked upset. Shelley recalled the scene in the Cork courtroom:

He was crying and he put his arms around me… He said to me, "I did it, I did it", and as he was saying, "I did it, I did it", I was saying, "You did what?", and he said, "I went too far". Then he let me go and just went back to his room.

Under cross-examination, Bailey's lawyer said to Shelley:

He is quite clear… that he never told you he did it in the context that you put it. What he said was, "they say" or "they said" that I did it, and I must suggest that you either forgot that or are leaving it out?

Shelley countered: *I am not forgetting it, I am not leaving it out.*

It would be an extraordinary thing for him to make an admission to you, wouldn't it?

It would be, I suppose, but I am not lying at all. I have no reason to lie.

Chapter 12

ON THE RUE TIQUETONNE

This, I thought, is the lair of a real investigator: a wide table with a dozen carefully marked files, newspaper clippings, a neat stack of correspondence, a bilingual French-English dictionary, a screen and a keyboard. That was one side of the room. The other side was a comfortable sitting area, a place for family and friends to come together. I had come to see Jean-Antoine Bloc, a retired engineer in his sixties, a man with a shaved head and spectacles, wearing a cardigan the day we met.

The Paris apartment he shared with his wife – a life-long friend of Marguerite Bouniol – served as the premises of the Sophie Justice Committee. The set-up suggested that roughly half of Bloc's time was dedicated to pursuing Sophie's killer. I liked Bloc the moment I saw him.

Bloc had co-authored a book on the murder which made a firm case for Bailey's guilt. Written in French, it was not stocked anywhere in Ireland. He asked me if I had met Bailey. I said I had, and noticed his eyes narrow. It put me on the back foot, but I knew Bloc was right to be sceptical about the intentions of anyone interested in writing or broadcasting about the murder.

Bloc and Jean-Pierre Gazeau, Marguerite Bouniol's brother, the chair of the Justice Committee, had done the hike from the Prairie to Sophie's place, and thought that a younger and fitter Bailey could have done it in as little as 36 minutes. But had Bailey and Sophie ever met? I asked Bloc what he thought. He placed his right index finger just under his eye and pulled the skin down slightly. It was the French expression, *mon oeil*, signalling incredulous disbelief, like saying 'my foot!' in English. Bloc was using the expression ironically. It was obvious to Bloc that the two had met, that Bailey had pursued Sophie. The most convincing evidence he had come across was from one of Sophie's colleagues, a filmmaker named Guy Girard. Sophie had mentioned Bailey's name to him a short time before her final trip to Ireland. The problem, said Bloc, was that the rules on hearsay meant that Girard's testimony would not be accepted in an Irish courtroom, whereas in France the same testimony would, in principle, stand.

Bloc took a dim view of the Irish DPP's analysis of the file. Bailey's scratches and the cut on his forehead were clearly caused by something other than cutting a tree and slaughtering turkeys. The gist of Bloc's argument was that the witness statements given by people drinking in the Galley bar on the night before the murder – people who had had a good view of Bailey's hands and forearms – had not been accurately assessed by the DPP; nor had any link been made between the ferocity of the attack on Sophie's face and skull, and the type of violence used by Bailey in his assaults on Jules Thomas. In any case, the DPP was beginning to fade from view. The French investigation was up and running, interviewing witnesses in Ireland, one of whom was a man called Sean Murray.

Bloc said that I should look into Murray. He had a petrol station that Sophie had visited on her way from Cork Airport to Toormore on the Friday before she was murdered. She had bought some fuel there. Only Sophie had not been alone in her hire car. Bloc had been to the petrol station himself, and had asked some questions. What was interesting, said Bloc, was that there was no doubt that the front passenger seat of Sophie's car had been pushed right back. I wrote down *Sean Murray* in my notebook.

I was overstaying my welcome, although Bloc was too polite to say so. He and his wife had things to do. There would be a meeting of the Justice Committee that very evening. I was invited to come back later and observe proceedings. When I did, there were 20 people gathered in Bloc's sitting room. I recognised Agnès Thomas, Sophie's best friend, and Alain Spilliaert, the Bouniol family lawyer, who also acted for the Justice Committee. Jean-Pierre Gazeau appeared on the screen of Bloc's computer. Gazeau was in Rio de Janeiro, as I understood it. There were comments along the lines of *Oh, lucky you*, and *I bet the weather's better over there than it is here*, but when the meeting started in earnest I felt a sharp pang of sadness. Once again, there was scant progress on the case to report. People filled this same room month after month, year after year, their hope for justice for poor Sophie ebbing and flowing – but mostly receding, as layer upon layer of dust settled on the case.

***

For the first 15 years or so after the murder, Marguerite Bouniol was the voice and the face of the campaign to secure justice for her daughter. Initially she had pushed Ireland to put Ian Bailey on trial for Sophie's murder. Later – when Ireland and the DPP looked like a poor bet – she tried to get the French Republic to honour its responsibility properly to investigate the crime. Sophie's mother had written dozens of letters – to presidents, to prosecutors, to members of different parliaments. Many went unanswered. Now, Marguerite Bouniol was frail. The baton had passed to the man with whom I had an appointment on the Rue Tiquetonne, the handsome street in the second arrondissement of Paris where Sophie had grown up.

I rang the bell. Pierre-Louis Baudey-Vignaud came to the door to meet me. We walked upstairs. He explained that his grandparents were in their house in the village of Combret, in the Lozère, so the apartment was empty. The autumn light fractured pleasantly into the stairway through a sheet of stained glass. "Where are the others?" asked Pierre-Louis. He was wearing a blue blazer and a shirt and tie. He appeared anxious. He had agreed to an interview with MacIntyre and Sheridan for their documentary, which by now was their joint project. The idea was to do the interview there, in Sophie's childhood home. The two men were slightly late, caught in the city's traffic, which meant I had a few minutes to talk with Pierre-Louis alone.

Pierre-Louis led me into the sitting room. A mantelpiece held a large number of framed photos. I recognised Bertrand, Sophie's brother, who lived in Paris. There was Stéphane, the younger brother, who was based in the United States. Photos of children, Pierre-Louis among them. Old photos of the Bouniols on holiday, squinting in the sunshine. I guessed Georges, Sophie's father, had been behind the camera most of the time. Marguerite looked sensible, practical, her slender arms around her children. Of course, there were photos of Sophie, ones I had seen in newspapers and magazines. Next to the mantelpiece, a painting. I recognised it straight away – *Les Champs Blancs*, the big abstract canvas that gave Sophie the name for her documentary production company.

People wondered why Pierre-Louis had not sold the whitewashed house at Toormore. It was a place visited by evil, so why had he not got rid of the thing? Pierre-Louis had worked in real estate, after all. He was in a good position to organise a sale.

Pierre-Louis said he kept it because of what it meant to his mother. It was the only place he went to with her and, staying in the house, it felt like being with her again. Sophie's camel coat still hung on a rack in the hall. Sometimes his own daughter, also called Sophie, would take the coat off the peg and try it on, in the way any little girl would put on an adult garment for amusement. In the kitchen, there was a tin of Sophie's favourite loose-leaf tea. The tin was nearly full to the brim, precisely as it had been in December 1996. If you took the lid off, you could smell the aroma.

"My stepfather, Daniel, wanted to sell the house," Pierre-Louis said, "but my father said, listen, it's your mother's house." This was the first time I heard him say *Maman*, the first time I heard him say the name he used with her and, when he did, his voice cracked very slightly. "Give it some time. Then you can decide if you are going to keep it or not. We're not going to sell it straight away."

Pierre-Louis and Pierre, his father, went together to the shallow valley at Toormore in the summer of 1999. Pierre had never been there before. "We were going to see if I felt okay in the house. It was an important moment, but I did feel okay there." Of course, Pierre-Louis knew how the Guards had found the house, with blood smeared on the rear door. Sometimes it was difficult for him, he would be having breakfast with his wife and he would look out of the window, and imagine his mother's blood splattered here and there, but would not say anything to his wife, he would keep it all in, because otherwise she would get upset.

"It's like being handicapped. I live it like a handicap."

Thirty-six minutes over the hill. A short drive down the Kealfadda Road and then a left up toward Durrus and Bantry. An even shorter distance if you went up the Kealfadda Road on the north side and looped round from there. That's where he lived. Pierre-Louis had seen Bailey three times. Each time had been traumatic. One time he saw Bailey, he had felt so bad he had wanted to cut his holiday short. Pierre-Louis looked down at the floor. There was not much more to say about it.

The crew set up the camera. Pierre-Louis took a seat by the window of the sitting room. Down on the Rue Tiquetonne, tourists had started perusing the lunchtime menus chalked up on boards outside a row of restaurants. I looked at Pierre-Louis: dark hair, neatly trimmed beard, hands clasped firmly together. Jim Sheridan asked him how the investigation was going. Pierre-Louis said that he had recently met the Guards in Ireland. They had told him that the case was still open, but they weren't necessarily pursuing it actively. They were waiting for new findings. That was a surprising position to take, but there was not much Pierre-Louis could do to change things. Meanwhile, in France, he had a meeting with Patrick Gachon, the investigating magistrate, every six months. So maybe next year, 2016, Gachon would deliver his findings, then there would be an assessment of holding a trial, which might have to be *in absentia*, although France would do what it could to make the suspect come to France for questioning in the meantime.

Pierre-Louis counted through the years. "This takes us to 2018, 2019. Maybe we'll have justice in 2020." He paused.

"It's a long time."

***

In August 2001, Ian Bailey had received a three-month suspended sentence at Skibbereen District Court for assaulting Jules Thomas at their home.

At that time, Bailey had a leg in plaster as he had ruptured his Achilles tendon. He had been snoozing on the sofa and it appeared Thomas woke him up. An argument ensued, and Bailey lashed out at Thomas with one of the crutches he was using. Thomas suffered injuries to an eye, a serious cut to her lip, damage to her cheekbone and bruising on her arms and legs. Once again, Thomas needed hospital treatment. This time, the Guards got involved. Soon after the attack, Bailey was arrested at Cork Airport with a couple of suitcases and a plane ticket to Britain. He served three weeks in prison, as he was unable to raise the bail money.

At Bailey's civil action in Dublin in 2014-2015, I had seen the barrister acting for An Garda Síochána and the Irish state read out excerpts from Bailey's diary that seemed to show he was in a fragile psychological condition in the years leading up to Sophie's murder. By contrast, the legal team defending the newspapers against Bailey's charge of libel at the Cork District Court back in 2003 had concentrated on what Bailey had written in the same diaries about his attacks on his partner.

The court heard that the assault of Jules Thomas in May 1996 had started in the car. This was the beating that had drawn the Guards' attention to Bailey in the immediate aftermath of Sophie's murder. On this occasion, Bailey had been driving. *She began to assault me. I tried to push her away… It was just something that happened in the heat of the moment, a hand came up to scratch me and I was pushing her away… As I have said, there was no thought of premeditation.* About the 2001 attack, Bailey said in court in Cork, under cross-examination: *I was trying to get away from the sofa and out of the room, and she at one point got hold of the crutch… My recollection was that she pulled it, she pulled it towards her.*

You get a sense of how incredulous the barrister was when he heard those words. He countered sarcastically: *It was really almost self-induced, her pulling of the crutch and it hit her face, is that it?* After beating Thomas with the crutch, he kicked her with the leg that was in plaster. Still Bailey downplayed the assault. It was *over in a second* and – in his telling – was almost involuntary: *I did let the crutch go and it did strike her… As I have said, it was something that just blew up, it occurred.* When the barrister asked Bailey if trying to leave the country via Cork Airport was an attempt on his part to get away in the event of a prosecution, Bailey replied: *Oh, absolutely not.*

The excerpts from Bailey's diaries were nothing short of shocking: *I am an animal on two feet,* he wrote. About the assault in May 1996: *One act of whiskey-induced madness, coupled and cracked, and in an act of such awful violence, I severely damaged you and made you feel that death was near… As I lay and write, I know there is something badly wrong with me… I am afraid for myself, a cowardly fear. That although I damaged and made grief your life, I have destroyed my own destiny and future to the point where I can see, in destroying you, I destroyed me. And only time will tell but, in doing what I did, I am damned to hell.*

There was another excerpt from Bailey's diary that caught my eye. It had nothing to do with violence, nothing about being damned to hell, or about being an animal, or about feeling that death was near. But I thought it was relevant, somehow. In 1994, Bailey wrote:

I absolutely need mental stimulation and unfortunately I cannot get it from Jules. She is fine as a sexual partner, but as a soulmate I feel little in common. I am often taken by brighter young things.

***

Bailey and Thomas had a party up at the Prairie one night in the summer of 1993, an impromptu kind of thing. There was a bit of music in one of the pubs in Schull, some good *craic*, and Jules Thomas issued a kind of general invitation to the musicians to come back to the Prairie to continue the fun.

There was a woman, Colette, in the crowd that night who had driven down from the town of Baltimore with a man named Ronnie, who was one of the musicians. Colette was from Manchester, 24 years old, and had been in Ireland for about a month working as a waitress.

Back at the Prairie, there were a few more drinks and, when the party was over, Ronnie said that it was a long drive back to Baltimore, he did not feel like getting behind the wheel. Thomas suggested that they stay the night. Colette told the Guards: *I thought I was staying in the house where the party was… Ian, who I had not spoken to, told me there was another house in the grounds, and it might be quieter.* Bailey was talking about the 'studio'.

Bailey walked Colette and Ronnie over to the studio and showed them a double bed upstairs. *At this stage, Ian may have thought that Ronnie and I were going into the same bed.* Ronnie had recently got engaged, and neither Colette nor Ronnie was comfortable with the proposed arrangement with the double bed, so Ronnie went back to the cottage to sleep there. Colette got into the double bed at about 4am. *About an hour later, I was awoken from my sleep as I realised that there was someone in the bed beside me. I could feel a hand covering over me. This hand was then on my leg. When I felt the hand on my leg, I did not know who was there. There was no light on in the room at the time. I moved across to get out of the bed and then the door of the room opened and Jules came in. I went to grab my clothes, and Jules shouted at me and wanted to know what I was doing in bed with Ian.*

It was only then that Colette realised who had got into her bed. *I said to Jules I had no idea it was him that was there… I saw that the upper half of Ian was naked and the bedclothes were pulled over the bottom part of his body so I could not see. Ian then shouted back at Jules and said, "What are you doing here disturbing me", and they began shouting at each other and I left.*

Colette ran up to the cottage with her clothes and shoes and got dressed there. Some five minutes later, Thomas returned to the cottage and made Colette a cup of coffee. She offered Colette a cigarette and apologised for Bailey's conduct. While the two women were having the cup of coffee, *Ian was stamping around outside roaring and shouting. I could not make out what he was saying. He was deranged. Jules then said that Ian had done worse to her and she lifted up her skirt… There were bruises up and down her legs. Then she lifted up her top… and her lower ribs were black and blue. Ian was still stumbling around the garden but was only shouting the odd thing by now.*

Colette told the Guards that Bailey did not apologise himself for his behaviour, nor offer any explanation. In fact, she had only spoken to Bailey the one time, when he took her and Ronnie over to the studio. During the party Colette only had a vague memory of seeing Bailey, kind of in the background, as Colette put it, which made Bailey's alleged uninvited appearance in her bed and his wandering hands all the more difficult to understand.

***

The document drawn up by the Office of the Director of Public Prosecutions setting out their grounds for not prosecuting Bailey was titled an *Analysis of the Evidence to Link Ian Bailey to the Sophie Toscan du Plantier Murder*. This was the text that Bailey was insistent that I read. I hardly needed his encouragement. Some things struck me immediately as odd. First of all, the DPP thought that Bailey's *voluntary provision of fingerprints and a specimen of his blood is objectively indicative of his innocence*. It is true that Bailey swiftly volunteered a hair sample to the Guards (as did Jules Thomas), and did so very much in a spirit of cooperation with the ongoing investigation. But the DPP was taking its argument too far. Accepting a routine request for samples that could be used to check DNA was not the first thing you would imagine a guilty man doing, but it was surely not *objectively indicative* of Bailey's innocence, it seemed to me.

It turned out that the DPP had asked the Guards for a copy of a tape of an interview that Caroline Mangez, the journalist dispatched to Ireland in early 1997 by *Paris Match* magazine, had made with Bailey and Thomas. In the interview, Thomas told Mangez that she thought her arrest was (in the DPP's words) "biased" and that she had been "press-ganged". *On tape, Jules Thomas sounds credible and convincing... She states in the interview with apparent conviction that she is convinced of his innocence.*

Concerning Bailey, the DPP listened to what he had to say to Mangez – that he had nothing to do with the killing, that he had been "stitched up" by the Gardaí, that he was "disoriented" during his first arrest, that the Gardaí were determined to find evidence to convict him even though he was innocent. They also concluded that *on tape, Bailey sounds credible and convincing.*

What I found strange was this: I could understand the DPP saying in effect that, we are working in our office in Dublin, we review the evidence in the Garda file and we react to it, but we don't – as a French investigating magistrate would do – travel and conduct key interviews and take stock of a suspect for ourselves. I could also understand the DPP wanting to use every avenue available to them under the Irish system to find out about Bailey and try to understand why the Guards were so sure that he was the murderer. But this was an uncomfortable middle ground – listening to a tape a single journalist had made, presumably aware that other journalists would have recorded their own interviews with Bailey, and using it to arrive at such a determined conclusion, that

Bailey was "credible" and "convincing". Surely it was for a jury to decide this, after hearing and seeing Bailey – as with any other suspect accused of such a serious crime – respond to several days of cross-examination?

Jean-Antoine Bloc had been amazed at the way in which Bailey had been able to deflect the accusation that he had repeatedly confessed to the crime. But the DPP saw it very differently. Bailey said to the news editor Helen Callanan, "Yes, I did it. I killed her to resurrect my career as a journalist" – to the DPP, *his remarks to her reek of sarcasm, not veracity*. Equally, when Bailey said to Richard Shelley, "I did it… I went too far", the DPP reasoned: *An objective assessment of the alleged conversation… does not demonstrate that the conversation was about the murder*, adding that *it is a matter of indisputable fact that Bailey has on other occasions consistently and publicly proclaimed his innocence*. Conclusion: *On an overall basis, the Shelley evidence is dangerously unreliable*.

Regarding the admission made to young Malachi Reed, the DPP's view was that it was "abundantly" clear that Malachi was not upset immediately after getting the lift home from Bailey; *however, following his conversation with Garda Kelleher* [the following day] *he became upset and turned a conversation, which had not apparently up until then alarmed him, into something sinister*. Here I thought the DPP was making the mistake of ascribing adult behaviour to a child. Yes, this situation might be odd if we were discussing a grown man, but Malachi was only 14 when the incident occurred. Why would he not process Bailey's comments in his own way, and in his own time? The section on these pieces of testimony had been given the title, *Alleged Informal Admissions by Bailey*, which probably told you all you needed to know about how the DPP viewed them.

The DPP reserved its most scathing assessment for James Camier, the organic vegetable seller, who claimed that Jules Thomas told him on the morning of the murder that Ian Bailey was investigating the crime. The DPP made great play of the fact that the first time Camier made a statement to the Guards was on 21st September

1998, approaching two years after the event, and that Camier did not mention the murder to any other shoppers or passers-by that morning. The DPP noted: *The most charitable interpretation that one can attribute to the Camier evidence is that it is wholly unreliable.* Meanwhile, the DPP appeared to be perplexed by the evidence of Pádraig Beirne, calling it "strange", since the 'pick-up' photo of Sophie that Beirne claimed that Bailey offered him (saying that she had been a "good-looking woman") was not mentioned by Bailey to Michael McSweeney. Then again, it occurred to me, McSweeney's main objective at that time was to get usable images of the crime scene, and nothing more. This was the service he provided as a photographer, so was it really so "strange" that there was no talk with Bailey of a 'pick-up' photo?

I did agree with the DPP about a couple of things. The nature and location of the scratches on Bailey's hands and forearms were not evenly recalled by the Guards who interviewed him, nor, for instance, by the two shop assistants at Lowertown Creamery on Christmas Eve. On the other hand, the DPP did not go into much detail regarding the witnesses who saw Bailey in the Galley bar on the night of the murder, which was a key complaint of Jean-Antoine Bloc and the Sophie Justice Committee. That surprised me. What I read was a rather lofty after-the-facts assessment of what could have happened: *Common sense dictates the real possibility of being scratched during such an operation* [cutting a Christmas tree].

The DPP inevitably responded to the testimony of the Guards' one-time 'star' witness, Marie Farrell. I had to remind myself that the DPP had drawn up its report before both the Cork libel trial and, most importantly, before Farrell's dramatic recanting of the significant sighting of Ian Bailey at Kealfadda Bridge on the night of the murder. What struck me was that the Dublin-based author of the report had simply got it wrong when he wrote: *Even if the identification was definite, this would be of little probative value given the location was not even indirectly en route between the scene of the murder and Bailey's home.* He had got it wrong because the location was precisely this – it was "indirectly en route". A better geographical description would be difficult to find. (There was a slightly shorter route by paved road that Bailey could have taken via the northern side of the Mizen peninsula.)

But the author of the DPP report was bang on the money when it came to the implication of Farrell refusing to identify the man she was with that night. This was the fundamental problem with the Farrell evidence: *For all we know the person might refute the suggestion that the man on the road was Bailey.*

Chapter 13

HURLEY'S GARAGE

It was the morning of 12th December 2015. I had arranged to meet Ian Bailey to spend a few days with him. I needed to discover something crucial and new about the case or, otherwise, see some familiar evidence from a fresh, illuminating perspective.

But how likely was that? I had come close to cancelling my trip that day across the Irish Sea from Liverpool John Lennon Airport. I felt I was going round in circles. The evidence against Bailey when taken together – the scratches on his face and forehead the morning after the killing; his unusual alibi; the suggestion that as a reporter he knew 'too much' about the crime; and his 'confessions' – were reason enough to make him the principal suspect. However, with no identified trace of foreign DNA at the crime scene, the Guards had failed to land a knockout blow. It was stalemate.

By what looked like a happy coincidence, Bailey was going to drop off Jules Thomas at Cork Airport at the same time as I was flying in to meet him. Thomas was going away to see some relatives in England and do a spot of Christmas shopping. With Thomas in the air, the plan was that I would hire a car and follow Bailey in his vehicle back to their cottage. I would be spending time in his company on his home turf, so to speak. How freely would Bailey talk without Jules Thomas around?

It turned out that a violent piece of weather named Storm Desmond had other ideas. My plane bobbed and lurched in the turbulent air as it came in to land. The day before, an Irish TV weather reporter's warning about Storm Desmond's likely force had earned her a moment of fame when a clip of her frantic on-air performance went viral. Much rain had already fallen; the roads were waterlogged and the River Lee in Cork was apparently in danger of bursting its banks.

I left the car park in my hire car only to find Bailey marooned in his ancient Volvo at the side of a slip road. "I can't get it to start," said Bailey. "I think it's got a flooded engine." He abandoned the Volvo, looking glum. An expensive repair job was the last thing he needed.

Bailey struck up a conversation with a taxi driver outside Arrivals who offered to put him in touch with a mechanic. I watched Bailey and the taxi driver from a distance. Bailey had a gift for putting people at their ease. I had seen this during the court case in Dublin. Here he was in a casual conversation with a man of his own age. The taxi driver was giving Bailey's rusty vehicle a quick inspection. Bailey appeared cheerful, approachable, but not needy – friendly, but not over-friendly. Put simply, people warmed to him. Outside Cork Airport, stinging rain lashing my cheeks, I found myself envying Bailey for his easy rapport with strangers.

Bailey's mobile rang. It was Jules Thomas calling from inside the terminal. Her flight had been cancelled because of the storm and her trip was now off. As we waited for Thomas to come back out of the building, Bailey appeared to perk up. The mechanic had arrived, checked the damage and agreed to fix the Volvo, which would be ready to be picked up in a couple of days. For the meantime, Bailey had figured out a decent Plan B. "We'll all go back home in your car," he said to me. "And we'll stop for a spot of lunch in Skib."

I pointed my rental, a shiny new SUV, in the direction of the town of Skibbereen, a journey of about an hour and a quarter. From her seat in the back, Thomas kept her eyes fixed on the bristling hedgerows and soaked meadows, separated by tiny variations in shades of dark green. Bailey pushed his seat back as far as it would go to give his six-foot-four-inch frame more room. Conversation turned to the investigation in France. Bailey asked if I had heard anything after the French detectives' visit to County Cork the previous September. I told him I had heard nothing. The investigation was pretty much hermetically sealed, as far as I could tell. Nothing was being leaked to the French press.

We spoke about Patrick Gachon, the current investigating magistrate assigned to the case. He would send his findings to the prosecution service, which was the next level up. If Gachon found that Bailey should stand trial for the murder of Sophie Toscan du Plantier, the prosecutor would almost certainly order a trial. Bailey said that he had heard a rumour that magistrate Gachon was moving to another post and was likely to leave before filing his report on the Toscan du Plantier affair. If true, this round of criminal justice musical chairs would likely buy Bailey some time, while no doubt exasperating Sophie's family and supporters. But the key question was, would the appointment of a new investigating magistrate affect the outcome?

Bailey told me he was worried. Looking back, I think he knew then that it was only a matter of time before the French authorities would set up a trial. "I just can't think about it," said Bailey, shaking his head. Jules Thomas said that the little they knew about how the police operated in France came from *Spiral*, a moody French cop show that had recently been a minor hit on TV.

In Skibbereen, we had lunch in a pub with commentary from an English football match blaring out of speakers on the walls. Bailey wolfed down a meal served on two large, steaming plates, his appetite apparently undimmed. Thomas, her elegant raincoat laid carefully over an unoccupied chair, ate her soup slowly. I went to the bar to settle the bill and when I came back, it looked like Bailey's concern about his decrepit Volvo had completely lifted. He asked me:

"Did you ever speak with Sean Murray?"

"No. I haven't been to see him yet," I replied. Contacting Sean Murray was on my to-do list. Murray's witness statement was unusual in that it did not relate to him seeing or hearing anything out of the ordinary on the Mizen peninsula. It concerned a sighting at a petrol station right here in Skibbereen, well away from the crime scene. When I met Bailey and Thomas in Dublin, within the first hour of our first conversation, Bailey had referenced Murray and his petrol station as an interesting lead that needed following up. I had dutifully jotted down *petrol station witness* in my notebook, not thinking much more about it. Jean-Antoine Bloc had said to me pretty much the same thing. Back in the day, however, the Guards had appeared to ignore Sean Murray's testimony altogether, with one Guard dismissing it as a "red herring".

"You fancy going there now? He's bound to be working on a Saturday."

My mind was racing ahead as we walked out of the pub to grab some supplies at a nearby supermarket, a quick errand before calling on Sean Murray. I thought: Bailey has invited me to go and see a witness; he is clearly encouraging me to talk to Murray in particular. Why?

The car park was full and there were people with shopping and dogs on long leashes and children running here and there. I manoeuvred my car an inch at a time out of its tight parking space, craning my head out of the window as I did so. A rental from Avis, as it happened, and, as ever, I was minded I could get lumped with a hefty bill for scratches. Better safe than sorry.

Bailey teased me for my indecisive reversing:

"There you are, Mr Bean again!"

We arrived at our destination in under 10 minutes.

Sean Murray sold used cars at Hurley's Garage, a car showroom next to a muddy lot crammed with vehicles, their asking prices glued to their windscreens. Hurley's Garage also doubled as a petrol station, and in 1996 Sean Murray had been manning the pumps in the run-up to Christmas.

In the last days of December, Murray contacted the Guards after seeing a television news item on the murder of Sophie Toscan du Plantier. Garda Flor O'Driscoll paid Murray a visit at the garage on 3rd January 1997 and took a statement from him.

My name is Sean Murray and I am a salesman at Hurley's Garage, Ilen Street, Skibbereen. I wish to state that before Christmas, most likely Friday the 20th between 2pm and 3pm a car called to the pumps for petrol. The car was a Ford Fiesta. It was blue or grey. It had a '96 Reg. The Reg. may have had CE or C in it. I am sure that this car was a Fiesta and that it was a hired car because the hub caps were missing. I am in the motor trade and I would recognise a hired car.

The driver of this car fitted the description of the murder victim in Schull. She had longish shoulder length hair tied in a ponytail. Her hair was gold blonde. She was an attractive woman with very little makeup. Murray added that the woman looked like the one he had seen in photos on TV, and would have been in her late thirties or early forties.

The car approached from the town side. There was a gent sitting in the passenger seat. As the car was parked on the r/h side of the pump this gent's seat would have been next to the pump. I asked the lady what she wanted. She did not appear to understand. At this point the gent said something to her. She then smiled and said "full, please" to me. I filled the car with unleaded petrol. The gent handed the money to me through the passenger window. I don't think the car took much petrol. I think he may have given me a 10 pound note and that the bill was an even tenner. I noted the gent in the car was tall. His head was nearly touching the roof. The gent was around the same age or might have been a bit older than the lady. He was wearing a medium coloured jacket with the collar turned up. I did not get a very good look at his features. He was not a heavy man but he was tall. He had medium length dark hair. Due to his height I did not see much of the top of his head. He could have had a beard. He did not speak to me but looked Irish. The car drove off in the Schull direction.

Having thought about it I am quite sure about a number of things. The car was a Fiesta and was a self-drive [i.e. a manual, not an automatic]. *I remember thinking these may have been persons home for Christmas. The driver was French without a doubt. The car came from the town side and drove off towards Schull. I have a strong feeling it was the Friday before Christmas.*

What was puzzling was that a CCTV camera at Cork Airport had snapped Sophie on the afternoon of 20th December 1996 emerging into the main concourse pushing a trolley containing a large amount of baggage, but clearly alone. The CCTV images corroborated the story provided by Sophie's family and friends that she had flown to Ireland from Paris without a travel companion. Indeed, it was seen as a fundamental and tragic irony of the case that she had not managed to persuade a friend – Agnès Thomas, for instance – to go with her. So, where did the man Sean Murray said he saw in Sophie's car fit into things? When the Guards processed Murray's statement they appear to have dismissed it because it did not fit into the narrative swiftly established in the days after Sophie's murder that she was travelling solo. There are a couple of other factors: Murray also said that the Ford Fiesta was "blue or grey", whereas in fact it was silver – not a huge difference, but a difference, nonetheless. Also, the Ford Fiesta did have hubcaps.

On the other hand, Sophie's grieving family recovered the rental outside her holiday cottage with the passenger seat pushed right back, as if it had been moved to accommodate someone tall. The Guards had noted the same thing. It seemed unusual. When hire cars are cleaned for the next customer, the seats are routinely put in a neutral position – neither too far forward, nor too far back. Also, a sticker on one of the windows of the rental vehicle advertised *Avis – We Try Harder*. If his customer in the afternoon of 20th December 1996 had indeed been Sophie Toscan du Plantier, Sean Murray was quite right that the Ford Fiesta he topped up with fuel had been a "hired car". The thing is, Murray had spotted the car was a rental, but he gave the wrong reason.

The existence of a couple of peripheral errors in Sean Murray's statement seems understandable given the volume of customers passing through the gas station on a Friday afternoon. Even if there had been hardly any customers, how could he have got every detail right? Indeed, you would be suspicious if he *had* got every detail right. Ultimately, Sean Murray's witness statement is compelling because you can readily understand why the core elements of his sighting that December afternoon were memorable. (Also, if the woman was Sophie, Murray was slightly wrong with the timing, since Sophie had only picked up the keys to her car at Cork Airport at around 2:30 pm.)

Reading his statement, you can see why this transaction stuck in his mind: the then middle-aged Murray had spoken with a strikingly pretty woman driving a car who was clearly foreign, and the woman had been confused when Murray had asked her what she wanted. How many times a day would that have happened out of the tourist season? Next to her sat a passenger whose stature was remarkable in Ireland; this particularly tall man explained to the pretty foreign woman the simple question that Sean Murray, the petrol pump attendant, had asked her, the same question he asked dozens of customers every day, and which presumably almost everyone else understood at first hearing. Why would the secondary errors invalidate the central recollection which was unusual both for the attractiveness of the woman in the car and the misunderstanding about the simple question?

In the weeks after Sean Murray's testimony, there was another important issue for the Guards: Marie Farrell, the Schull shopkeeper, had signed a statement – later retracted, of course – saying that she had seen Ian Bailey walking at Kealfadda Bridge in the early hours of the morning of Monday, 23rd December 1996. The bridge was about a third of the way between Sophie's holiday home at Toormore and Bailey's cottage at the Prairie, even though it was not on the most direct route between the two properties. Ian Bailey had a shaky alibi for his whereabouts that night, putting Farrell's testimony at the heart of the Guards' case against him. In this context, Sean Murray's statement was not so much a "red herring", as a Guard had described it, as an unwelcome complication for the investigation, since Murray had not had a clear view of the face of the man on Sophie's passenger seat.

"This was the pump, this one here," said Sean Murray, a grey-haired man of average height, several years older than Ian Bailey. Bailey, Murray and I were sheltering from the tail end of Storm Desmond under a corrugated iron roof above the double set of petrol pumps. I was struck that Murray spoke clearly, knew what he saw that day, knew what he didn't see, and stuck to his story.

Sophie had approached from the town, according to Murray's testimony. When I read his statement the first time, I had reached for a road map. I couldn't work it out. That wasn't the route I had taken driving west from Cork. Then I realised that in 1996 the Skibbereen bypass had not yet been built. Everyone driving from Cork Airport to the Mizen peninsula had to drive through Skibbereen town centre. There was, of course, a chance that the mystery male passenger had been picked up there. Or he could have approached Sophie in Cork Airport in the Arrivals hall, where there were always people coming and going, or at any point along the route.

Murray and Bailey looked comfortable talking together – no surprise there. But they were acquaintances rather than friends; Ian Bailey regularly bought his fuel at Hurley's Garage when he was in Skibbereen and, in the years since the murder, Bailey had established a casual contact with Sean Murray. In September 2015, Murray had told Bailey that the French detectives had requested an interview with him. Sean Murray said that he told the French fellas (investigating magistrate Gachon and the travelling French detectives) what he had told the Guards all those years ago. That the man in the passenger seat appeared to explain to the lady driving the car what Murray had meant – meaning how much fuel – when he asked her what she wanted. The man had passed Murray the lady's £10 note. There was no change given. Then the car drove off.

"Did you hear the man speak?" I asked Sean Murray.

Murray said that, yes, he heard him speak, but very briefly.

"Could he have been from continental Europe? Say, German, Italian, French or something like that?"

"No," replied Murray, "he was Irish or English."

"But it was getting dark, so you didn't get a good view of him, right?"

Murray and Bailey started to say the same thing at once, that it hadn't been dark if the car had come in at around three in the afternoon.

"What time is it now?" asked Bailey. We all looked at our watches. It was 3:30pm.

"It's still light," said Bailey. Murray nodded in agreement. In another eight days, on 20th December 2015 – precisely 19 years after Sophie Toscan du Plantier drove to her holiday cottage for the last time – the sun would set a few minutes earlier than today. The 20th December would be almost the shortest day in the year, in fact, but the difference compared to 12th December would be negligible. Since there was a bit of daylight now, there would have been daylight when Sophie passed this way.

Our conversation came to a natural break. Sean Murray was not wearing a coat despite the storm; it was a mild winter's day, but my guess was that Murray wanted to be back inside his showroom. I glanced at Jules Thomas in profile in my car, her back straight as a rod, sitting perfectly still and looking ahead, not towards the petrol pumps where we were standing. Over the years, some commentators on the case had written to the effect that she was a handsome woman. Sometimes comments on Thomas's looks were followed by judgments on her past relationships. Thomas had had three daughters with two different men before meeting and setting up home with Ian Bailey. John Montague, the Irish-American poet, who lived part of the year near Schull until his death in 2016 – and whose 2000 *New Yorker* piece on the Sophie Toscan du Plantier case raised its international profile, and got me interested – wrote that

Thomas's *love life* [had] *been mildly untraditional, but eccentric behaviour is generally tolerated here.*

In Montague's piece, Bailey came across as suspicious, anxious to please and difficult to like. The Englishman did gardening work for the Irish-American Montague, whose Irish side was alert to – and perhaps even enjoyed – the historical irony of an Englishman doing the planting and the weeding for an Irishman, rather than the other way round.

"Like I say," said Sean Murray, summing up, "what I told those French people was what I told the Guards."

"Was it me in the car?" asked Bailey.

The question was sudden and unexpected. It was blurted out. I watched for Sean Murray's reaction.

Murray, good-humoured, half a smile on his lips, looked at Bailey, hands on his hips, pretending to size him up, like he hadn't seen him before. Then he winked at me. The wink was a surprise, given the circumstances. We were talking about a murder, weren't we? Actually, that wasn't quite right. *I* was thinking about a murder, the raw violence of the attack on Sophie Toscan du Plantier was in the back of my mind all the time. Murray, meanwhile, was talking about *and only about* what he had seen that day – the lady in the car and the strikingly tall fellow who handed him the money. His testimony began and ended there. This was a man who had contacted the Guards because it was his duty as a citizen. His mind wasn't racing ahead, making assumptions, joining up the dots without being asked to do so.

It occurred to me that Sean Murray was the perfect witness.

Bailey was waiting for the answer to his question. So was I.

But no, Sean Murray wasn't going to be drawn, clearly wasn't going to say definitively that Sophie's passenger wasn't Ian Bailey:

"I don't know who it was, but he spoke like he was Irish or English, not from Europe." The man's face had been mostly hidden. Murray had given the cops the best description he could. That was it.

Bailey, Thomas and I drove away from the petrol pumps at

Hurley's Garage and took the Schull road. We didn't speak much. The sun, for the most part obscured by clouds the colour of dishwater, had by now dropped very low in the sky. From time to time narrow shafts of light showed up at the grimy edges of my windscreen. I wondered: was it Sophie who Sean Murray saw at the petrol pump that Friday afternoon prior to Christmas in 1996? If it hadn't been Sophie, who else could it have been? And who was the man in the seat beside her? I wondered if Bailey and Thomas were asking themselves the same questions. Or perhaps their minds were occupied by something else entirely?

There is a moment on the Schull road, 10 minutes out of Skibbereen, when the landscape opens up; you see the scattered, jagged islands of Roaringwater Bay on your left, on your right the distant mountains of County Cork and County Kerry. If you disregard the rash of bungalows on the hillsides and the traffic flashing by, it has been the same view, more or less, for tens of thousands of years.

I thought to myself: One day, when this is all over, I'll come back here with the family. Get out on the water in a boat, maybe. Do some hiking. See the bigger picture. Actually, see any other picture that doesn't have a murder in it.

I dropped Bailey and Thomas off at their cottage at the Prairie, and drove back to my hotel in Schull. By this time, Storm Desmond was quietening down. In the spaces between the townlands it was now pitch black. Low on the horizon, the arc of the Fastnet light gleamed every few seconds and then dissolved. The air smelled of brine. In the first light of morning, there would be local people on the beaches harvesting blackish kelp spewed up by the violent swell of Roaringwater Bay. The smooth, glistening strands of kelp would be Storm Desmond's silver lining.

The next day, a Sunday, I returned to the Prairie for an early dinner invitation. Bailey and Thomas had cooked a roast: a large, juicy cut of beef selected by Bailey at the supermarket in Skibbereen the previous day. It was my contribution to the meal.

There were roast potatoes, parsnips, carrots, Yorkshire pudding and stuffing. Apart from the beef, most of what they served on the pine dining table in their narrow kitchen came from their own tiny farm. In the summer, said Thomas, they had far more garlic, courgettes and onions than they could eat themselves. In a good year, they harvested a thousand heads of lettuce, most sold to restaurants and B&Bs. A shelf lined with jars of jam labelled 'Old Bailey's Preserve' stood above the cooker. Eventually the jam would end up on the couple's stall at Schull farmers' market.

The little kitchen felt stuffy, the door to the yard shut tight against the cold. The oven was still burning, emanating heat, and the air reeked of beef stock. Bailey wore a bottle-green padded waistcoat – one of those waistcoats with lots of pockets and zips. He looked like a gentleman farmer. We finished dinner.

"People say we're lucky. But it's not luck. We chose this," said Thomas, gesturing at the leftover meat and vegetables.

"It's a millionaire's lifestyle on the breadline," said Bailey, smiling, as Thomas got up to move next door to the sitting room to watch a bit of television.

Bailey suggested I switch on my audio recorder. He offered to tell me about how he came to journalism. It all kicked off in England in the 1970s. It started with a swarm of bees.

Chapter 14

THE HUNCH

In his final year of primary school, with his family now living in Gloucester, Ian Bailey passed the 'Eleven-plus' – a written test to identify academically bright children – and was offered a place at The Crypt, a local grammar school. He had already begun writing poems at age seven or eight. At age 15, he paid a call to the office of the *Gloucester Citizen*, interested in becoming a journalist. The editor took a shine to the boy and gave him some gentle encouragement.

On one morning not long afterwards, the sky above the playground of The Crypt darkened. It was pandemonium. A swarm of bees had appeared from nowhere. Bailey's reflex was to call the editor at the *Gloucester Citizen*.

"The newspaper man had opened my eyes to what a story was. So I rang him and that evening there was a report on the front page with me interviewed." After the incident with the bees had been forgotten, the precocious Bailey started sending in short pieces 'on spec' – school play reviews, reports on cricket matches – and the editor ran them. "I was still at school, cheques were coming in and I didn't know what to do with them, I hadn't even got a bank account."

When Bailey left The Crypt, he had already decided on his future career path. There were no openings at the *Gloucester Citizen*, but he found an apprenticeship at a news service in Gloucester, studying journalism at college part-time. His boss at the news service told me that he could hardly believe that Bailey was only 18 when he came for his interview. He was tall, broad-shouldered, had the physique of a rugby player. He appeared ambitious. Most of all, he was supremely confident.

Bailey wrote good copy, but things started to come apart: he got bored with the district court reporting which was the bread-and-butter of the agency. He was easily tempted to press events where there were drinks and company on offer. According to one journalist who knew him well, Bailey was good-looking and popular with other journalists working the same beat, but they learned not to talk too openly about the leads they were pursuing when Bailey was around, as he was not above pinching their stories. One day, Bailey's boss – a young man himself – opened the door of the office to find the place pretty much trashed. Bailey had hosted a party there the previous night.

Subsequently, still in his early twenties, Bailey quit the agency in Gloucester and set up his own news service in the nearby town of Cheltenham, in direct competition with his former employer. He also entered into a short-lived marriage with another journalist living locally, named Sarah Limbrick. Before the marriage came apart, Bailey and Limbrick set up home in a comfortable detached house with stables – Limbrick's parents were considered wealthy, they owned several properties.

His fledgling news service was ticking over nicely. In Cheltenham, Bailey cornered the local market in stories on the comings and goings of Prince Charles and Princess Anne, who both had estates in this part of England – polo matches, various horsey events, the openings of village fêtes, that kind of thing. But Bailey had difficulty controlling his temper when he was with his wife. He threw objects around when he got angry – chairs and other pieces of furniture.

His eventual divorce from Limbrick was "acrimonious", according to Bailey. It was at the time of the separation from Limbrick that Bailey's initially promising career started to wane, according to the journalist who knew him well, the same one who had kept her mouth shut around the charming Ian Bailey, for fear that he might steal her story ideas.

It was now pitch dark outside. In the moments when the wind died down – a wind loaded with moisture and the smells of turf and brine – it was perfectly quiet. That was when I was aware of Bailey's heavy, laboured breathing. I looked at him in his olive-green jacket with its myriad zips and pockets, big hands resting on the pine dining table, and I decided to skip over his failures, his missteps. No need to bring them up. This was not what he wanted to discuss. Who would?

Anyway, Bailey's journalism had some high points: The most memorable story he'd reported on was as a stringer for the prestigious *Sunday Times* 'Insight' team. This was the case of KGB spy Geoffrey Prime, which hit the headlines in the early 1980s. Genteel Cheltenham, with its rows of pretty Victorian houses and its horse racing, is also the home of the Government Communications Headquarters – better known by its acronym GCHQ – the UK government's surveillance and intelligence body. During this period, people in Cheltenham hardly spoke about what went on in the large, ring-shaped GCHQ building on the outskirts of town dubbed the 'Doughnut' – but, of course, everyone knew.

"One day a spy scandal broke at the heart of GCHQ," said Bailey, warming to his theme, stretching out his large frame in his chair. "A mole had compromised America's satellite systems, channeling information to the Soviets."

Prime, a former RAF sergeant with an aptitude for languages, had copied a vast number of documents and passed them on to his Soviet handlers. Most damaging of all, said Bailey, when workers at GCHQ and their counterparts in the United States cracked Russian ciphers after a couple of decades trying to do so, Prime passed on the news – destroying the code-breakers' advances. Bailey told me that Geoffrey Prime could easily have been caught sooner: In 1973, Prime's then wife found a large sum of money hidden at their home. Prime confessed to her that the money had been acquired as a result of his collaboration with the KGB. Mrs Prime told a neighbour, a Miss Barsby, about her husband's spying. Miss Barsby threatened to call the police but, in the end, she did not. Coincidentally, Prime's routine vetting check was due later the same year and Miss Barsby was interviewed by some GCHQ officers. However, Miss Barsby didn't like the officers' tone of voice, and decided not to tell them about Prime's confession to his wife. Geoffrey Prime had ridden his luck – for a while.

"It was serious investigative journalism, and it was exciting," said Bailey, referring to his work on the Geoffrey Prime affair.

"I liked doing investigations. I was inspired by *All The President's Men* [a 1974 non-fiction book by Carl Bernstein and Bob Woodward, two of the journalists investigating the Watergate break-in and ensuing scandal]." Indeed, the young Bailey was so inspired by *All The President's Men* he said he read the book cover to cover three times.

"Watergate was a major ongoing saga. I've always believed that investigative journalism is the top end of journalism. Everything else is fluff."

We agreed that before Bernstein and Woodward exposed the Watergate scandal, it was impossible to believe that the President of the United States could be so corrupt. Watergate changed all that. Now anyone, it seemed, was capable of anything.

The door to the sitting room was ajar and we could hear the ebb and flow of music and bursts of applause from the television, which Jules Thomas had switched on. We were still at the kitchen table. Thomas would not be able to hear much of what we were saying. It felt odd, this moment. My conversation with Bailey felt normal. I should not have been surprised – Bailey had a rational side that was engaging, even nicely professorial. The nine years' age difference between us, and the fact he had spent longer pitching stories to newspapers than I had, gave him a sort of natural authority. In any case, I was beginning to forget why I was in his home, what my purpose was.

"What happens is that you have hunches, and then you set out to see if they're correct," said Bailey.

Then he asked me: "Do you have strong hunches when you're doing a story?"

"Sure, Ian, at the beginning, but then, well, you find you're never quite as sure as you thought you were…" My voice trailed off.

I was slightly taken aback by Bailey's question, but I tried not to show it. This seemed like a good moment to pause the audio recorder as Bailey said he was keen to dig out a few mementos from his schooldays. We got up and passed through the sitting room to a small, low-beamed library that ran off it. Thomas was watching *Strictly Come Dancing: The Results Show* against the background of the sound of the wind buffeting the window panes on this exposed, west-facing side of the farmhouse. According to Thomas, the cottage was "put up in a few weeks" in the mid-1920s following Ireland's independence. The new state distributed land to farmers who had previously been tenants on vast estates, but some of the houses in this period were built with corners cut. Consequently, the property Bailey and Thomas shared was a comprehensive compendium of design flaws, starting with its flimsy foundations.

Bailey looked for the cardboard folder he had in mind. I glanced around the library. There was a photo of Bailey in a graduation pose, his skin pale against the black of his gown and mortar board. It marked his award of a Law degree from University College Cork in 2011. (His dissertation was titled *Fair or Foul? The European Arrest Warrant – 'Justice Sans Frontier'* [sic] *– An Instrument of Use Open to Abuse?*) On the shelves I saw a couple of French grammar books, books on tort law, European Union law. And there was another one with *How to Play Poker and Win* printed on its spine.

In one of the folders there were a few press clippings, paper yellowish with age, ink smudgy, old-fashioned advertisements filling up the pages.

"Here it is!" said Bailey, satisfied that he had found what he was looking for. He held up a bundle of programmes for school plays put on at The Crypt in the early 1970s. One of these in particular caught Bailey's attention. It was a programme for a production of George Bernard Shaw's *Pygmalion*. Down towards the bottom of the cast list I read: *A Sarcastic Bystander – Ian K. Bailey*.

"That's what I was then," said Bailey. "So what's changed?"

We went back through the sitting room where Jules Thomas was now dozing in front of the television. The same dancing show was still on. Back in the kitchen, Bailey resumed his story. He told me about his first trip to Ireland. By now, Bailey was working on and off in Fleet Street for a range of titles, commuting from Cheltenham to London, sleeping on friends' sofas in the capital. Judging by his clippings, Bailey hadn't managed to establish himself with regular commissions at any of the national newspapers.

"One day a friend in London said to me, 'You must come across to Ireland to meet a *seanchaí*, a traditional Irish storyteller'." A *seanchaí* is always a man and is usually quite an old one. He typically tells long, folksy, gently amusing anecdotes perched on a bar stool, often with a cup of tea in his hand. The *seanchaí* in question, Pat Murphy, lived near Crookhaven, the village right at the end of the Mizen peninsula. Bailey told me Murphy had been a journalist, too, and traveled widely in Europe, lived in Berlin between the wars, spoke half a dozen languages. From a reporting perspective, Murphy had consistently been at the right place at the right time. He also certainly knew how to tell a story. Bailey was spellbound.

Bailey made more visits to Ireland over the next few years, thanks to flourishing contacts with Irish people in London, who provided local introductions. In London, in his early thirties, Bailey told me he was "burned out" with the business of being a freelance reporter. London was anonymous too, it lacked the human touch. I thought back to the helpful taxi driver at Cork Airport the previous day. Would that exchange have been as likely outside the revolving doors of Arrivals at Heathrow or Luton? In rural Ireland when you crossed someone's path, even if you didn't know them, it was always 'hello' and 'good morning'. Bailey truly loved that aspect of life in Ireland.

Bailey also wanted to try his hand at writing poetry, and do it seriously. "I wanted to experience new things so I could write about them. This would be my material. And I was ready to do anything." In short, Bailey was reinventing himself.

During the proceedings of Bailey's case against the Irish state in 2014, I had seen the defence barrister portray Bailey as someone whose life was going seriously downhill at this point. In 1991, a divorce and a career behind him, he came over to Ireland to start a new life. While working on a farm in the south-east of the country, he got back to his digs to find his employer had packed his bags. He never found out the reason. Bailey had gone from ambitious investigative journalist to a stint as a human scarecrow. He was writing poems about the crows that landed on the dirt of a tilled field, which he was paid to keep away.

Bailey drifted west back to Schull, where he had been storing some winter clothes – "and this might sound odd," added Bailey – he found a job at a fish factory, with accommodation thrown in. "They wanted someone to run the floor who wasn't related to anyone. And I was used to handling fish. You might ask why go from journalism on Fleet Street to a fish factory? Back in Gloucester when I was a boy, I had a Saturday job at the fish stall in the market. I'd take fish home, and no one knew how to cook it. My mother was a butcher's wife, after all." The young Ian had a go at preparing the fish himself. "And that's where my love of cooking comes from."

In winter, fishing boats would come into Schull full of herring, and the catch was sent straight down a chute. The job was to separate the female fish from the male fish, splitting open the bellies of the female herring to extract the roe, which was being bought by the Japanese. There was even an expert from Japan walking the factory floor, checking the quality of the roe.

The fish factory was a rough-and-tumble sort of environment, known for its fist-fights and fallings-out. But, as often as not, grievances were buried with a drink or two at Regan's bar above the harbour. When the fish workers were in, Regan's stank so much of fish that other townsfolk gave the place a wide berth. However, not everyone at the factory liked the idea of having an English foreman. And Bailey didn't have the most auspicious start:

"On my first day my name was announced over the sound system, but the acoustics were bad and 'Ian Bailey' came across as 'Ian Paisley' [a Northern Irish politician known for his uncompromising pro-Union views]."

"One guy turned to me and he said, 'You fuckin' English bollox,' and I said, 'It's Mister Bollox to you'." This was after the worst of the Troubles, but they were still rumbling on, and there was – and still is – a strong undercurrent of Republican sentiment in County Cork. In any case, Bailey had arrived at the fish factory at the tail end of the tradition of exporting roe to Japan. When Bailey's first winter season ended, the factory closed down.

But in his single winter season at the fish factory, Bailey started to find some of the material he was looking for. He wrote long poems written for performance in pubs and bars in the *seanchaí* tradition. Sometimes he would accompany these with beats on a *bodhrán*, the Irish drum.

"Do you still know any poems?" I asked.

Yes, he did. "It's fixed," he said, jabbing the forefinger of his right hand at his temple. "I fixed it here." His tone had become suddenly harsh, but he composed himself to recite.

I wrote down a fragment. Bailey's verse sets the scene. A fishing boat has come into dock with 40, 60, maybe 100 tons of catch. This is a good day. The men and women at the factory are paid by volume, this is piece work. The glistening fish slide down the chute onto the factory floor.

"…Here they come, boys,
Stand back in awe
And watch the slaughter, and
If the man from Tokyo says 'yes'
To catches full of gold
Then Christmas time will be less cold…"

In the spring of 1992, with the fish factory closed, Bailey worked in farmers' fields, did gardening for wealthy blow-ins and second-homeowners who wanted to keep their properties neat and tidy while they were away. The fish factory gave Bailey a helping hand in another way. One day Jules Thomas came in looking for fish to buy. They got into conversation. Bailey had seen Thomas around and about Schull – "I was aware of her", he said to me – and accepted her offer of digs in the 'studio'. This was the small, run-down dwelling close to Thomas's cottage. The studio was, frankly, difficult to rent out. It was the property where Thomas did much of her painting and the structure that would feature in his account of his movements in the dark, freezing early hours of 23rd December 1996.

Quickly, Bailey and Thomas became an "item", and in time, and as their relationship blossomed, Bailey moved into the farmhouse where Thomas lived with her three daughters – at that time they were two teenagers and a 10-year-old. Thomas said that she appreciated having a man about the house again. Still, it was practically a hand-to-mouth existence for the couple.

Bailey was now mixing casual farm and gardening jobs with a couple of stints on 'schemes' – back-to-work initiatives, one as a press officer of an environmental charity, another on a community film project in Skibbereen, where Bailey was tasked with helping to write the script. The idea of the film project was to give local people an insight into the workings of the film world. The result, a 'short' rather than a full-length feature, was called *Changing Tides*. It told the story of a fisherman who had gone missing at sea, turning on the local belief that a body would be washed up on the 10th day after the drowning. The writing, filming and production occupied Bailey on and off from April to September 1995. It had a public screening at a community centre in Skibbereen.

"It was never going to win an Oscar," Bailey said to me, deadpan.

Nevertheless, the *Changing Tides* project had renowned British film producer David (now, Lord) Puttnam as patron. Puttnam had a holiday home in West Cork and he gave the project the faintest coating of Hollywood gold dust. *Changing Tides* helped Ian Bailey believe he could make a living from writing again. "By 1996, I decided to go back to full-time journalism," said Bailey.

Later that year many local people were looking forward to the release of the film *Michael Collins*, directed by Neil Jordan, with Liam Neeson in the title role of the man who in County Cork they still call the 'Big Fella'. "I had the inside track on *Michael Collins*," said Bailey. In October 1996, he took Thomas to the film's premiere in Cork City and did a big piece on the movie, spread across two pages of the *Examiner*. This made him proud. Several general interest features followed in the *Sunday Tribune*. Bailey was phoning on Wednesday and selling ideas for the next Sunday. With a fresh injection of self-confidence, his writing was, finally, back on track.

The upturn in Bailey's journalistic fortunes proved to be short-lived. The fallout after the murder of Sophie Toscan du Plantier changed everything. "There was a headline, 'Newsman Chief Suspect'," said Bailey. "Our house was under siege [by journalists and photographers]." Bailey had sold stories to Irish newspapers about the Sophie case – one speculated about Sophie's private life, another raised the possibility that a jealous lover had ordered her killing, still others discussed the physical details of the murder – and he had collaborated with journalists working for French titles such as *Paris Match*. He had made a useful and pleasant connection with one of the French journalists, the young staff reporter from *Paris Match* named Caroline Mangez. But after Sophie's delicate, freckled face gradually disappeared from the front pages and from television news items, Ian Bailey found he was mostly unemployable.

We were going over old ground here. I paused my voice recorder. Bailey looked down at the grains and knots on his dining table as he recounted his professional demise in the wake of the murder of Sophie Toscan du Plantier.

In the end, he did not get a single franc out of the bigwigs at *Paris Match*, what with him being their local fixer and at the same time the principal suspect in the case. Other journalists covering the case whispered that he was the man the Guards were saying had committed the crime. Bailey's contacts at the *Sunday Tribune* said there was no money to pay him anymore. He had no luck placing stories elsewhere, either.

Bailey paused to reflect on this state of affairs. He had repeatedly referred to himself and his companion as two of the "victims" in the Sophie murder case.

My voice recorder was now on again.

"In France some people say that you knew Sophie Toscan du Plantier," I said to Bailey. "They are adamant about it." I mentioned Sophie's friend Guy Girard, who recalled that Sophie had mentioned to him in December 1996 that, a short time earlier, she had been approached by a writer in Ireland named "Ian Bailey" who was working on the theme of violence. The genre of the writing was not specified, but plausibly it might have been a film script or treatment.

Bailey replied levelly: "I did not know her. I was never introduced to her. I know that it has been said by others that I was introduced to her. Untrue. A lie."

He added: "She might have had knowledge of me, I don't know, from poetry or music in bars." Bailey's tone was firm; I had the impression he wanted to show me he was speaking on the record.

In April 1995, Ian Bailey had some gardening work at the house owned by Alfie Lyons and Shirley Foster. It was Easter; the schools were out. From where he was standing in Lyons' garden, Bailey recalled seeing a couple of young boys chasing sheep in the field below. These boys were Pierre-Louis, and Carlo, Daniel's younger son from his second marriage. Sophie was the only adult in the house on this occasion; she had come to Ireland with her son and her stepson.

"I could see somebody at a distance in the kitchen," said Bailey.

I had stood on the same spot and had checked the line of vision for myself. I mentioned nothing of this to Bailey, of course. As Bailey said, there was a view into the kitchen of Sophie's house. Anyone standing in the kitchen – washing up, preparing food, whatever – looking out could keep an eye on what was happening in the field, which is where Pierre-Louis and Carlo were playing. I wondered if this had been the moment when Bailey's attraction to Sophie had crystallised.

I asked Bailey if he knew at the time what Sophie Toscan du Plantier did for a living.

"I heard she worked in television." Alfie Lyons had told him this.

It was late now. Enough talking for one evening.

"You know, the [Toscan du Plantier/Bouniol] family was told from very early on that the Gardaí knew who had done it. This whole thing has been based on a dirty, rotten, stinking lie." Bailey said that the Guards said much the same thing to locals on the Mizen peninsula. As a result, some people would applaud ironically when he left bars and pubs. Others ignored him on the street, refused to frequent his stall at Schull farmers' market. The animosity towards him finally dissipated, but it took many years.

"They said, 'Have no doubt. That fucking Ian Bailey bollox is the murderer'. And unless the murderer is found, there will always be a question mark hanging over me."

***

On the Monday morning, I went back to the Prairie and offered Jules Thomas a ride to the repair shop near Cork Airport where the couple's Volvo was waiting to be collected. She was to go on from there to see her daughter, Virginia, who had recently had a baby. While Thomas packed, Bailey seemed to be at a loose end. I suggested we go for a drive.

We took the road up Hunt's Hill; the houses over at Toormore are the same ones whose lights Bailey said he had admired in the frosty early hours of the night Sophie met her death. Further away, across Bantry Bay, you can see the Sheep's Head peninsula – a place of contrasts, as they say in tourist brochures. Amongst the comfortable vacation homes belonging to London showbiz folk are a couple of former poorhouses, dark holes for windows, in ruins now.

Half an hour later we got to Bantry, a place with its own French connection: in 1979 an oil tanker owned by the French company Total exploded at the oil terminal on nearby Whiddy Island with the loss of 50 lives, including those of 42 French workers. In Bantry town centre, basically whiling away the time, we were having a coffee at a table outside a café when a local man approached Bailey. Apropos of nothing at all he explained to Bailey that he was having problems with a fellow in the bar he frequented. Whenever he set eyes on this fellow, it made his blood boil. It looked as if the man was looking for some advice. Bailey nodded sympathetically as he listened to the story. "I understand perfectly," Bailey told the man. "I've been through the same thing. I recommend taking fish oil." The man seemed satisfied with Bailey's tip and walked off, smiling.

Next, Bailey and I went into a shop selling stationery and novelty items – rows of jokey trinkets for hen parties, that kind of thing. There were three or four computers against a wall. Bailey said he needed to check his emails; there was a problem with reception at the Prairie, so he couldn't do it there. After a couple of minutes, I glanced over at the computers and saw Bailey examining the results of a Google search of himself.

By mid-afternoon, I had Jules Thomas beside me in my hire car. This time it was Bailey who had stayed at home. Thomas and I set off for the car repair shop. Just outside the town of Bandon we got caught in what passes for rush-hour traffic in these parts. Waiting in line for a traffic light to turn green, I asked Thomas about her memory of the night of the 22nd to 23rd December 1996, the time of the murder. Thomas told me that she and Bailey drove home after drinking and socialising at the Galley bar in Schull. They took a detour to see the lights glimmering in the clear night across Bantry Bay. Overlooking the dark, wintry scene Bailey told Thomas that he had a premonition. He didn't explain what those bad feelings were. He asked her if she wanted to get out of the car but she replied no, it was too cold. The couple arrived home at about 1:30am. I asked Thomas when she went to bed.

"I suppose it would have been about two o'clock."

Bailey had been drinking beer and whiskey at the Galley, reciting poems and playing the *bodhrán*. Thomas had had about three small bottles of white wine over the evening. Before she went to bed she took some analgesics for period pain.

"Then Ian went to the studio?"

"No. Ian went downstairs to write at the kitchen table, came back to bed and then, say around 6am, he went to the studio to write up his article."

That coincided pretty much with the statement that Thomas had given the Guards, except that Thomas had Bailey going to the studio earlier than he claimed. For a moment, I wondered if Thomas thought I was trying to catch her out by suggesting that Bailey had gone to the studio before the kitchen.

"Jules," I asked, "you know how you went to bed at about two o'clock, when is it that you got up?"

Thomas said it was difficult to remember, it all happened so long ago.

"But, let's say how long before Ian got the call from Eddie Cassidy at the *Examiner* saying that the body of a foreign person had been found over at Toormore? Would it have been three or four hours before Cassidy called?"

Thomas said yes, maybe three or four hours.

"And you were asleep all that time, from the moment you felt

Ian get up to when you woke in the morning, a few hours before Cassidy called."

Thomas said that this was right.

We approached a traffic light on red and I came to a halt and put the car into neutral. I glanced at Jules in the seat next to me, her profile as handsome as ever, her back as straight as ever, staring straight ahead into the wet night.

It struck me that the comment that Bailey had made to several people that he had no real alibi for the night of the murder, turned on the fact that his partner had slept soundly from 2am until 8:30am at the very earliest. Thomas's account of Bailey's movements that night was merely Bailey's own account of what he had done.

"And, Jules, about the cut that people say they saw on Ian's forehead…"

"Oh, it wasn't really a cut, more like a little nick, really, just under the hairline."

The word "nick" was the same one that Bailey used when he described the incident with the turkey on the afternoon of 22nd December 1996. I had heard Thomas using the word "nick" in the courtroom in Dublin in 2014 when she was being cross-examined by the defence barrister during Bailey's civil case. In court, she had also located it "just under the hairline". However, in her initial statement to the Guards, Thomas had described the cut on her partner's forehead as a "scratch" that was "fresh". She also told the Guards that the wound had not been there the previous day. I asked Thomas if she saw the turkey flaring up and scratching Bailey, or if he had mentioned at the time that there had been a bit of an accident with one of the turkeys, but Thomas didn't seem to understand the question, and didn't reply.

I dropped Thomas off at the repair shop and said goodbye. Then I drove to my hotel, a place that markets itself as a venue for wedding receptions and fancy birthday parties. This Monday night in mid-December it was virtually deserted. In my room, the heating was on high and I couldn't find a way to turn it down. I was just about to give a call to the reception when something occurred to me.

I really should have thought about it sooner. I was due to leave Ireland in a few hours. How had I missed this?

At Hurley's Garage in Skibbereen two days earlier, Ian Bailey had introduced me to Sean Murray. Murray had told the Guards that he had filled the Ford Fiesta rental driven by a woman who he later recognised as Sophie Toscan du Plantier with an even £10 of fuel. The woman had not understood when Murray had asked her what she wanted. A tall man with medium-length dark hair in the passenger seat, his face obscured, had explained to the woman what Sean Murray had meant. From the way he talked, he was either Irish or English. Then the woman had passed a £10 note in payment to the male passenger, who then handed it to Murray. When Sophie's family later examined her rental car, they noticed that the passenger seat had been pushed right back, as you would do to accommodate a tall person. At Hurley's Garage, Bailey had asked Sean Murray: "Was it me in the car?"

Murray had refused to be drawn. He had not either confirmed it was, or was not, Ian Bailey in the passenger seat. But why did Bailey need to get Murray to say that it wasn't him in Sophie's Ford Fiesta? Why had he not simply said where and with whom he had been on that Friday, 20th December 1996, between 3 and 3.30 in the afternoon? Why did Bailey feel it necessary for Sean Murray to rule him out of the picture, when he might well be able to do it himself?

Back home, I called Jean-Antoine Bloc of the Sophie Justice Committee. Did Bloc have a few minutes to talk?

He did.

"I have a hunch," I began.

Chapter 15

BACK TO THE PRAIRIE

"Go on," said Jean-Antoine Bloc.

I cleared my throat. I had to explain my argument carefully. Bloc was a man who had dedicated many years to trying to find and expose Sophie's killer. He was polite, but he clearly would not suffer fools gladly. "When you look at the file of witness statements taken by the Guards, and look at the way people express themselves, what do you see?"

Bloc did not reply.

"Well, you see no-one is afraid to talk to the Guards. You see this in the language people use in their statements. It's fluid, it's unrestrained. At least that is what it was like in the late 1990s. These cops often came from the same, or similar, communities. They saw them at Mass, they saw them in bars, they saw them on the street. They were approachable. Not like some of the *gendarmes* you have in France. A *gendarme* could be from the other end of the country. In fact, I think they often are from the other end of the country, and that is precisely how the system is set up, to keep them distant and remote. French people don't approach policemen as readily as Irish approach the Guards. So, like I say, in France people are often

178

wary of the *gendarmes*, but in Ireland it's different, or at least it was then…"

I paused for a second, but Bloc stayed silent. I carried on.

"It's different in Ireland because everyone – *everyone* – who had some snippet of information, some tiny lead, appears to have come forward and spoken to the Guards. There's just one exception as far as I can see."

"Who's that?" Bloc asked.

"The passenger in Sophie's car on the Friday at Hurley's Garage. He's the only one who didn't come forward. And yet Sean Murray is sure he was Irish or English."

My hunch was this: the man on the passenger seat of Sophie's hire car would have seen Sophie's photo everywhere, on television and on the front page of newspapers. It is unthinkable that he somehow did not find out about the murder since it was the lead item on the TV news for days and was the main story in every newspaper. It is also unthinkable that, after sharing a car journey a couple of days before she was killed, the mystery passenger did not realise that the woman driving was the victim. Even if he had been a married man requiring a degree of discretion, he would surely have approached the Guards, if only to take himself out of the frame. It was a hunch that required an impeccable witness – and Sean Murray of Hurley's Garage was that impeccable witness.

"So why didn't he call the Guards?" I ask Bloc.

Jean-Antoine Bloc didn't say anything immediately, he didn't have to. He knew where my hunch was going: the man who Sean Murray had seen next to Sophie in her Ford Fiesta rental was either her killer, or one of her killers. The very tall man with dark hair on the passenger seat was not merely a person of interest in the case, he was likely directly culpable in the murder of Sophie Toscan du Plantier.

I went back to my file and checked Bailey's statements to the Guards in the months and years following the murder. I also searched several hundred pages of cross-examination from his civil case at the High Court in Dublin in late 2014 when he took the witness stand. There it was: Bailey had indeed been asked where he had been, and with whom, from midday on Friday, 20th December 1996 to 10am on the Monday when Sophie's body was discovered – and Bailey had given an answer of sorts for the Friday afternoon. It was in the questionnaire he and many other locals on the Mizen had completed at the request of the Gardaí.

Jules Thomas had also filled in a questionnaire. The Guards had been astute in starting the timeframe for the questionnaire on the day Sophie arrived in Ireland. Bailey and Thomas completed their questionnaires when a couple of Guards came to visit them at the Prairie on 14th January 1997. At that point, Sean Murray's evidence had already been collected by the Guards, but there was never, it seems, a time when the Guards felt that Murray's sighting of a man in the passenger seat of Sophie's hire car was considered important. This meant that when Ian Bailey explained his whereabouts on the Friday before the murder, it was ostensibly treated as the least valuable part of his version of his movements. In reality, Bailey's movements on Friday, 20th December only mattered if Sean Murray's evidence mattered – and for a long time Murray's testimony had barely mattered at all.

After all these years, did Bailey have a verifiable alibi for the Friday afternoon?

I booked another plane ticket to Cork. It would soon be time to sit down at Ian Bailey's pine dining table and turn on the voice recorder again.

***

When the Office of the Irish Director of Public Prosecutions, the DPP, took its decision in 2001 that *a prosecution against Bailey is not warranted by the evidence*, the grounds for the decision made no mention of Sean Murray's testimony, even though it had been given within two weeks of the murder.

This left open the possibility – unlikely, but a possibility nonetheless – that the DPP's office had not even received Murray's sworn statement. (There were a few isolated cases where the DPP noted that it had to chase up the Guards for a copy of one or other document.) In any event, in its decision the DPP had warned against what it perceived as the unreliability of much of the visual evidence that the Guards had produced in their case against Ian Bailey. At the top of the pile of unreliable evidence was Marie Farrell's sighting of a mysterious man at Kealfadda Bridge at 3am on 23rd December 1996. Farrell's sighting had formed the cornerstone of the Garda case against Ian Bailey, until she withdrew her testimony claiming a number of Guards had encouraged her falsely to identify the man at Kealfadda Bridge as Ian Bailey.

The DPP had surely been right to wonder who Farrell's companion was and what, if anything, he had seen that night. However, even if he had been located, there were other difficulties. Farrell and her companion – if he existed – would probably have been tired (we know Farrell had worked a long day on 22nd December and had already driven to Cork City and back). It was also the middle of the night, and in a moving vehicle, the headlights would only have illuminated the man in the long dark coat at the side of the road for the very briefest of moments. Under those conditions, how could anyone make a sufficiently reliable identification? From the first time I heard about the Farrell evidence, I sensed any barrister defending Bailey worth his salt would have torn it apart.

There were other examples of visual evidence that, reading between the lines, had exasperated the DPP. For instance, the statement given by Prairie resident Louise Kennedy to the Guards, claiming she saw smoke rising from a bonfire next to the studio cottage on St Stephen's Day (26th December) 1996, was given nearly four months after the murder. The supposition was that Bailey could have lit this bonfire to destroy incriminating evidence. The day after Christmas was a strange day to burn things, as well. (Bailey said Kennedy was mistaken, that the bonfire had been lit earlier in the month.) Whatever: the testimony in this case was supplied too long after the event to be reliable, according to the DPP.

Meanwhile, Sean Murray had told me he had spoken to the "French fellas" – Gachon and his team – when they asked for an interview with him. The *juge d'instruction* – the investigating magistrate – thus had a direct opportunity to assess Murray and his recollection of the afternoon of Friday, 20th December 1996. The French had obviously spotted the relevance of the sighting of the man in Sophie's passenger seat, otherwise they would not have requested to speak with Murray. Gachon presumably did not share the DPP's generally dim view of visual evidence in the Sophie case. Still, I wondered just how important they thought Murray's testimony was.

***

I flew back to Cork Airport at the end of January 2016. I once again picked up the keys to my hire car at the Avis desk, and headed west. I was excited that day. I could have quizzed Bailey over the phone, but I needed to see his reaction with my own eyes. I had to be here.

Fortunately, Bailey never turned down an interview.

After a night's sleep in Schull, I drove to the Prairie the long way, via Crookhaven. The route was a geographical roll-call of the Sophie case. I left my hotel and drove along Main Street, where Marie Farrell had made a sighting of Ian Bailey wearing a long black coat on Saturday, 21st December 1996, at the same time as Sophie Toscan du Plantier was browsing the local shops. There was Brosnan's Spar supermarket, where Ian Bailey allegedly saw Sophie walking down the aisle, and there was the Galley pub. A mile or so further on I came to Airhill, where Farrell said she saw Bailey attempting to thumb a lift early in the morning of Sunday, 22nd December. Then the turn-off for the single-track road up Hunt's Hill. Kealfadda Bridge – a low, small thing, its diminutive dimensions out of all proportion with its notoriety – appeared next. Nearby, the smooth, weather-beaten stones of the Altar Wedge tomb, built thousands of years ago for a person or persons unknown, looms on a low cliff overlooking the churn of the Atlantic Ocean. The Altar Wedge is not part of our story, strictly speaking, but it is more of a monument than Kealfadda Bridge, and Josephine Hellen guessed that Sophie's murderer had tossed the axe she kept in her porch into the foamy waters hereabouts.

Father Cashman's church in Goleen occupies a plot a bit further on, set back from the water, the location for the Bouniols' memorial Mass each December. And how could I forget that in the little village of Goleen on the morning of 23rd December 1996, James Camier said that Jules Thomas approached his organic fruit and veg stall and mentioned that a Frenchwoman had been murdered in Toormore? The countryside got rockier, rougher, and the hedgerows petered out. There were no more trees. When Sophie had seen the old dry stone walls demarcating the wide fields at the tip of the Mizen, she had thought of lace draped across the land.

I came to Barleycove Beach and stopped in an almost empty car park, the same one that Marie Farrell might or might not have visited with her mystery companion on the night of the murder. That day, the white surf broke hard on the deserted sands. Here, the road forked. The cliffs of Mizen Head were straight ahead; a left turn took me to Crookhaven.

At O'Sullivan's, 'The Most Southerly Pub In Ireland', I turned down the offer of its Most Southerly Pint and ordered a clam chowder, which was delicious, and I spent a few minutes chatting with Dermot O'Sullivan, who remembered Sophie from her visits, although it was really his parents Billy and Angela who had known her. Billy could speak decent French from a period working in France, and Sophie and Billy would sometimes speak a bit of French together. On 22nd December 1996, Billy had invited Sophie to come over for a drink on Christmas Day, if she was still around then.

O'Sullivan's is a fine place for a drink or a bite to eat, and I could see why Sophie liked coming here. But there might have been another reason for Sophie to have trekked out to Crookhaven. That other reason was the next thing on my list, the very last thing. I got back into my car to drive in the direction of the Prairie. A low shaft of sunlight caught the surface of the rippled water in the inlet, a natural harbour that would be crammed with yachts and yachtsmen in the summer season. In winter, it was the preserve of lobster pots and wooden boats with outboard motors covered with tarps, their paint peeling.

I could hardly leave this a moment longer. I did not *want* to leave it a moment longer. I felt that the day was working up to something important, a conclusion one way or another. If Bailey had a solid alibi for the afternoon of Friday, 20th December 1996, he could make a decisive step to rule himself out of the investigation. It would be something tangible to take to the Bouniols and the Justice Committee. Perhaps not the news they wanted to hear – certainly not anything near what they would have expected – but it could be a potential breakthrough nonetheless.

In truth, over the past weeks I had let my mind race ahead: if Bailey had an alibi for the time Sean Murray made his sighting at the petrol pump, he had to move fast. He had to get the French cops to pay attention to the logic of the argument that the man in Sophie's passenger was hiding the darkest of secrets. The French criminal justice machinery was moving, albeit slowly. The French might well decide to try Ian Bailey. Time was not on his side.

Of course, I had my doubts about Bailey. There was a lot of circumstantial evidence stacked up against him. He came across as almost off-the-scale suspicious. But Sean Murray's testimony was potentially the ultimate trump card to pull out to demonstrate Bailey's innocence – literally, a get-out-of-jail card. Moreover, if the French side were really planning to put Bailey on trial, a miscarriage of justice could potentially be thwarted. My part in solving the case would surely be recognised. It would be a fine conclusion to my involvement – something to brag about to family and friends, an anecdote to top all anecdotes. The anticipation of the moment was already giving me a warm feeling inside. If all this worked out, I would have been cultivating a relationship with an innocent man, not a murderer. Bailey's life had been blighted, and I would be instrumental in turning things around for him, and Jules Thomas, too.

That added up to a lot of 'ifs'. Also, I had yet to hear what Bailey had to say.

In the meantime, there was one more thing to do. It was a kind of pilgrimage, and it would only take five minutes.

Bad weather and bad planning had meant I had not seen the Fastnet Rock before today, only its beam. I knew the best view of the Fastnet was from here, the south side of the Crookhaven peninsula. Barring actually getting out onto the water, I could not have been physically closer to the rock. I stared at it, about six miles away as the crow flies. The Fastnet Rock had fascinated Sophie. Its outline was startlingly jagged – a spiky black island out of the imagination of a child. From where I was standing, the pale lighthouse, perched on one side of the rock, not quite at its centre, was pencil-thin. In a way, I *had* seen it before. The Fastnet Rock was a dead-ringer for the forbidding sea rock depicted in Tintin's cartoon adventure *The Black Island*, *L'Île Noire* in its French-language original, albeit that the only construction on Hergé's cartoon island is an off-centre castle, rather than a lighthouse.

In the late 1930s, the Belgian illustrator Hergé had created a scary island that Tintin and his pet dog Milou, Snowy in English, would visit in an effort to apprehend a group of counterfeiters. They had to overcome their fear and apprehension to do so. I remember the cover of the book: the boy detective Tintin has his hand on the tiller of a boat of the type I had seen in Crookhaven harbour. You don't see Tintin's face, but Snowy is looking at his master as if he's terrified. Of course, it all works out in the end – it has to, this is one of the earliest books in the Tintin series and the young hero has to live another day. It struck me that one message of Hergé's *L'Île Noire* could be: *Deal with your fears. They might not be as bad as you think.* It was a neat lesson for children. It was a neat lesson for adults, too.

On top of that, Hergé was a masterful illustrator. Long before I ever met Bailey, long before I knew precisely where the Fastnet Rock was, I hammered a nail into the wall of my sons' bedroom. I had found a poster that I thought they might like, and got it framed. The artwork was the cover of a cartoon book. It was Hergé's image of *L'Île Noire*.

Ian Bailey was on his own at the Prairie when I called. Jules was out somewhere. By now, the watery light was fading. I set up my voice recorder, laid out a page of notes on the table. Bailey put my habitual gift of a couple of bottles of Bordeaux on a sideboard.

"Ian, I wanted to start by asking you about something that Sean Murray said. Or, rather, I wanted to run a theory past you."

"Okay," Bailey said, opening his palms in a gesture that indicated that he was listening, and I should tell him what the theory was. What I told him was an edited version of what I had told Jean-Antoine Bloc over the phone.

"Right," I said, "well, you know there are hundreds of witness statements. The Garda file you gave me has, I think, 670 of them. That tells me that the Guards had no problem to get people to approach them, to give their evidence, even for the most minor thing. There is just one exception. It's the man Sean Murray saw in Sophie's passenger seat. He was Irish or English, according to Sean, but he did not go to the Guards. But this man sitting next to Sophie must have found out about the murder, it's unthinkable that he didn't…"

Bailey was looking at me quite intently. Sometimes he looked at me obliquely when doing interviews, or seemed transfixed by the bumps and lines on the wooden dining table, where we always sat together to discuss the case, or the ups and downs of his life, or his poetry, or whatever. Not this time. This time he was looking straight at me.

"The man in the passenger seat murdered Sophie. If he had something to hide that prevented him from going to the Guards, then it can only be that. He murdered her or, minimum, he took part in her murder."

I paused briefly, but Bailey said nothing.

"Ian, if you have an alibi for the middle of the afternoon of Friday, 20th December it cannot be you. You are ruled out. Do you see what I mean? Where were you?"

The questionnaire that Bailey filled in just after the murder is vague. Bailey wrote that he was *at home during the morning and afternoon, gardening and writing.* For her part, Jules Thomas wrote: *Friday, possibly went shopping in Schull.*

There was more. At around 10pm on the evening of 20th December, Bailey and Jules Thomas went to hear the band 'The Three Fellows' play at a bar in Schull. Only there weren't three fellows there that night. One didn't show, so there were just two fellows playing. Would this jog Bailey's memory?

I asked Bailey: "Ian, try to think back. In the evening, you and Jules went out and there was this band 'The Three Fellows'. They were on at the Courtyard. You told the Guards that only two of them showed up. You said that it was a quiet night. You left the bar at midnight and drove home. So try to think back, what were you doing before you went to the Courtyard?"

I was anxious, but hopeful. Bailey might well have had the key to exiting what he often called his "nightmare", right there and then. He had told me several times that the cloud of suspicion hanging over him had blighted his life, and his partner's life, too. His health had suffered. His career in journalism had been thwarted. Thanks to the European Arrest Warrant, he was effectively unable to leave the Republic of Ireland. He did not even attend his mother's funeral in England for fear of arrest. So this was worth it. It was worth trying to remember any scrap of information, anything at all.

"I know it's a long time ago, but try thinking about 'The Three Fellows' who were only two fellows and then maybe work backwards chronologically from there."

Bailey looked at me hard, mouth slightly open. It was a quizzical look. There was surprise there, too. He stiffened slightly, enough to be perceptible. He did not remember 'The Three Fellows'. He did not recall writing anything about them in the questionnaire, either.

"I don't remember what I was doing that day. I suppose I was here. But, you know what? I'm not even going to try to remember."

You know what? I'm not even going to try to remember.

"And anyway," said Bailey, "It doesn't matter. You were there. You heard Sean Murray say it wasn't me in the car."

You heard Sean Murray say it wasn't me in the car.

But that's not what Sean Murray said at all. I was certain about it. I remembered the conversation very well. When Bailey asked Murray point-blank if it was him in the car with Sophie, Murray replied by saying that it was someone Irish or English. He had pointedly refused to confirm that it was not Ian Bailey in the car that day.

For a split second, I did not know what to do or say. Or, rather, I knew I could do one of two things. I could challenge Bailey, sitting there staring at me across the pine dining table. *Ian*, I could say, *you're bullshitting me. You know as well as I do that Sean Murray did not confirm that it wasn't you in the car with Sophie. You asked him to, but he didn't do it.*

Or I could note his answer down. Stay in the game. Swallow my pride, in a way. Remain a "supporter". I knew that if I challenged Bailey about Murray's comments, I wouldn't be able to come back, his door at the Prairie would be shut forever. No more contact, no more questions. Equally, if I didn't challenge Bailey here and now about his version of what Sean Murray had said, I wouldn't get a second chance to confront him on this specific subject, meaning I wouldn't get a second chance to confront him about his attempt to get me to believe that Sean Murray had said something he had not. But everything else – all other topics – would still be open.

It struck me that Bailey might have slipped up. He took a risk in encouraging me to see Sean Murray and it did not work out quite how he expected. Murray did not say what Bailey had wanted him to say. Murray had been his own man, so to speak, he had not been minded to take suggestions from Ian Bailey. The fact that Bailey had been keen to interrupt his journey home to see Murray with me was a clear flag that Murray was important to the story. He was important in the search for Sophie's killer, regardless of what the Guards had thought.

I had to process all of this information quickly. I had to maintain a poker face, so to speak. It was an effort; I am not much of an actor.

At the Prairie in that precise moment, with Ian Bailey staring intently at me, I knew this: Bailey might well slip up again. I was in this for the long haul, after all.

That was what decided it for me: I was playing the longest of games.

I tried not to show that I knew that the man opposite me had made a mistake. I played dumb. I was Mr Bean again.

You have to be careful. You cannot assume that everyone will act and respond in the way you think reasonable and logical. We are all different, after all, and sometimes those differences can be stark. Having said that, it made no sense for Bailey to refuse to try to remember what he was doing on the afternoon Sophie Toscan du Plantier flew into Cork Airport for the last time. Bailey was in it up to his neck, with the French investigation gathering pace. What do they say about the drowning man? He grabs at straws. Bailey ignored the straw I offered him; he turned down the chance to try to carve out a meaningful alibi. His refusal would have made some sense if my idea was fanciful, or useless. But he did not suggest either of those things. He did not refute or rubbish my argument that the man in the passenger seat was the killer. He just shut up shop and closed down the interview.

I felt stunned looking at him across his pine dining table. I invented a reason for leaving his cottage quickly – a phone call I needed to make, some family issue. I wanted out of this country kitchen. I wanted away from Bailey.

Was Ian Bailey the man Sean Murray saw in Sophie's hire car? He had time enough that day to get to Cork Airport, or any other point on Sophie's route, and get a ride back to Schull with her. That meant he knew Sophie – his claim they had never met was a lie. If Bailey was the man in the passenger seat, it meant he killed her or was a party to her killing. That was what I thought, it was the hunch I had explained to Jean-Antoine Bloc. Emotionally, my view of Bailey had shifted. Intellectually, I still needed to process the exchange with Bailey, put it in a wider context, and keep digging.

I was playing a long game.

Before I left, Bailey scurried off to get me something. It was a copy of a document he had printed off for me. He said it was a short text he had drawn up for his legal team. Something he had written about himself. A piece of reading for my journey home. I might find it interesting. At the top of the first page I saw the title, underlined and in bold print: *Who Is Ian K. Bailey?*

Chapter 16

ANOTHER COUNTRY

In the summer of 2016, Bailey's worst fear materialised. The French authorities decided to prosecute him. The timeframe was anything but clear, though. I spoke with a French journalist who told me that she was sceptical that a trial would be held any time soon. France, and Paris in particular, had been hit by a number of bloody terrorist attacks. Justice urgently needed to be served for these crimes – there had been dozens of victims. Moreover, the French journalist said that it was not difficult to understand why prosecutors prioritised trials where the suspects were already in remand. This pushed the Sophie case down the queue, so to speak.

In the meantime, the French applied to serve the European Arrest Warrant for a second time, but the Irish judiciary rejected it again. It became clear that any trial of Bailey would be highly unusual – as Pierre-Louis had predicted, it would almost certainly be *in absentia*.

Another two years passed. The killing was always at the back of my mind, fused with a regret that I could not see a way of penetrating the fog of the case. The mystery of what happened that frozen night at Toormore would steal into my thoughts unbidden – when I was gazing out of a train window, sitting in a dull meeting, waiting to pay at a supermarket checkout.

Then, on a January day in 2019, I unexpectedly received a news alert with the date of Bailey's trial for murder. The trial was going to be held at the Paris Criminal Court in the last week of May that same year. Suddenly, the Sophie case was all I could think about. Bailey had been right about one thing: there was now a new investigating magistrate − a woman named Nathalie Turquey had replaced Patrick Gachon. I started to read the case file again. I thought of Bailey's claustrophobic cottage at the Prairie, the choppy vista of Roaringwater Bay, the sad granite cross with *SOPHIE* chiselled into it, the dissolving gleam of the Fastnet light. Nothing was going to keep me away from the trial in Paris.

I arranged to meet Donal MacIntyre and Jim Sheridan there. They would have a camera team in Paris, and another trailing Bailey, for the duration of the proceedings. The day before the trial was due to open, I was packing my case, getting ready to travel to France. MacIntyre called me. He had been talking with Sheridan. They had a proposal. Would I accept playing prosecutor with Bailey? He meant, asking Bailey the questions that the prosecutor would be asking the vacant dock in the courtroom, the empty space where Bailey should have been. Taking notes and putting those same questions to Bailey over the phone outside the courthouse.

MacIntyre was offering me the chance to play the bad cop.

Bad cop, good cop, whichever. I did not need asking twice.

***

I walked along the left bank of the River Seine towards the old courthouse on the Île de la Cité. The Seine was ash green and the water swirled here and there making me think that there were whirlpools beneath its surface. Most people, though, were looking up rather than down. Six weeks earlier, the Cathedral of Notre-Dame, France's most venerated religious site, had suffered a disastrous fire. Tourists lined the quayside to take photos of the wounded roof of the cathedral. Some were taking selfies with the charred hulk of the building in the background. A few were smiling, as you conventionally do when you take a selfie. Others projected a neutral expression or mild sadness. On the roads, the Monday morning traffic advanced at the pace of a crawl. I took my photo quickly. I had business elsewhere.

A newspaper kiosk outside the courthouse had a poster advertising a gossipy monthly magazine. It caught my eye. The magazine had the smiling, elderly and lately very creased face of actor Alain Delon on its cover. Underneath there was a headline: *If it hadn't been for the women in my life, I'd have turned into a rogue.*

Alain Delon was part of Sophie's circle, the French film crowd of the 1980s and 1990s, and a near-contemporary of Sophie's husband, Daniel Toscan du Plantier. I had once come across a black-and-white photo of Sophie, Daniel, Alain Delon and a woman whom I did not recognise – one of the women, I presume, without whose company he would have turned into a rogue. In this photo, Alain Delon, Sophie and the other woman were looking at Daniel as if he was in the midst of telling a wonderful anecdote, their faces on the very cusp of a laugh. The image was redolent of desire and of high summer. It was redolent, too, of wealth and ease and glamour – glamour of a slightly dated kind.

The photo had been taken in a meadow and from a low position, so that blades of grass made long arcs in the background. Some of the blades of grass were close to the lens, too, and pleasantly out of focus. There may even have been a bee buzzing in the frame, suggesting that nature itself was alert to Daniel's wit. Sophie's freckles were prominent, and the sun caught wisps of her blond hair, tied back behind her head, as she smiled at Daniel, who was in profile with his trademark bushy, salt-and-pepper moustache.

I reckoned that Sophie would have been in her early thirties at the time of that photo. I wondered if at that point she had gone to Ireland and bought her holiday home, or if the whitewashed house at Toormore loomed ahead of her. The photo was poignant, no doubt about it. It was poignant in the way that radiant images of people who die young always are.

Sixteen years separated Sophie and Daniel. In every photo, the age difference was palpable. Daniel, too, had died young, relatively speaking. With Sophie buried in a graveyard close to his country home, and an Irish police investigation ongoing, Daniel had said that there was a devil in the hills of southern Ireland.

Daniel died without ever finding out who the devil was.

***

My mobile phone rang. The name 'Bailey' appeared on the screen.

"Ian, hello, how are you?"

Ian Bailey said he did not feel so bad, under the circumstances. His partner, Jules Thomas, was not taking it too well, however. She was under a ton of stress. Still, Bailey told me that he and Thomas were ready for whatever the French criminal justice system threw at them.

"What will be, will be, that's my attitude" said Bailey. "Anyway, are you in the court? Has it begun yet?"

"No, they're only beginning after lunch…"

Ian Bailey, incredulous: "What? They haven't even started?"

Bailey and his Irish legal team had called this a "show-trial" and a "farce". The crux of their argument was that Ireland's Director of Public Prosecutions had long ago decided that putting Bailey in the dock for the murder of Sophie Toscan du Plantier was *not warranted by the evidence*. So why should a foreign power now be able to hold a trial for the same crime? Bailey's French lawyer had opined a few days earlier that a "miscarriage of justice is about to happen". Bailey said many times that he would never get a fair hearing in France. His view was that the French had already decided he was guilty.

For anyone used to murder trials in Ireland, England, the

United States and elsewhere, it seemed odd that this one was due to last a single working week. Actually, it was even less than this, since Thursday was a public holiday in France and so the court would be shut that day. Now I was telling Bailey that the French were not even getting the thing going on the morning of the first day. That meant that there would be a grand total of three and a half days of court time for the coldest of cold-case murder trials. Bailey had consistently said that he wanted to clear his name in a trial in Ireland. He never wished for this trial in France. His lawyers had unsuccessfully tried to prevent the Irish authorities from cooperating with the French investigators. That was why it seemed strange to me that he appeared aggrieved that the French did not seem to want to get the proceedings started quickly that day.

"No, Ian, it's due to open at 2:30. I'm outside the courthouse now. The press officer is going to give the foreign journalists a briefing in a minute or two. Can I call you back?"

I hung up and took my seat at a table at the back of Les Deux Palais, a brasserie directly opposite the courthouse. The interior had marble columns and gold-leaf mouldings and the waiters wore black bow ties and starched aprons. The court's press officer told the overseas reporters that this trial was unusual, although not unique. It was not unique because in very rare cases, historically rare cases, defendants had been tried in France without being present in court. France's penal code laid down that on such occasions there would be no jury. Instead, a presiding judge and two other judges handed down their verdict and a sentence, if appropriate. In this scenario, the sentence could not be appealed.

Once I had been driving through the sodden fields of County Cork, my windscreen wipers on at full speed. It was difficult to see the road in front of the car and I had Bailey in the passenger seat. He had said to me: "Here just about everyone has come to realise I'm innocent". He was surely stretching it to say "just about everyone" in County Cork but, as was habitual for me at that time, back in 2015, I didn't much feel like challenging him. In any case, in 2015 we had only ever talked about the *possibility* of a trial being held in France. For years, nobody could tell if a trial in Paris was a done deal and was just about to be announced, or if it would be shelved and never materialise. Anyway, what Bailey had not needed to say in the car that day, and what I am sure he did not say, was that a majority of people in France familiar with the case thought very differently.

All the members of the Bouniol family I had met had said that Bailey had killed Sophie. Sophie's mother, Marguerite Bouniol, had named Bailey as her daughter's murderer several times on French television. She said it was her *intime conviction*, her 'deep-seated conviction', that Bailey was guilty. In using the term *intime conviction*, Marguerite Bouniol was referencing the standard of proof in the French Penal Code applying to criminal trials in France. It is equivalent to a member of the jury asking herself: I have heard all the evidence and have given it due consideration, now what do I believe in my heart? If Ian Bailey had been put on trial in Ireland, the jury would have had to assess whether the prosecution had made its case 'beyond reasonable doubt'. Both 'deep-seated conviction' and 'beyond reasonable doubt' contain a degree of subjectivity. For instance, 'beyond reasonable doubt' does not define what would be an 'unreasonable' doubt. Neither approach is entirely objective. Sophie's mother had looked at the evidence available to her and believed in her heart that Ian Bailey had killed Sophie.

At Les Deux Palais, the press officer, an affable young man with a perfectly trimmed beard and a well-cut dark blue suit, wound up his presentation by informing the foreign journalists that Ian Bailey could be found not guilty, or one of the following: guilty of manslaughter; guilty of murder; or guilty of pre-meditated murder. Half a dozen pages of my notebook were already full of scribblings of this and that about *Bailey* and this and that about *Sophie*, although the press officer was careful always to refer to the victim as *Madame Toscan du Plantier*. Bailey was *Monsieur Bailey*. The six syllables of *Toscan du Plantier* were a mouthful. *Sophie* was a very nice name.

Not for the first time, *Bailey* and *Sophie* rhymed in my mind in a way that made me feel uneasy.

***

I returned to the street outside Les Deux Palais, now busier than ever. I phoned Bailey back, but I could barely hear him when he said to me:

"Anyway, I wanted to ask you, how are we going to do it? There's young Colm who'll be getting here in a minute. Are you going to call him, or do we call you?"

Colm was a cameraman hired by Jim Sheridan to shadow Bailey at his cottage at the Prairie for as many hours in the day as Bailey accepted, which turned out to be most of the hours in all of the days. Bailey had always been an enthusiastic performer when a camera was pointed in his direction. Jim Sheridan and Donal MacIntyre, the bosses of the documentary on the Sophie case I was helping out with, had a camera team here in Paris, too. When we got down to the serious stuff this week, the idea was that the two cameras would be filming at the same time – one would be on Sheridan and me, the other one would be on Bailey.

"And how often are you thinking of doing it?" said Bailey. "What I'd like is morning and evening. Two calls a day." I sensed excitement in his voice. Not a hint of trepidation, it seemed.

"Sure, Ian, that's what we'll be aiming for. Of course, in the end it's up to Jim and Donal."

I had not talked with Ian Bailey in a long while, not for something like a year. I would be spending a bit more time with him on the phone over the next five days, getting reacquainted. I suppose that was why it occurred to me that I should not close that morning's conversation too quickly. It would appear too impersonal. I needed to be sure of his trust.

"Ian, I just thought of something. The last time we spoke when I wasn't at home or at your place in Ireland, I was in Madrid, on a bus with my wife and kids, and you said where exactly and I replied that we were headed to the Atocha Station…"

"…the Café-Bar Atocha!"

"Yes, that was it. You said that the best place you'd ever eaten, the best place anywhere, was a restaurant near the Atocha Station…"

"Hold on a minute."

The line went quiet at the other end. I guessed Bailey had gone off to do something or to get something.

"Here it is. A saucer with *Café-Bar Atocha* on it."

I imagined a small saucer of the type scattered across the tables at Les Deux Palais. I imagined Bailey holding it up to catch the light and admiring the Café-Bar Atocha's logo or crest or intertwined initials or whatever.

"Did you ever get to eat there, at the Café-Bar Atocha? Did you ever go?"

"No, Ian, I didn't."

Bailey said I should have gone. He said he had had a steak there, a very fine one, washed down with plenty of Spanish red.

Bailey's tone suddenly appeared melancholy. Thanks to France's determined efforts at extradition and specifically the piece of paperwork named the European Arrest Warrant, Bailey had been unable to leave the Republic of Ireland for the past 10 years. That ruled out a return visit to the dining room of the Café-Bar Atocha. The fact that Ian Bailey was to all intents and purposes broke was undeniably a factor, too. As things stood, he rarely left County Cork.

Bailey said there was something else he wanted to tell me, before I ran off to the courthouse.

"What's that, Ian?"

"I'm pleased it's you."

"How do you mean?"

"I'm pleased it's you, Nick. It's fitting. You were the one who told me that the French were going to hold the trial. I got the news from you. You broke it to me. Do you remember?"

Yes. I told him I remembered. It had been almost three years earlier. The news had come through to me from a contact in France and I instinctively dialled Bailey's number to tip him off, before the mass of Irish journalists started ringing for a quote, which turned out to be about 15 minutes after my call. In those 15 minutes, Bailey had been able to compose his thoughts and work out what to say to them. This is what he had told me. Later, I wondered if I had done the right thing in calling Bailey that day. But my concern was short-lived. Bailey was innocent until proven guilty. He deserved the same rights and treatment as anyone else who had not been convicted of a crime.

"So I'm glad you're there now, at the trial. I'm glad you'll be the one letting me know how it's going."

I recognised something in Ian Bailey's tone of voice when he told me that he was happy that I would be giving him updates from outside the courthouse – *informing* him, that seemed to be the gist of what he was saying. Bailey had several times told me I was his "supporter" and I had not denied it, or put it into some sort of context for him, or anything else. Perhaps I should have done. I was about to play prosecutor with Bailey over the phone. Things were going to get complicated from now on in. I wondered if Bailey suspected anything.

***

I made some notes to set the scene for Bailey: *Room has dark wood panelling and a very high ceiling. You would have taken your seat in the glass-fronted defendant's box. To your left is the panel of three judges, all dressed in black gowns. Directly in front of you are the benches where the family is sitting, with Pierre-Louis closest to you, five or six metres away, close enough to smell his aftershave, if he is using any. To your right you have the journalists and the public gallery. There is a gendarme standing next to the defendant's box. They switch every hour or so. Sometimes they stifle a yawn. You see, with you not there, the gendarme assigned to keep an eye on you does not have much to do. A moulding on the wall above the judges shows an ornamental set of scales of justice, framed by a dagger and the palm of a hand, dismembered. There is a single eye above the set of scales, an all-seeing eye.*

A French journalist sitting on the same bench told me the single eye on the set of scales – the Eye of Providence – was a Masonic symbol. The palm of the dismembered hand had two fingers bent backwards. I thought of Sophie's almost dismembered finger on the frigid ground outside her Irish house. I asked the French journalist if the two bent fingers were a Masonic symbol, too, but the journalist shrugged, he had no idea. Bailey's trial *in absentia* would be one of the last ones held in this place. A new criminal court on the outskirts of Paris was due to replace it. Would the new courthouse have room for these mouldings with their half-known, half-forgotten meanings? I supposed not.

Rays of sunlight passing through a pair of high windows picked out particles of dust, rising and falling. I thought: people had been sentenced to death by guillotine in this courtroom.

The presiding judge was a woman with large glasses named Frédérique Aline. Her spectacles gave her an owlish look. Aline was flanked by two other judges – a strikingly young-looking woman, and an older man. The prosecutor for the Republic was a bearded middle-aged man with dark hair called Jean-Pierre Bonthoux. He wore a red cloak with a fur sash, and he was seated in a comfortable-looking chair on a raised platform to the right of the three judges, I spotted Alain Spilliaert, the lawyer I had met at a meeting of the Sophie Justice Committee, next to Marie Dosé, the lead barrister for the Bouniol family. They were sitting just in front of the Bouniols. Ian Bailey, as widely predicted, had nobody representing him in court.

Judge Aline read out the indictment. *On the night of 22nd December 1996, Ian Bailey made his way to the house occupied by Sophie Toscan du Plantier...* Then the details of the murder: violent, grim, brutal. I glanced to my right: Sophie's family immobile, for the most part staring straight ahead. Sophie's parents were desolate. Her mother had entered the courtroom in a wheelchair. She looked terribly frail. I knew she had been in bad health. Sophie's father, grey hair perfectly combed, dark suit, was in tears. There were the Bouniols on Sophie's father's side, and the Gazeaus on her mother's side. Sophie's favourite aunt Marie-Madeleine Opalka was dressed in black, wearing a large hat. She seemed to be breathing with difficulty.

Pierre-Louis, Sophie's son, looked smart, but drained and anxious. A week earlier, he had made an emotional appeal at the gate of the church in Goleen for the Irish witnesses to travel to France, to play their part in the trial. Pierre-Louis's words were broadcast on television and reported widely in the country's newspapers. *I was eight years old when I first came here and 15 years old when my mother was brutally killed*, he had said. Pierre-Louis spoke of his mother's affection for Ireland, her love of her corner of the Mizen. *It is time today to turn one of the saddest pages of your history, and the darkest page of mine. I could have given up my mother's dream, I could have abandoned this country, I could have chosen not to bring my children here, I could have believed in curses, in a kind of predestination, I could have been afraid, but I'm here. This land must find peace again. My mother Sophie is not a ghost. She was a woman. She was a victim of human cruelty and violence, which has no place here.*

For 20 years, I have trusted you. Don't betray me, and don't betray yourselves.

The clerk of court read out a long list of Irish witnesses, announcing the outcome in each case: "No news... We did not hear back... He said he would come maybe... Did not have a valid passport... Did not reply... Unknown... Did not reply... Address incomplete... Not known at this address... Did not reply." The court had written to Saffron and Virginia, Jules Thomas's eldest daughters. Neither had written back.

Marie Farrell and Jules Thomas had been asked to give their testimony in Paris. So had Fenella Thomas, who had told the Guards that Jules Thomas and Ian Bailey had left the cottage at the Prairie for a couple of hours on the morning of 23rd December

1996, flatly contradicting her mother's and Bailey's account of their movements at that time. Embarrassingly, a couple of the witnesses had been dead for several years, and yet the French authorities had still mailed the letters. No Guards were going to attend – the case was still open in Ireland, so this was surely the reason. I asked around and it seemed that two Irish witnesses out of a list of 24 would appear before the court. I had heard that the witnesses would have to buy their flights and pay for their accommodation in Paris, and then apply for reimbursement. Perhaps this arrangement put some off. They also had not been given much notice, apparently. Others, maybe, were not pleased that the trial was being held in a foreign jurisdiction. I did not know. But I could see Pierre-Louis. He looked downcast.

The indictment took an hour and a half to read out. A few things were clear. Firstly, the French treated Bailey's "alleged informal admissions", to use the expression coined by the Irish DPP, as confessions pure and simple. Secondly, they thought Bailey's alibi was nonsensical. Thirdly, the French had salvaged something from the early statements made by Marie Farrell, although they appeared to have glossed over the contradiction between Farrell identifying a man of medium stature outside her shop on Saturday, 21st December 1996, and the fact that Bailey was very tall. They must have come to the conclusion that Farrell had been telling the truth when she identified Bailey at Kealfadda Bridge in the early hours of the night of the murder. They certainly placed no importance on Farrell's subsequent retraction. Fourthly, the presence of scratches on Bailey's hands and forearms, and the wound on his forehead, were evidence of his culpability.

But what about motive? Why did Bailey kill Sophie, if this is what happened? Could the French court establish a tangible connection between murderer and victim?

Marie Dosé, the barrister acting for the Bouniols and the Justice Committee, rose to speak to outline the case against Ian Bailey as she saw it. That is a good thing, I thought. Here is a criminal justice system that gives an outlet to the victim's family. That did not mean that the *partie civile* was necessarily able to see to it that justice was done and that the punishment properly fitted the crime. But at least the victim's loved ones were there, represented by their own lawyers, and they could make their views known and their voice heard.

I was thinking these lofty, blue-sky thoughts when Marie Dosé made an abrupt switch from speaking about the murder and its awful circumstances. Dosé, black-gowned, said that she was "scandalised" that there was an Irish film crew sending text messages to Ian Bailey on the progress of the trial and filming his reactions at home in Ireland. Dosé named the production company at fault – it was the one headed by Donal MacIntyre – and she then looked towards the press seats and the public gallery. Dosé's voice reached a crescendo as she denounced – well, as she denounced *me*, since I was the one taking notes in the courtroom in order to grill Bailey on the phone later on.

People started to look around for the culprit. When Judge Aline had asked if Bailey was in court, nobody had glanced up to see if the defendant was about to make a dramatic, last-gasp entrance. Now it was different. *Who was this person?* Some people in the room were muttering and shaking their heads in disapproval. As a diversionary tactic, I started to peer around like everyone else, pretending to look for the Bailey message-relayer lurking in the Parisian courtroom. I was worried, too. Dosé's appeal to the judge was framed in a way that suggested Aline could take action against the person informing Bailey.

However, what Dosé said about the messaging was not true. Nobody was sending any text messages or updates, which would have made little sense, since it would have removed the potential of surprising Bailey over the phone. Otherwise, though, Dosé's description of our activities was correct. Judge Aline said she did not welcome Dosé's news, but pointed out that the press were ultimately free to report the proceedings in any way they saw fit. Aline said that there was therefore nothing she could do about it.

I breathed an extremely discreet sigh of relief. Then I thought, oh no, if Dosé was offended, that likely meant that Sophie's family and friends were opposed to us filming Bailey's reactions in Ireland. It must have come from them. What to me was a chance to grill Bailey, to discover the truth, looked to the French like a way of giving a presumed murderer the oxygen of publicity. Jean-Antoine Bloc had greeted me warmly outside the courthouse, but I wondered what the implications of this public shaming might be.

***

"Ian," I said into the phone, "they said you bashed her head in with a stone and then a cavity block, they said you struck her 40 or 50 times".

There I was, the bad cop.

"They said I bashed her head in?"

"Yes, that's correct."

Bailey said it was all wrong. None of it was true.

"They spoke a lot about Marie Farrell. They are placing you at Kealfadda Bridge."

There had been a French detective giving evidence. He had been one of the team that went over to Ireland to interview witnesses. I was fairly sure he was the grim-faced man I had seen in the car on the lane leading to Sophie's house. A cop with experience of investigating cold cases. The detective had set the scene by saying that Ireland was a Catholic country and Schull was a place where everyone knew everyone else. He said that in Paris it would be banal for a woman to spend the night with a man other than her husband. Not so in Ireland.

He told the court that Farrell had stuck by her statement until 2005. Her story from then on was that the Guards strongly encouraged her to say it was Bailey at Kealfadda Bridge. Farrell had been under pressure from the Guards for nine years. Bailey had put a lot of pressure on her, too. Farrell was a woman who had cheated on her husband, the French detective had said. He added that Farrell had even tried to commit suicide, which was news to me. I did not mention this last detail to Bailey.

"Absolute terrible fucking bollocks, but never mind," said Bailey. He appeared to be getting annoyed on the other end of the line. I wasn't sure why; after all, Marie Farrell had switched sides. "Haven't they read the DPP's critique from 2001?"

The phone connection was poor. Bailey could barely hear me. I started to tell him about the photos. I told him that they were terrible, awful, heart-breaking. I would have liked to have seen his reaction, looked into his eyes at that moment, but we could barely hear each other. In the end, I had to cut the conversation short, and I passed the phone to Jim Sheridan.

I will never forget seeing the photos of Sophie's body. Nothing can really prepare you.

There was a large screen in the courtroom. At first, it showed images of journalists and observers sitting in an overspill room in the courthouse. People wandering in and out, a bit less formal than in the courtroom itself. The screen suddenly turned a deep shade of blue. We were about to see something else. They were getting something ready for us. Pierre-Louis helped his parents file out of the courtroom, guiding his grandmother into her wheelchair. Marie-Madeleine Opalka followed, as did all of Sophie's family and friends. But Bertrand Bouniol, Sophie's brother, stayed in the room, as did Jean-Antoine Bloc and a couple of other Justice Committee members.

Her eyes were closed. Her face was outrageously bloodied. I could not really identify her features, her mouth in particular. There was blood on the stony ground all around her head, pools of it. Bloodied brambles nearby. How could this much blood spill from a slender body? In some photos, there was the blue of the winter sky at the top, and the red of blood everywhere else. I said a prayer for her soul.

Anyone who saw this would surely have looked away quickly.

Nobody's gaze would voluntarily settle on the outcome of this monstrous act. Any of the people who saw the terrible scene – Shirley Foster, Alfie Lyons, the Hellens – they would have looked only long enough to make an identification. Surely only the murderer would have rested his eyes on this sight and lingered?

Her leggings or perhaps her nightdress, or perhaps both, had caught on some barbed wire. There was a gate, also bloodied. The gate was one of the items from the crime scene that, amazingly, the Guards had lost. It was put into storage and then one day it was gone. A big, six-bar gate. How on earth had that gone astray?

Nobody in the courtroom gave us any explanations for the photos, what they demonstrated, how to interpret them. Some showed the inside of Sophie's house. A pair of black boots at the foot of the stairs next to a jacket. A mattress with white sheets on a brown rug. Sophie's handbag left on the floor. A book lying open. Then more blood: this time, on one of the doors to the house. Those were the drops of blood Alfie Lyons had spotted. Presumably, this was the back door to the house.

Finally, a photo of a small car, Sophie's hire car from the Avis counter at Cork Airport, with its passenger seat pushed right back.

Chapter 17

THE VIEW FROM HUNT'S HILL

Much of the second and third days of Bailey's murder trial were taken up with the evidence against Bailey being read out in court – witness statements, Garda memos, the shifting sands of Bailey's alibi for the night in question, and an analysis of how much he knew about the murder, and when. It was especially interesting to hear the evidence that Sophie knew Bailey or, at least, that Bailey had tried to contact her. This was a vital part of the case against Bailey, and Bailey knew it: if the two of them had never met, there was essentially neither motive nor opportunity.

A film director named Guy Girard who used to work with Sophie told investigators that in November 1996, Sophie mentioned to him the name Ian Bailey, or 'Eoin' (his occasional pen name) Bailey. Girard thought that Sophie was referring to Edwin Baily, a French film director and producer, but Sophie said that she did not know Edwin Baily, although she had heard of him. She was talking about someone else – about Ian Bailey, a writer who lived in Ireland. Girard was sure that Sophie brought up the name of Bailey, the Irish-based writer, again. Girard could not recall the precise details of what Sophie had said to him on this second occasion, but he was sure their conversation had taken place on 19th December 1996, that is to say the day before Sophie left for Ireland.

What intrigued me about Girard's testimony was the misunderstanding about the name – the surnames 'Bailey' and 'Baily' are almost identical, and the first names (Edwin and Ian/ Eoin) are rather similar when you say them out loud. It's the kind of brief conversation that would stick in your head for that very reason, precisely because of the curious mix-up. Since Sophie would have had to repeat Ian/Eoin Bailey's name to differentiate it from that of the similarly named Frenchman, there was little chance that Girard would have misheard it. Equally, the fact that both Sophie and Girard recognised the name Edwin Baily, but only Sophie knew who Ian/Eoin Bailey was, meant that it was entirely logical for Sophie to offer Girard a brief description of the Bailey who lived in Ireland.

With Sean Murray, something along the same lines happened: when Murray asked Sophie if she wanted the tank of her hire car filling up, Sophie didn't understand, which was unusual (since what else could Murray have been asking her?). This minor but unlikely misunderstanding on the part of an unusually pretty driver crystallised the exchange in Murray's memory.

Girard's first piece of testimony was given in 1999. However, in an interview with investigators in 2008, which struck me as a long time after the event, he recalled a few more details. Girard said that Sophie *did* say she knew Ian Bailey and that he – like her – was interested in the "theme of violence". Sophie, coincidentally, had an interest in the output of the so-called Viennese Actionists, a loose group of avant-garde performance artists active in Austria in the late 1960s. The Actionists' work often featured destruction and violence, occasionally contravening decency laws, placing them at the extreme end of the counter-culture of the time. According to Guy Girard, the day before she set off for Ireland, Sophie mentioned to him that she had a book for Bailey (meaning, a book she was intending to take to Ireland and give to him).

Secondly, Sophie's cousin, Alexandra Lewy – the woman Sophie had gone house-hunting in Ireland with – recalled that several days before her last trip to Ireland, Sophie had received a telephone call at the office of Les Champs Blancs, Sophie's documentary production company. Lewy understood the caller to be a man from the area where Sophie's Irish house was located. According to Lewy, the man who called claimed to Sophie that he was a freelance journalist and writer, and wanted to meet her "for cultural purposes". Sophie had appeared surprised by the call and had wanted to know how the man had found out her telephone number. Lewy said that the man had not wanted to give an explanation, but that Sophie had not appeared worried about it, putting his attitude down to "Irish eccentricities". Lewy did not remember Sophie mentioning the name of the caller.

Thirdly, there was the testimony of Paul Webster, formerly the Paris correspondent for *The Guardian* newspaper. Webster had appeared as a witness for the defence in Bailey's libel action in Cork in 2003. He had told the court then that Bailey had called him early in 1997 to talk about the Sophie Toscan du Plantier case, and Bailey had mentioned that he had known the victim prior to her death. Webster – who had died in the meantime – had been adamant that Bailey had told him he had known Sophie.

In the courtroom, we heard directly from a fourth witness. The evidence she gave was entirely new to me. I quizzed Bailey about it.

"Ian, Sophie's best friend, a lady called Agnès Thomas, said that a few days or maybe a couple of weeks before her last journey to Ireland, Sophie had told her that she got a phone call from someone living close by wanting to discuss a poetry project with her." Agnès Thomas had added that Sophie had said that the person wanting to meet her was a "weird guy".

"It certainly wasn't me, if that's what the implication is. It's a load of bollocks," Bailey said.

"She was certain about it. The only thing is that she blacked it out of her mind, and she only recalled the conversation many years later." Agnès Thomas had told the court that the Justice Committee had held a meeting to celebrate Sophie's life and achievements and the reminiscences had triggered the memory. She had involuntarily buried the story about the "weird guy" under a pile of grief.

"Ah, yeah, yeah, yeah, of course she did," Bailey said, his tone sarcastic.

"Did you make that call to Sophie?" I asked Bailey.

"Me? That's a load of bollocks. The only indication was that Alfie Lyons said he had a French neighbour. We were never introduced, it's a load of nonsense."

I moved swiftly along. The French had commissioned a character profile from a clinical psychiatrist and a psychologist. The duo had worked from Bailey's writings and other reports. I gave Bailey the highlights.

"Narcissistic, impulsive, egotistical and you need recognition. Any response to that? If you were here, what would you have said?"

"Well, I would dispute the whole thing. The idea of a psychologist who hasn't met me going through my writings, which might have been altered, is once more an example of, well, I don't know, words fail me... Am I narcissistic, what does that mean? Does it mean I'm in love with myself?"

"Well, I think narcissism is, like, putting yourself at the centre of things."

"I would dispute that as a lot of poppycock."

"They said alcohol made you violent, but that's on record, isn't it?"

I meant Bailey's multiple attacks on Jules Thomas.

"I did drink whiskey, I did drink spirits, and so did she, and so we did have unfortunate domestic incidents, all alcohol-fuelled, and I haven't touched spirits in what, 20 years, a long, long time... But talking to other people, it's [domestic violence] not that uncommon, when you're in a relationship and it's very intense, very highly charged."

I returned to my notes. "You take pleasure from being the centre of attention and you like to provoke?"

"No, but maybe some of the writing, one of the things a writer does is write things that are not provocative exactly… but no, I think this is a load of old bollocks."

"Wouldn't you like to be here to tell them that?"

"No, no, no, Nick, no…"

"But can you see where I'm coming from?"

"No, if I was there it would have made no difference. I believe I've been convicted in advance."

"Conclusion: borderline psychological disorder without being psychotic. That's what the court was left with."

"It's just such a crock of *merde*, and that's probably not a very good response."

"Do you recognise any of it?"

"I may have been impulsive in the past but I'm not impulsive now. Is it a crime to be impulsive?"

"Have you learned from things you've done?"

"You learn, you grow up. If you're wise, you learn from your mistakes and you don't make them again. Isn't youth a bit impulsive?"

After a pause, Bailey added: "I've probably got a bag of regrets".

But Bailey was warming to the theme of narcissism. "I don't think I'm particularly narcissistic, but I'm a performance poet. I had 120 people [listening to the poems] in Ballydehob the other day and I was the centre of attention. When you're performing, you're in the zone."

Bailey said that if we were going to go down that avenue, we would need to lock up every singer who ever got up on a stage.

"What do feel like when they don't like your poems?"

"Well, I've never had any negative response, apart from one or two buffoons."

"You can't please everyone all the time, I suppose."

I decided to change tack.

"Ian, they keep coming back to it, they keep talking about Hunt's Hill."

I tell Bailey that, as he was well aware, it was all on the record. The details had been read out in the courtroom. The drinks he had at the Galley bar on the evening before the murder, the poems he read out, his turn playing the *bodhrán* with his sleeves rolled up. He left the Galley with Jules, and they drove up Hunt's Hill. According to what Jules Thomas had told the Guards, a statement she had disputed, Bailey had got out of the car and looked out over the valley to where Alfie Lyons and Sophie lived.

"Where I stopped there is no view of the houses of Alfie Lyons, Sophie and the other house."

"Did you go that way that night?"

Bailey adopted the kind of tone that sometimes people use with a child who fails to grasp something very simple: "There are two ways back, over the flat and over the hill. At the point where I stopped, there is no view of the valley below."

Bailey made a slight pause. "Even so, you tell me, even if I had stopped where there is a view, what's the connection, what's the point?"

I replied by saying that the court had laboured the point: Bailey had stopped where he could see Alfie Lyon's place and Sophie's place and he had had a premonition that something bad was going to happen.

Bailey, levelly: "How is this an evidential piece that I murdered somebody that I didn't know and didn't have anything to do with?"

I don't play snooker but I think the relevant metaphor is that you are 'snookered'. There was no way out. There was no proof that they had met. It was an insurmountable obstacle. The evidence offered by Guy Girard, Alexandra Lewy, and Agnès Thomas would be considered hearsay in an Irish court. On top of that, their evidence had been tendered after Bailey's name had entered the public domain as the only suspect in Sophie's murder. In other words, when they gave their witness statements, they would already

212

have been aware of Ian Bailey and his connection to the case. I told Bailey it was up to the court to decide on that.

"So on Friday afternoon I'll find out that I have been convicted of a crime I had nothing to do with. I'm sure they'll have it over and done with. I know the French quite well, they like their weekends, they like their wine."

"Ian, the psychologists had some other findings. They were looking at your writings. What came out was this idea of sexual obsession, of you being a pervert. How does that make you feel?"

"The whole thing's a load of bollocks." I heard a slamming or clattering sound in the background. "How do I feel?"

"Does it surprise you?"

"No, well I knew it was coming but, you know, it's almost *infra dignitatem*, it's almost below my dignity to address such accusations, but you should just talk to the people who know me. Jules probably knows me better than anyone. You know, Nick, I can't really answer that at the moment."

I paused for a few seconds. I was finding that I had to be careful – I could pause and Bailey would take it as a prompt to say he was tired and didn't want any more questions, or I could pause and he would carry on. This time, Bailey carried on.

"No, I'm not a pervert and no, I'm not a murderer. I might be a bit eccentric, but if that's a crime, everybody should watch out."

"It came up in court that…"

Bailey cut me off. "What do you want me to say, Nick? Put it into one simple question and I'll try to answer it."

"Sorry?"

"One simple question and I'll try to answer."

"Are you a sexual predator?"

"No, of course not. Absolute nonsense and a fantasy."

I passed the phone to Jim Sheridan, the 'good cop' in the telephone routine. Bailey told Sheridan he was suffering from "BCOS", which it turned out stood for "Bailey Case Overload Syndrome".

Nonetheless, Sheridan wanted to ask Bailey for a quick clarification on the topic of masturbation: "Ian, they are talking about your diaries. They're saying you calculated how many times you had knocked one off. What was it? Fifteen thousand times or thirty thousand times?"

That was it. Three days of the trial gone. I had not had the chance to tell Bailey about the two witnesses who travelled from Ireland – his neighbour, Amanda Reed, had spoken about her son, Malachi, and his reaction to Bailey telling him he had murdered Sophie, and his former friend and workmate, Bill Fuller, who had also witnessed what appeared to be a confession on Bailey's part. It was odd, they were the 'Irish witnesses' in my head and in my notes, but they both spoke with English accents when they took the stand. I wondered how many of the French people in the courtroom had noticed this.

When I was much younger, I had visited the famous La Coupole brasserie on the Left Bank with a young woman on my arm, arriving by metro. The waiters were older chaps who chatted away with each other conspiratorially when they weren't serving up vast seafood platters. Two young wide-eyed tourists. The waiters greeted us with an expression between a smirk and a frown. I hovered my finger over the second-cheapest bottle of rosé on the wine list. We ate French onion soup and probably the chicken. I worked out an acceptable tip to the nearest franc.

That night, passing again through the revolving door of La Coupole but this time with half a ton of camera equipment and a kind of louche swagger that screamed, at least in my mind, *true crime documentary*, the maître d' greeted the four of us like long-lost friends. The older chaps waiting on the tables leant forwards with their hands behind their backs in a way that suggested our choices from the menu were fascinating. We ordered oysters, the best steaks and four bottles of premium Bordeaux.

***

The Thursday of the trial week was the Feast of the Ascension, a public holiday in France. Jim Sheridan, Donal MacIntyre and I had come with our camera crew to a café in the trendy Marais district of Paris to film some more of our telephone conversations with Bailey with a suitably Parisian backdrop. The old courthouse, four miles away on the Île de la Cité, had meanwhile shut up shop for the day, its vast courtyard now the preserve of pigeons.

I had most of the day to prepare, but still I was feeling nervous. This would be my last chance to grill Bailey on the details of the prosecution case. Through the window of the café, I saw a group of wiry, Mediterranean men playing boules in the evening half-light, some crouching over the spinning silver balls, some standing upright with their hands on their hips. Every couple of minutes, small, boxy cars formed a tight, impatient queue at a traffic light. From time to time, a motorbike screeched. Paris no doubt had much edgier filming locations, but this one served the purpose.

My objective was to press Bailey on the specifics, and be as detailed as possible. I needed to keep speaking to him in the way a prosecutor would, but I needed to ramp up the intensity. I also had to keep him talking for as long as possible. MacIntyre and I had agreed that I would start with a soft-ball question to make Bailey feel comfortable, to massage his ego a bit. I was using MacIntyre's mobile phone. It was a different phone this time. The screen was pitted and rough where the glass had shattered. The cameraman in the café started filming as the call connected. Colm, our man at the other end, said "Hi" and passed the call to Bailey.

"Is that Ian?"

"Nick!" exclaimed Bailey.

I asked Bailey how he was. He said he had been running some errand or other, to take his mind off things. I said that in the circumstances, that was quite understandable.

I asked Bailey if he had any questions for me, before we began. Also, would he like me quickly to describe the courtroom to him? I wanted to tell him how distraught Sophie's parents had looked, how determined Pierre-Louis had appeared. He really needed to know that, in my view.

Bailey, flatly: "No, that is a detail at this stage I would not be interested in. Just ask me questions. Hit me with your questions."

"So, Ian, I'm going to take this more or less chronologically, Monday to Wednesday and let you know what the charges against you are – if that's okay with you – except I'd like to begin with something that came up yesterday that left me scratching my head. It's about the testimony of a man called Patrick Lowney…"

"Absolutely fucking not at all, it's a nasty piece of malicious shite that was invented, made up. It never happened. It's just preposterous and it's a load of fucking bollocks, Nick."

I wrote down in my notebook: *Denies it.*

"But Ian, it struck me your defence team could have made something of this, had they been there. It just feels like something where a defence barrister could have scored some serious points."

I was not sure if a theoretical defence barrister would have chalked up points or not, but Bailey's habit of dismissing all the arguments against him as "bollocks" underscored the weakness of any attempt to conduct a proxy murder trial by mobile phone. In any case, what we had heard in court was this: Patrick Lowney had gone to the Guards in October 2000 saying that in May of the same year a man had called him, not giving his name, to see if he could develop a roll of film discreetly. Lowney lived in Clonakilty, a town on the Cork road some 35 miles from Schull. It was apparently well known in the area that Lowney had a darkroom. You could go to Lowney's place and you could have him make your prints there and then, and he would do it quickly. No need to post off your spent roll of film and wait a week or two; no need to drop into a shop on Schull Main Street.

Anyway, the caller had shown up at Lowney's house under an hour later, more or less the time it would have taken to drive there from Bailey's place, if you put your foot down. When the Guards subsequently showed Lowney pictures of a few men, including the long-term suspect in the Sophie murder, Lowney identified the man who appeared on his doorstep with the undeveloped roll of film with 24 exposures as Ian Bailey.

"In fact, Ian, there was a bit of an awkward moment in the courtroom because they had summoned Patrick Lowney as a witness, they even had him down on the list of people to give evidence to the court. But then a court clerk announced that Lowney had died a couple of years ago…"

"Like I said, it's complete and utter bollocks."

"So the court heard you both went into the darkroom and you stayed with Lowney until the film was developed. At the beginning, seven or eight family-type images appeared. But the other shots were of a woman outside, lying on the ground. It looked like she was fully clothed. The ground was stony and there was a gate nearby, and what appeared to be briars. The tips of the photographer's shoes were showing in a couple of the pictures. Lowney started to look at the photos and you became uneasy, and you grabbed them, even though the paper was still a bit wet. You grabbed them all. You took the negatives away, too."

I told Bailey that, according to Lowney, in some of the shots there was also an item of clothing, dark in colour, caught on the gate. The court had already seen some blue material hanging off the lower bars of the gate near Sophie's body in the police photos of the crime scene. That seemed to clinch it: if Lowney's testimony stood up in court, who could the woman on the ground be, other than Sophie?

"In any case Ian, I don't get it. I can't get my head around it, and nor can Jim or Donal…"

I looked down at my notes. I could feel the heat of the light of the camera on my brow.

"So, Ian, in the year 2000 everyone in County Cork knew you. I remember once we were in a supermarket in Skib, I'm talking about a few years ago now, 2015 it must have been, and we were buying a shoulder of beef and a few other things, and everyone recognised you. There were people in the supermarket nudging each other and pointing as you walked by. Quite a few people came up to you and smiled and said hello as well…"

I wanted to imply that Bailey was a kind of celebrity, and that I had seen this with my own eyes. Bailey was famous and he was infamous and he was notorious but of those three descriptors, the one that fitted best was *famous*. By then, by the time I went to the supermarket with him in Skibbereen, Bailey had partly shed the carapace of infamy that came with being the only suspect in a brutal murder. Even though his fame rested entirely on his notoriety, it was in some tangible way also divorced from it. In County Cork, Bailey had simply become a famous face with a half-plummy, half-northern English accent which sounded exotic to people in these parts. It seemed to me that this was due to the fact that Bailey had never been put on trial in Ireland. As such, he was innocent until proven guilty. He had to be given the benefit of the doubt.

Bailey was somebody you saw on the TV news from time to time, a face in the papers, comparable to a second-tier politician or character actor past his use-by date. He had aged, for sure, but he still cut an imposing presence among the locals, even though he was now a bit stooped and his movements had slowed. He hardly looked like a danger to the general public. When Bailey was out and about, he had nice manners, even if there was something vaguely reptilian about him.

What I felt in the café in the Marais and what I had felt quite keenly that day in the supermarket in Skibbereen, was that Ian Bailey loved – no, more than that, he *gloried* in public attention. And this had always made me wonder: was it possible – not likely, but just about possible – that Ian Bailey was not the killer, but he wanted fame and recognition so badly that he was prepared to behave, and even delight in behaving, in an ultra-suspicious manner? He would even admit to the crime to keep himself in the frame, to remain centre-stage. No sane person would do this, of course.

You could put it another way: only a supremely unkind and

unfeeling person would boast, untruthfully, about killing somebody in the sure knowledge that the effect would be to rub salt in the deep wounds of the murdered person's family and friends. It would also waste police time and resources and hamper the search for the real killer. And yet, this was the minimum that Ian Bailey was guilty of. He was guilty of wanting celebrity so much he would accept being thought of as a murderer to achieve it – and if Sophie's family suffered immeasurably in the process, that was too bad. That was why I had wanted to describe to him how distraught Sophie's parents and son had looked, how deeply and atrociously they had suffered. I wanted to drag him here, and I wanted him to see it.

Otherwise, Bailey was a murderer, and his confessions were testament to just how difficult it was for Bailey to keep the knowledge of his heinous crime entirely to himself.

It was one thing or the other.

"…You were famous and so it's curious that Patrick Lowney didn't know who you were the minute you arrived at his house. Then it looks like he took six months to approach the Guards about it. Another thing: why would somebody who committed a crime as serious as this risk incriminating himself? It makes no sense. I just can't get my head around it."

It would have to be a murderer desperate for attention, indeed *absolutely desperate for attention*. That much was undeniable.

Bailey repeated that it was all bollocks. It was the Guards trying to stitch him up again.

As far as Patrick Lowney's testimony was concerned, there was no hard evidence left – not a single image, no negatives, nothing. The sole witness had passed on. It was, in fact, a perfect dead end. It brought us nowhere.

"Ian, I'd like to talk about the night of the murder. The court is asking questions about your whereabouts."

It was quiet at the other end of the line. In the café, between the light of the camera and the old wooden bar there was a couple in my field of vision, hands clasped across a narrow table, their bodies leaning in symmetrically, the kind of couple – young, it goes without saying – who appear oblivious of everything and everyone around them.

"I'm not going to ask you about Hunt's Hill again. Sorry for banging on about it yesterday. You didn't see the lights on at Alfie Lyons' place. You didn't have a premonition or a foreboding or anything else."

Bailey said he had a supply of sleeping tablets, which he had considered dipping into the previous day. "But I didn't take them as I was rather upset when I went to bed. I've learned not to take sleeping tablets if you're rather upset."

I let Bailey get his complaint off his chest. Now Hunt's Hill was off the agenda – well, almost. Bailey had had the idea of taking Colm the cameraman out to show him exactly where he and Jules had stopped on the night of the murder, but low cloud and mist had rolled in so they had put it off for another day. I had taken the single-track road over Hunt's Hill with Bailey in 2015. Obviously, Colm would stop precisely where Bailey told him to. It proved nothing.

"Oh, sorry, I forgot to ask, who was driving that night?"

"It was me. I was driving."

"Right, Ian, I've got it. So you and Jules get home. Did you go straight to bed?"

"We left the Galley bar at, I think, around about midnight. We came home, Jules went to bed, I had a story I had to deliver to the *Sunday Tribune* on the Monday, although as it turned out I didn't have to deliver it on the Monday, I had until the Tuesday."

"When did you find out you had an extension for that?"

"I think I found out about that on the Monday when I rang through, because they said they were going to have a copytaker on the Tuesday." At the time, the *Sunday Tribune* employed someone to type up stories that were dictated by telephone.

"The thing is this. I hadn't written the story and at some point in the night I got up, I left the bed in which Jules was sleeping, I went down to the kitchen and I handwrote the story, which was about the internet coming into West Cork. Then I went back to bed. In the morning, when the morning light had come, I think about 9 o'clock or thereabouts, I went down to the studio house where I have my office and telephone. I thought I was going to have to get it [the story about the internet] faxed, but I spoke to somebody at the *Tribune*, they said, we have a copytaker coming in on Tuesday morning, and I think I filed the story on the Tuesday morning."

"So you actually went to sleep? Because if you went to the studio at 9am after writing it longhand sometime in the night, that left plenty of time to go to sleep, doesn't it?"

"Listen, what happened is, after we got home, I went to bed, I'm not sure at what time, with Jules, and had it in my mind, it was sort of worrying me, and very often it wasn't uncommon of me, if I had a writing idea, to get up in the middle of the night and go down and write. Apparently there was nothing weird about that, okay?"

Bailey appeared to be getting angry. "So, I don't know what time it was, I got up and I went down and I spent about 40 minutes I think, maybe half an hour, at the kitchen table, handwriting the story, I left it there and the following morning I got up about 9 o'clock. I made two cups of coffee, Jules was still asleep, I drank one and left one by her bedside. I went down to the studio at about 9:00 or 9:30, it was certainly getting light, then I rang through to the *Tribune* at 10:30, maybe 11:00, and I was told don't worry, tomorrow there will be a copytaker on…"

I briefly thought of the testimony of Fenella Thomas, Jules Thomas's youngest daughter. According to her, Bailey and her mother had left the cottage for a couple of hours on the morning after the murder.

"I came back to the Prairie cottage, I think it might have been at about 11 o'clock. Jules was still in bed snoozing, I think. Then she got up. We were going to go over to Skibbereen as we had a turkey to deliver. The plan was we were going to go over to Skibbereen to do our Christmas shop, and then the call came through from Eddie Cassidy, and so what happened was, I said to Jules we'd better go

221

out. We went and found the scene, I was given bare bones detail, but I do know the area. Then I met a lady called Shirley Foster who was coming down from the end of the *boreen* [country lane], where both the Fosters and Sophie lived. She said, 'What are you doing here?' And I said, 'I'm here on behalf of the *Examiner*, have you seen the Guards anywhere?' She said there are Guards at the end of the lane. She then drove on to Schull and we then drove along the *boreen*…"

I said that the version that had been presented in court was a bit different.

"You got back from the pub and Jules took a couple of painkillers."

"And well she might have done! They were for menstrual pain."

"There was tossing and turning in the bed. What was on your mind, Ian?"

Bailey denied he was tossing and turning. He said he went to bed and then he went to sleep.

"You got up an hour later and she doesn't remember anything else because she took the painkillers. They are saying that in temperatures of no more than three degrees, you left the house in the middle of the night and not at 9am."

"A total lot of fucking bollocks. What I told you is what happened. They are putting their twists on it, of course."

I told Bailey that this was not true. "It's from a statement that Jules made. They've constructed their case from her statements."

"Well, I think you're going to have to talk to Jules about the statements she made because I know this, Nick, she disputed the statements that were taken from her by the fuckers on her first arrest."

When she was under arrest, Jules Thomas had told the Guards that Bailey got up after about an hour of his tossing and turning and had left the bedroom. Earlier, he had told her that he might go over to Alfie Lyons' place. This happened when they had stopped at a point on Hunt's Hill where they had a clear view over Toormore.

Thomas said Bailey had said he had a premonition. Thomas fell asleep and the next she knew it was morning, about 9 or 9:30, and there was Bailey at her bedside with a cup of coffee.

"They say that it didn't happen like that. They say you got up an hour after you and Jules went to bed, so at 2:30 or so, and then you went to Sophie's place, possibly via the studio. They say that the maximum temperature in the studio, the absolute maximum, that night would have been three degrees celsius, although it was probably lower..."

There is a pause at the other end of the line.

"If it was three degrees when you got to the studio, how many degrees was it when you left? How many degrees was it, Ian, when you'd finished typing up the piece?"

Bailey said nothing. I carried on.

"Ian, the court's position is that no sane person would have gone to the freezing studio in the night to type a newspaper article. They don't believe that you would have left your warm house to do it. They're just not buying it."

The thing was, and this was not something I was going to say to Bailey then – perhaps it wasn't something I would say to Bailey ever – but this was a part of his story that I *could* believe. I am not saying that I necessarily think it did happen like that, in the way that Bailey had claimed. You could argue that Ian Bailey was the only suspect in the murder of Sophie Toscan du Plantier – the last man standing, if you will – partly because of his unusual and extreme behaviour. Bailey was, perhaps, a man capable of anything. That was what you heard people say. This meant that he was capable of serious violence.

However, it seemed to me that you could not have it both ways: if Bailey was capable of anything, really *anything*, up to and including a brutal and violent killing, it held true that he was capable of taking a simple and innocuous decision that was supremely counter-intuitive. Specifically, he was capable of deciding to leave a place of comfort on a freezing cold night to carry out a task in a

223

place of significantly less comfort, when it was doubtful there was a pressing need to do so.

You see this same strangeness in one of several episodes involving Ian Bailey as recounted by Marie Farrell. After Farrell had identified Ian Bailey as the man at Kealfadda Bridge, Bailey had visited Farrell's knitwear shop in Schull and had – at least in Farrell's version of events prior to her recanting her evidence – intimidated her. However, Bailey had also started spouting poetry, *his own poetry*, a fairly light-hearted piece of verse about a couple of Guards investigating the case who were about to lose their pensions. Farrell had been surprised that part of Bailey's opening gambit in her shop was to recite one of his own poems. This was a detail she never retracted.

As I say, the man seemed capable of anything.

Bailey: "Look, I'm getting tired. Move on to the next question."

"All right. Let's talk about the following day, 23rd December."

I wanted to talk about the morning after the murder – what Bailey said to whom, and when. But it was clear that Bailey was fed up with this whole prosecutor set-up.

While I was speaking, Jim Sheridan sat down next to me. The camera turned slightly to bring Sheridan into the frame. I handed Sheridan the mobile phone and breathed in deeply. What Sheridan said to Bailey was a blur. Sheridan was humouring him, this much was clear. He knew how to do that, he had a knack for finding the right words and he knew how to keep Bailey on board. We joked that none of us would ever lose Bailey. After all, here was a man who loved the limelight and could not bear to be without it. But there was always a risk he would get irritated with us – with me, specifically – to the extent he would not give me any more interviews, or speak to me again.

After 20 minutes or so, I asked Sheridan for the phone back. We had been on the phone with Bailey for an hour. The sun had set. The boules players had packed up and gone home.

"Last question," said Bailey. "I'm tired, I'm hungry and I'm horny, I'm not worried about the horny bit, I can handle that myself, but I've got a steak over there with some lovely buttered potatoes."

I had a choice to make: I had two sheets of paper with notes on the café table. One described the evidence of Arianna Boarina, a piece of testimony unusual for a number of reasons, a testimony I was anxious to pursue. Arianna Boarina's witness statement concerned what she saw in the Bailey-Thomas household in the immediate aftermath of the murder. The problem was that at this point Bailey had shut up shop with me as far as talking about the day after the murder was concerned.

I turned to the other sheet of paper.

Chapter 18

THE VERDICT

"Ian, I know you're tired, but I wanted to ask you about what one of the French cops said to the judges. It was one of the cops lurking at the end of your drive when the French came over to investigate in 2015. A chap called Roehrig. Like I said the other day, you might recognise him if you were here – stocky, broad-shouldered, not a tall man, short black hair, every inch a cop, if you see what I mean…"

I knew I needed to get to the point, and I was starting to ramble.

"So, anyway, there he is describing Paris as an anonymous big city, the kind of place that you can live in for years and never know your neighbours. Well, then he goes on to say that Schull and Goleen and the Mizen are just the opposite. Over where you live, everyone knows everyone else."

I put it to Bailey that the prosecutor would have asked him if he had known Sophie Bouniol.

Bailey, now distinctly weary: "I've told you this before, I never met her. I was at Alfie Lyons' place once doing gardening and I saw her. But that's all. I never met her."

"Ian, this detective, Roehrig, he said something else, as well. He said that at any event you would have known *about* Sophie. In fact, he said of Sophie Bouniol, *when she walked around Schull, everyone knew who it was*. And she was beautiful, she was French, she worked in the film business, she was cultured, she was artistic…"

I was speeding up. He had to hear me out.

"…and so she was the kind of person you would have necessarily gravitated to."

I put it to Bailey that he had tried to meet Sophie Bouniol.

He said he had not, that he never did any such thing. He never made an attempt to meet her.

"But Ian, it's a reasonable question. They're saying over here that you tried to get to know Sophie Bouniol. You must have done. She was exactly what you wanted. She was a pull that you never could have resisted."

Bailey replied that the only way he had become aware of her *"visage*, her face" was through photos published after the crime. "I can say absolutely, honestly that I did not see her around Schull. The answer to the question is, *Non, non, non!*"

Not for the first time, I wondered why Bailey sometimes peppered his replies with words in French. I kept at it: "I'm trying to say where they are coming from. She was beautiful, she was artistic, she was a free spirit, she worked in the film business…"

"I know where they are coming from, they are trying to put me in the frame. It was said I had been introduced to her – wrong! On one occasion I was gardening for Alfie Lyons, I think in April 1995, the house was occupied, she was there and had two children with her. Jules dropped me off, I did some work for Alfie Lyons, I came down and I saw someone in the house, I guess in what was the kitchen. I wouldn't be able to identify them, I didn't know who they were."

Bailey was not answering the question.

"So if you didn't, why didn't you?"

"I'm tired. I'm going to bed."

"Talk tomorrow, Ian."

***

We finished filming at the café and a waiter cleared our plates and glasses away. We were sitting outside, on a tight strip of pavement under a scarlet-red awning. It was a mild evening. Paris hummed all around; far-off sirens wailed and faded away.

I thought about the two witnesses who had travelled to Paris from West Cork. Judge Aline had instructed Amanda Reed, like all the witnesses, to "speak without hatred or fear, the whole truth and nothing but the truth". I was sitting next to an English court correspondent who whispered, "But this is hearsay!", and I took her point. It did seem a bit odd that we were hearing about Bailey's alleged confession to Malachi Reed – *I went up there and smashed her brains in with a rock* – from his mother. She said Malachi had not told her straight away because he had been afraid she would be angry with him for accepting a lift from Bailey when he appeared drunk. Amanda Reed said her son had not wanted to attend the trial because "he just found everything so difficult in the past [but] he's not going back on his word". Malachi Reed's name had been splashed across the newspapers during Bailey's 2003 libel trial, and he had not enjoyed it.

Bill Fuller took the stand next. He told the court about his recollection of Bailey's curious second-person rant: *You fancied her, you went up there to try and see what you could get... You stove something into the back of her head and you realised you went too far and you had to finish her off.* Fuller said that it was "common knowledge" that his former friend would sometimes speak about himself in the second or third person. "When we were working together he only spoke about women and sex," Fuller added. When doing gardening Bailey "was clumsy and rushed things". He was good at digging but not at operating machinery.

Fuller said that Bailey was very happy with the £900 he had made from journalism after the murder, and was only sad there was not more money to be made. Fuller added that Bailey had claimed to him that he had had dinner with Sophie Toscan du Plantier a couple of times at his cottage. I underlined in my notebook this comment about Bailey having supposedly eaten with Sophie at the Prairie. I had come across it before in a statement Fuller had made to the Guards. I was not sure what to make of it. I could readily believe that Bailey had made up the story of dining with Sophie and was just showing off to a mate. In fact, it seemed certain not to be true. Why Bailey would do such a thing – let his mind wander into an obvious fantasy and then say it out loud in company – I did not know.

Back in the café, MacIntyre said he had a call coming through from Colm, the cameraman stationed with Bailey. He listened for a moment and then said "No!" in a voice signalling disbelief. "Say that again... so Ian's wondering what would happen if he pleads guilty to a crime of passion?"

This was indeed the gist of it. Ian Bailey had decided not to go straight to bed after all. He had had a drink or two at the cottage and was floating the idea with Colm, with the camera unfortunately switched off, that he could say to the French that, yes, he did it, he killed Sophie, but it was a crime of passion. Foreigners are sometimes under the impression that the notion of *le crime passionnel* – crimes of passion – are still on the statute book in France and treated with a dizzying Gallic leniency. The French penal code of 1810, dating from the time of Napoleon, permitted the murders of an unfaithful wife and her lover at the hand of her husband, but the husband needed to catch them in the act in the matrimonial home, and he needed to exact revenge on the spot. However, this old penal code was repealed in the 1970s and replaced by a new one, which no longer made provision for avenging infidelity in the marital bed.

I got into an Uber with Sheridan to make sure he got back to his hotel safely. My head was spinning with possibilities as the electric-powered car glided across Bastille square. Could we really be that close? Could Bailey be about to admit to the killing, in a way that stood up to scrutiny? The images of Sophie's corpse in the courtroom flashed across my mind: the crushed skull, the blood covering the ground, all life extinguished from her pale body. I wanted the bastard who did that to pay the price. I had seen Sophie's poor parents take their seats on the hard benches in the old courthouse; I had seen them get up and leave when the moment came for the images of the crushed and bloodied body of their murdered daughter to flash up on the screen. No parent should have to go through what they had endured.

I asked Sheridan what he thought. He said Bailey needed to be the centre of attention. Had this been any kind of admission? No, he didn't think so.

It always seemed to come back to this one thing: Ian Bailey's thirst for notoriety.

We were, by all accounts, a day away from a verdict and all Bailey said to me on the phone was that the arguments in the Paris courthouse were a complete lie, a fabrication of the Guards, or a load of bollocks. If I had had a pound for each time Bailey had dismissed the evidence against him as "bollocks", I would have had enough cash to explore the priciest end of the wine list at Les Deux Palais. But Bailey's preoccupations were, frankly, about to be sidelined. The verdict and sentencing would soon put the French court in control of the narrative. For the whole day tomorrow the spotlight would shine hard on the Palais de Justice in Paris.

And another thing: crimes of passion – in France, or wherever – rest on one certain aspect: that the perpetrator knows his victim and loves her, or has loved her. There is, or was, a relationship between the two people. Meanwhile, Ian Bailey had always maintained he never met Sophie Toscan du Plantier.

So why was he now implying that he did?

***

The prosecutor for the Republic, Jean-Pierre Bonthoux, had not said very much thus far in the proceedings. He had queried a few things that several witnesses taking the stand had said, or had requested clarifications, but the task of dealing with the witnesses and coaxing information from them fell to Judge Aline. It was the morning of the Friday, the last day of the trial. It was time for Bonthoux to sum up the case for the prosecution. He rose from his chair, and cleared his throat. This was going to be his moment.

Looking at the rows of Bouniols and Gazeaus directly in front of him, Bonthoux said that it was largely thanks to them and their many years of efforts to keep the case in the public eye that the trial was taking place at all. For the family, the drama of the crime of Sophie's murder was alive every second of every minute. As for Bailey, "we feel he is both present and not present. He is there in the media. The French Republic has done nothing to deserve his defiance and his scorn."

Bonthoux was raising his voice now. The moment seemed cathartic.

"Bailey has no courage. Bailey is a coward. He says our system is unworthy. His contempt is intolerable. However, when he sued the newspapers, he lost. When he sued the Irish State and the Guards for wrongful arrest and corruption, he lost. In fact, Bailey has lost everywhere except in the matter of the European Arrest Warrant. What he does is he tries to obstruct justice, he tries to slow it down. Bailey…"

Bonthoux was now in full flow.

"…is mocking us! And let me be clear, nobody is helping us to change things."

I understood that comment to be a reference to the Irish Supreme Court, which had thrown out France's request that a European Arrest Warrant be served on Bailey. Maybe Bonthoux had the DPP in mind, too.

"No, I don't blame Bailey for howling at the moon. I don't blame him for being a dropout. I don't blame him for his 300 pages of obscenities. I don't blame him for being an alcoholic. I don't blame him for being a failed journalist or a failed gardener. This is about something much, much worse."

Bonthoux moved to the meat of his case. He said he had read

a few times – presumably he meant in reports outside France – that this was a "trial without proof". Bonthoux pointed out that the harvesting of DNA from a crime scene only just started in earnest in the 1990s. Today we could check each and every surface for DNA, but in 1996 this wasn't the case, and the Guards did not check the briars outside Sophie's home, for example. DNA was not an absolute proof, it remained one of a range of proofs. In the past – before the advent of DNA tracing – courts handed down guilty convictions anyway. All investigations, said the prosecutor, gather proof, particularly at the beginning. And in this case, since the very beginning, the evidence pointed in one direction only.

Bonthoux directed his venom at Bailey, but I knew the Irish DPP was not likely to come out of the prosecutor's summing-up unscathed. Bonthoux was scandalised that the DPP's internal report from 2001 was forwarded informally to the Supreme Court when it was considering France's first attempt at questioning Bailey via a European Arrest Warrant, despite the fact that the DPP's report was supposed to be confidential. The first time he saw it, Bonthoux said – the report was not signed, there was no letterhead – it was so one-sided he thought it was a document drafted by Bailey's own lawyers.

"They looked at each element of proof individually, and they tried to invalidate each one!" Every piece of evidence was worth zero, said Bonthoux, so there was no surprise when you added them up and you got another zero. Bonthoux found the DPP's approach difficult to understand. To take Bailey's scratches as an example. There were six witnesses, including the barman, who testified that on the evening before the murder, Bailey had had no scratches on his hands or on his forearms, and no wound on his forehead. The six witnesses were physically close to Bailey and the bar was well lit. Bonthoux said that, in this kind of situation, you would expect that 80% of people would remember close to nothing, and 20% would recall something. That meant that the majority of the drinkers in the Galley bar would have no firm recollection that night, no usable testimony, and anyone assessing the evidence should expect this. But the DPP's position paper only mentioned one witness in the bar who initially saw nothing, the man who subsequently returned to the Guards to say that Bailey indeed had some marks on one of his hands, although the witness in question could not remember which hand.

I had wondered the same thing when I read the DPP's paper. Why had the other witnesses in the bar who had been watching Bailey play the *bodrhán* and had clear recollections of their night out – and the man behind the bar who had served him his drinks – apparently been disregarded by the DPP? These witnesses had been clear that Bailey had no scratches or wounds that evening.

By now, Bonthoux's voice was resonating into every corner of the courtroom. The man was an excellent orator.

The prosecutor reminded the court that when the Guards first came calling at the Prairie after the crime, Bailey had said that on the evening of the murder he went on his own to the Courtyard and stayed there until closing time. Later Bailey changed his story, telling the Guards that he went to the Galley bar with Jules Thomas – which is what actually had happened. Why did he do that? The *bodhrán* playing and the poems must have stuck in his mind. Bonthoux's view was that Bailey only gave the Guards the correct version when he cast his mind back at the witnesses in the Galley, and that he had surely been recognised.

Bonthoux started to speed up, and I noticed that the two reporters sitting either side of me were taking notes in shorthand. I was struggling to keep up with Bonthoux's version of the night of the crime in my longhand. It was a version that rested on Jules Thomas's disputed statement taken at Bandon Garda station about the drive home from Schull on the night of the murder. I wrote:

They stop on Hunt's Hill because the moon is beautiful. Bailey points out Alfie's house. He says there's a light on there. But there wasn't. At nine-thirty they finished watching their film and they went to bed. The light was in Sophie's house. This is significant. Sophie was still active. This attracts his interest. There was no way he would confuse the two houses as he had worked for Alfie... Jules Thomas goes to bed. He says he wants to go out. He has a warm house but he goes to a shack, there's hardly any furniture in it and it's cold... We know he went out, because Marie Farrell's evidence is clear and precise...

Next Bonthoux said something that surprised me. He said that Marie Farrell was afraid from the outset, because she thought that maybe Bailey recognised *her* at Kealfadda Bridge. This had never occurred to me. It was a good point, and it was certainly possible. Bonthoux reminded the court that on the Mizen "everyone knows everyone else and they know what car they drive".

Bonthoux scoffed at the idea that Bailey's confessions – to Malachi Reed, Helen Callanan, the Shelleys and Bill Fuller – were some sort of "black humour". The prosecutor almost spat out his words: "Who would make jokes about such a terrible crime, still less if you were the main suspect". Furthermore, Bailey's confessions took place in his "comfort zone" – at home or in his car.

"We have a sexual motive," said Bonthoux, "although Sophie was not sexually assaulted."

At this, Sophie's father suddenly looked up, distraught. Pierre-Louis was staring at Bonthoux. I thought: this man has waited for this moment his entire adult life.

"They knew each other, and he got there and he made a proposition straight away. He hits her right there at the door. He hits her with a piece of slate or stone and then finds a cavity block... There is objective, material evidence against Bailey. This was an atrocious crime against a single woman. Here is a man who makes a mathematical calculation of his ejaculations. Need I say more?"

Bonthoux carried on: "He desired her for what she was, and he was the very opposite of her... Sophie endured two to three minutes of terror. The consequences were colossal. Her family has suffered for 22 years."

That suffering was visible in the courtroom, raw and undimmed. Before the speech of state prosecutor Bonthoux, Marie Dosé had summed up the sheer disgust that Sophie's family felt for Ian Bailey. My notes read: *Sophie was not some kind of easy lay… but he was turned on by her, she was exactly what excited him. He's a pervert. He wanted sex that night and he was blind drunk. Sophie saw him from the window of the kitchen and she opened the door because she recognised him. She was afraid of nothing. She did not give in. She ran to freedom, but he caught up with her. She fought to the end, but she could do nothing. The savagery, the bestiality, there are no words… this was violence like nothing else.*

"Let Ian Bailey tell us he is innocent! Let him do it here!"

What happened with Marie Farrell was "absolutely crazy", according to Dosé. "Bailey was never charged with harassing Marie Farrell. It's a scandal! Is that how you do it? You scare a witness? If he had tried doing that in France, he would be finished."

Dosé said: "Sophie was the first [in her generation] to drop out of college, first to get married, first to have a child, first to get divorced, first to die young."

We filed out of the courtroom. The judges would hand down their verdict before the end of the day. It was Bailey's version of a stitch-up by the cops and some ill-timed pieces of sarcasm versus Bonthoux's narrative of a violent narcissist who had already admitted to the murder several times. On the steps of the courthouse, Jim Sheridan approached Marie Dosé and told her that Ian Bailey had been talking about a crime of passion. The camera was rolling. Dosé glared at Sheridan. "Is that some kind of joke?" was all she had to say to Sheridan, shaking her head in disbelief as she walked away. In any case, the notion of a *crime passionnel* faded away almost as soon as it was aired: in my time following the case, Bailey never again said he had committed a crime of passion, or anything similar.

***

The judges' deliberations took five hours. In the early evening I got a message on my mobile phone, from the press officer, to say that the verdict was about to be announced. There was a hush in the panelled courtroom.

Judge Aline and her two colleagues returned to their places and handed down a guilty verdict, sentencing Ian Bailey to 25 years in prison for the murder of Sophie Toscan du Plantier. Everyone in the room had taken their seats, except Pierre-Louis, who stood, straight-backed, chin up, throughout. I listened to Judge Aline's voice as she read out the grounds for the verdict – it was a pleasant voice, with an easy authority – but my eyes were on Pierre-Louis. His own father was in the room, Sophie's first husband. I imagined this man's deep pride in his son at that moment. Pierre-Louis had engaged in a struggle that had occupied all his adult life. He had been courageous and determined. That was one thing. Secondly, he had constantly reminded the world of his mother's love and humanity. In so doing, he faced up to the peculiar indignity common to all, or almost all, murder victims: in public and in the media, the stories of their lives are told backwards. Sophie's name would forever be associated with the name of the man who crashed a slate against her skull, over and over again, until her features were barely recognisable. To fight against that dreadful association was like trying to hold back the tide. But Pierre-Louis had done what he could.

On the main concourse of the courthouse, cameras and microphones arranged in a tight semi-circle awaited Pierre-Louis, as he slowly descended the ancient stone stairs from the courtroom with his grandfather, Georges Bouniol. The old man was tearful, but he managed a weak smile. He left the building via a side exit, a family member supporting him on either side, leaving his grandson to talk alone to the media

Pierre-Louis took a deep breath. He said in French: "It's a victory after 22 years of waiting, 22 years of suffering, 22 years of asking questions. The judgement is very clear… We are going to keep on fighting so that justice is served, so that Bailey goes to jail in France, in Ireland, or somewhere else."

And then, Pierre-Louis addressed the reporters in English.

"Today everyone must know and understand that Ian Bailey is a murderer... He killed my mother 22 years ago." Ian Bailey was a "monster".

Pierre-Louis was happy with the verdict, he said, but most of all he was "at peace".

Pierre-Louis walked out of the Palais de Justice through the main door. On the steps, he lit a cigarette and inhaled. He flicked away the butt. He then walked off into the rest of his life. There would surely be more battles ahead, but this one was over. I watched him stride away, in his dark blue suit and black tie, with a silk pocket square. If the scene had replayed in a black and white movie, Sophie's son would have been the perfect fit for an old-fashioned film star.

Chapter 19

WHILE THE TAPE WAS RUNNING

I caught an Uber to the Gare du Nord, my head light after several glasses of red wine sunk in quick succession after our filming had wrapped. I was going home. The trial had given me some answers, but it had also left me with questions.

As for Ian Bailey, on receiving the news of his conviction and 25-year sentence, he said that he had been "bonfired" and felt "devastated". Still, the stress of being put on trial for murder in a courthouse 800 miles away had apparently set his creative juices flowing. His solicitor had given him strict instructions not to give interviews to the press, but those instructions did not seem to apply to a new poem he had just finished. "There is a full-force hurricane, storming, circulating, swirling, angry, aggressive and vengeful, around the outside of my head," recited Bailey, "yet because of beauty and love and thoughts of you, I remain calm in the eye of the hurricane".

Should I have questioned Bailey harder, and put him under more pressure? He had cursed me after our call from the café in the Marais. Bailey was an attention-seeker, but even *he* had limits. I knew if I had been more antagonistic, hoping to provoke him, I would have risked Bailey cutting off all contact with me. Instinctively I knew I had to stay in the game because I was far from being done with the Sophie story. I had to ensure that the door to Bailey's cottage on the Mizen would stay open, that he would keep on taking my calls. I just hoped that I had not made a mistake and crossed a line with him.

At the café in the Marais, with Ian Bailey on the other end of a phone line, I had hesitated with two sheets of paper on the table in front of me. One was labelled *You knew Sophie*, the other, *Arianna evidence*. They were two different lines of attack, but when Sheridan handed the phone back to me, Bailey had said he was very tired and would only take one more question.

I had told Bailey that – had he been in the dock – the prosecutor would have asked him if he had known Sophie Toscan du Plantier. If Bailey had been there and said no, that he had never met Sophie Toscan du Plantier – born plain Sophie Bouniol – the prosecutor simply would not have believed him.

Sounding weary, Bailey had said he had never met Sophie. He added that he had already told me many times that he had not known the victim. This was a crucial point: if Ian Bailey and Sophie Bouniol had never met, if they had never had a single conversation, it was always going to be difficult for the French authorities to establish a convincing motive for Bailey to turn up at Sophie's house the freezing night she was murdered. To put it crudely, if Bailey had knocked on Sophie's door in the early hours of 23rd December 1996 hoping to seduce her, at the very least she needed to have known who he was. She needed to have recognised him on the doorstep; there needed to have been some kind of rapport already in place between them. So that's why it was noteworthy that the French prosecutor had not managed to give the court compelling evidence that Bailey and Sophie had been acquainted. As far as motive was concerned, the prosecution had failed to land a knockout blow.

My train sped through Picardy. The sun had just set. Outside were broad fields of rapeseed and beet; vast, low warehouses; distant church spires. The man from the train's catering team offered me one of those miniature bottles of sparkling wine that make me feel a bit melancholy if I drink them on my own. I accepted the bottle anyway.

I thought back to the testimony of Paul Webster, the former *Guardian* correspondent in Paris, now deceased. The prosecutor had read out Webster's statement in a confident tone that suggested this was a key piece of evidence against Bailey. Now I was wondering why the prosecutor had appeared so sure. Webster was on record as stating that Bailey had called him about the case and had mentioned that he had known Sophie, albeit as an acquaintance rather than as a friend. Webster had been sure about what Bailey had told him. Webster's witness statement was the closest the prosecution had got to nailing it – to proving that there had been a connection between Bailey and Sophie, and so the germ of a motive.

I was starting to believe that Bailey's narcissistic personality sometimes gave him a sort of free pass not afforded to more conventional characters. The Webster testimony was a case in point: I could readily imagine Bailey having had nothing to do with Sophie's murder – not having met her beyond a swift 'hello' in Alfie Lyons' garden – but nonetheless *pretending* to have known her, so as to bolster his credentials with Webster, an established and successful reporter for a major newspaper. Bailey had an insatiable urge to be the centre of the story, and this was one aspect. He was also skint, which was another. I could see how Bailey might have thought he needed to exaggerate his role so that the *Guardian* journalist would take him seriously, while also making it more likely he would earn a few bob into the bargain.

My train carriage swayed gently. I closed my eyes and thought of the winding, pitted lane leading to Sophie's house. The French narrative put forward by members of the Sophie Justice Committee, Jean-Antoine Bloc among them, was that Bailey was a strong, physically fit man and would have had no problem hiking over the moonlit moor to Sophie's place. Bloc, the French detectives, and one of the Guards, had made the same hike to see for themselves. The consensus was that it would have taken a younger Bailey between 36 and 40 minutes to cross the stretch of moor on foot.

Was there some confirmation bias at play in the way the French had put together a narrative of the murder? It seemed to me that there was a risk that if you started with the certainty of the physical strength needed to commit the crime – particularly to lift and carry the concrete cavity block that the murderer dumped on Sophie's body – that knowledge, that *bias*, might weigh heavily on other assumptions you may make.

Just because Bailey, at age 39, had the physical capacity to hike briskly to Sophie's house that December night, did not mean that he would be *more likely* to choose to do so – it simply meant it was a possibility. After all, Bailey also had a car at his disposal. He could have pushed the car to the end of the drive and started it there, confident that he would not wake up Jules or her daughters in the cottage.

The French court had concluded that after their boozy night out in Schull, Bailey and Jules Thomas, with Bailey driving, had taken the slightly longer route back to their cottage in the Prairie via Hunt's Hill. This was, after all, the version of the story that Bailey had first given the Irish Guards, corroborated by Jules Thomas, so it was wholly uncontroversial. According to the French prosecutor, from a vantage point on the Hunt's Hill road, Bailey had seen the lights on in Sophie's house, and resolved to pay her a visit later in the night. My feeling was that if Bailey was the killer, he would have been in a hurry to see Sophie, in a hurry for sex, and going by car would have been much faster than walking. Either way, Marie Farrell could have spotted him stumbling by the side of the road at Kealfadda Bridge. He could have walked the whole circuit, meaning over the moor to Sophie's house, committing the murder, and then the longer return journey by road, in a little over two hours. Otherwise, he could have used his car and done the round trip in an hour or so. Farrell's sighting of Bailey at Kealfadda Bridge did not preclude the possibility that he had parked his car somewhere nearby.

The French prosecutor had sketched out the two possibilities – that Bailey went to Sophie's house by car *or* on foot – but he had placed more emphasis on the theory that Bailey had tramped across the moor. The panel of judges, meanwhile, had been a bit more circumspect in their verdict: Bailey had gone to Sophie's house that night "possibly on foot".

My train shot across the flat borderlands of France and Belgium. Something else occurred to me. If Bailey had driven to Sophie's house and returned via Kealfadda Bridge, where Marie Farrell said that she saw him at about 3am, he could have got back in his car and arrived home a few minutes later. That would have given him enough time to sleep a bit, write at his kitchen table, type up his newspaper article in the studio, or a combination of the three. Thus, Bailey might have gone to bed, got up again, done some writing in the cottage and, subsequently, at the time he suggested to the Guards – at about 9am – he could have gone to the studio. He could therefore have committed the crime *and gone to the studio, too*. It was not necessarily 'either or'.

I saw I had fallen into a trap of my own making when I had questioned Bailey over the phone. Like the French prosecutor, I had mocked the idea that Bailey might have spent time in the freezing studio that night or early in the morning. Like the prosecutor, I had become fixated with details like the precise air temperature in the hours before dawn on the morning of 23rd December, which suddenly, on the speeding train, felt almost irrelevant.

The cottage on the Prairie was cramped, and Thomas and one of her daughters were sleeping there. The other two daughters might return from their night out at any minute. In those circumstances, was it so inconceivable that Bailey – if indeed he was Sophie's killer – might have needed a place to gather his thoughts after the murder and compose himself? In this scenario, the studio was a logical place to go. You could also argue that it was the *only* place to go, since it was the one place where he was sure to be alone. This was another case of confirmation bias: if your starting point was that Bailey murdered Sophie and lied to cover his tracks, there was a risk that you would approach everything Bailey told you through that prism, imagining Bailey to be a compulsive liar, with an *entirely* fictitious alibi, rather than a *partly* fictitious one.

What had Dermot Dwyer, the Guard the French journalists had dubbed 'Columbo', said? *Even the biggest liar that ever walked tells the truth sometimes.*

This bias handed Ian Bailey an advantage. Much of his account of what he did on the night of the 22nd to 23rd December 1996 might be true – and so would be easy for Bailey to tell confidently and credibly – apart from the salient fact that he had, according to the French verdict, murdered Sophie.

Then there was the matter of the scratches on Bailey's hand and forearms.

Not every scratch is the same, after all.

My train began to slow, passing the backyards of a long line of redbrick houses, nearing its destination. I was thinking of Arianna Boarina the sheet of questions marked *Arianna evidence* that I almost quizzed Bailey about, when he accepted that one last question from me. Arianna's testimony came up in the prosecution case in the Paris courtroom and was included in the summing-up by the principal judge giving grounds for the guilty verdict. The judges had clearly considered that it was important.

In contrast, the Office of the Director of Public Prosecutions had made no reference to Arianna in its position paper arguing against putting Ian Bailey on trial in Ireland. In years of reporting on the murder, Arianna had passed under the radar of Irish and French journalists covering the case. None of them had sought her out, as far as I could tell. She had passed under my radar, too.

There had been hours of discussion in the Paris courtroom about Marie Farrell's testimony, just as Farrell had been a central, inescapable plank of the Sophie story in Ireland since almost the very beginning. However, Farrell's eye-catching pronouncements had the effect of putting other important pieces of evidence in the shade.

Sean Murray's sighting of a man in the front passenger seat of Sophie's hire car on the afternoon of 20th December 1996 was one such testimony. Like Arianna Boarina's testimony, it had been described in the indictment – which I had expected, because the French detectives had interviewed Murray about what he had seen, to check for themselves – but it had not been emphasised in any particular way. The position of the prosecutor, as I saw it, was that Bailey had likely been the man occupying Sophie's passenger seat, but he did not see Murray's sighting as being central to solving the case, in the way I did.

In Paris, Arianna Boarina's evidence had also not been stressed in any particular way, and yet Arianna mattered because she was an invited guest in the Bailey-Thomas household – at the dead centre of the storm, so to speak – the day after Sophie was murdered. It was Bailey, Jules Thomas, Jules's daughters Saffron, Virginia and Fenella – and Arianna – at home at the Prairie for Christmas that year. Thomas's three daughters had never, to the best of my knowledge, volunteered any incriminating information on Bailey's physical appearance or demeanour at home in the days after the crime – apart from Fenella's assertion that her mother and Bailey had left the cottage in her white Ford Fiesta on the morning after the crime (which both Thomas and Bailey denied). Arianna was, as far as I could tell, neutral, with nobody to side with, no agenda to defend. Her perspective was therefore unique.

Back home, it took me a half a morning on the internet to track Arianna down. She replied to my 'You don't know me, but…' email within the hour, accepting my request for the interview. She was living in California but was intending to go back to her home region in northern Italy with her two young children. Her plan was to spend time in Salò, a town on Lake Garda. After she arrived and settled in, we could meet. I form a quick impression of people when I sound them out for interviews, and Arianna was friendly and direct.

I booked a flight to Verona, the nearest city with an airport. In the meantime, I mailed Pierre-Louis. A catch-up, nothing more. I got no reply. I mailed Sophie's best friend Agnès Thomas; again, no reply. Ditto a couple of other colleagues of Sophie from the Parisian film production world. None wrote back.

It was a setback, but I understood why they had not answered my emails. I would probably have done the same. In particular, Pierre-Louis was a private person, and in his position, I would have drawn a line under cooperation with people in the media at that point. Ian Bailey had been found guilty, and Pierre-Louis's long struggle had entered a new phase – the fight to get Bailey extradited. He no longer had the same need to speak with journalists and authors to keep his mother's case in the public eye. I also recalled barrister Marie Dosé's anger at the notion that there were people in the courtroom keeping Bailey up to speed with proceedings. That anger came from the very people in the Sophie Justice Committee I admired for their tenacity and dedication. I had surely burned my bridges with those people, Jean-Antoine Bloc included.

I also felt I had disappointed Pierre-Louis. I had thought that Sheridan and MacIntyre's long hours of filming might have caught Bailey off guard, and maybe led to Bailey incriminating himself. That sticking close to Bailey and letting him speak for as long as he wanted might well shed light on some aspect of the crime. That was the gist of what I told Pierre-Louis when we had first met, and I supposed the reason that he had agreed to the interview on camera in his grandparents' apartment. I had told Pierre-Louis what I thought was possible – that Bailey might well put his foot in it, give himself away on tape, if he indeed was the murderer. In hindsight, this appeared a brazen act of over-selling. As far as I knew, the filming had not thus far produced a tangible result that we could hold up to Sophie's son. Had I been naïve in thinking that it might?

That was my mood in the late summer of 2019 – a self-pity that I had lost my access to Sophie's friends and family, mixed with a dull anxiety that the truth of what happened at Sophie's holiday home that cold, moonlit night over two decades ago was out of reach, and might stay that way forever.

***

Before I flew to Verona, MacIntyre asked me to make a transcript of the interview we had filmed with Pierre-Louis in Sophie's parents' apartment in Paris in 2015. I clicked on a link to see the rushes. In the video, I was off-camera, interpreting from French to English. Jim Sheridan was asking Pierre-Louis the questions. Much of the interview concerned the ins and outs of the criminal justice system in France. Back then, there had been no guarantee that Bailey would ever be tried in France – indeed, it had seemed quite unlikely. Pierre-Louis's tone seemed flat, resigned, as if he himself did not believe he would ever get his day in court.

At one point, Sheridan asked Pierre-Louis about his memories of his mother. I watched Pierre-Louis's eyes well up with tears on my computer screen. He paused before he responded to Sheridan's question. I typed down his reply.

"It's been 20 years since I lost my mother and the memories change over time. Now, it is really difficult for me to think of a specific moment with my mother when we were there [on the Mizen peninsula]… I have a very good memory, but the thing is I think that my brain, and it's involuntary, blocks recollections that are too intense, to stop my emotions from being too painful."

Pierre-Louis then spoke about his mother's love of Ireland. My own memory of the interview was that it ended there and then. I had a tear welling up in my own eye as Pierre-Louis was talking about his mother, which embarrassed me, as I was a mere observer, and this was not my family tragedy. When MacIntyre said "Cut", I walked up to Pierre-Louis and thanked him, and I think I patted him lightly on the shoulder. This is how I remembered the interview ending. But now I could see in the video that Pierre-Louis said something else, unprompted, with the camera still rolling. Maybe I missed this final comment while I was putting away my pen and notebook or discreetly wiping the tear from my eye. What Pierre-Louis said was:

"I went with her [to Ireland] several times and I got really bored at events, or places, where people recited poetry accompanied by a kind of simple music. I didn't understand a thing because it was in English. But I think what she wanted to show me is that people could be direct in their interactions, which happens in Ireland, and it's nice, but we have a bit less of this in France."

I rewound the sequence and played it again:

I went with her several times and I got really bored at events, or places, where people recited poetry accompanied by a kind of simple music.

Hold on. What had Bailey once said after dinner when I had interviewed him, years earlier? I looked for my notes, copied down from an audio recording.

It was December 2015. Sitting at his kitchen table, I had asked Bailey that day if he had known Sophie Toscan du Plantier. He said that he had not known her. He described any statement to the contrary as "a lie". He had seen her doing some gardening at Alfie Lyons' place, and that was all. Then he added:

"She might have had knowledge of me, I don't know, from poetry or music in bars."

If Bailey had known Sophie, if they had conversed, it might well have happened at a poetry reading, or at an evening of traditional music where someone will get up and play the *bodhrán* drum, or a combination of the two. An evening of music or poetry or both things together that the boy Pierre-Louis found tiresome, no fun at all. My assumption had been that when Sophie was in Ireland she was quite reclusive – apart from the O'Sullivans at their pub, cheese-maker Bill Hogan, the Ungerers at Three Castle Head, and her housekeeper, Josephine Hellen, Sophie appeared to know few people. She kept herself to herself. However, she loved poetry. If anything was going to prise Sophie away from the warmth of her Irish home, it had to be cultural or intellectual.

It seemed to add up.

Chapter 20

ARIANNA

The road to Salò skirted chained-up parking lots and abandoned camping sites. Inland, a solitary crow landed in a ploughed-up field of black soil. Far out on Lake Garda, flat and windless, a couple of sailboats appeared perfectly static, as in a watercolour.

I picked an empty café terrace on the town's promenade and took a seat in the shade. Arianna Boarina said she was surprised I had travelled to Italy with the sole intention of interviewing her. I supposed, in her mind, this upped the stakes a bit – for both of us.

When I showed Arianna a copy of the statement she had given to the Guards – a single A4 sheet printed on both sides and typed in a large font – she looked at it closely, as if it were a museum piece. It certainly belonged to a far-off time: Arianna had been 20 years old in 1996 when she accepted an invitation from her friend, Virginia Thomas, to spend Christmas at the cottage Virginia's mother shared with Ian Bailey on the Mizen. Arianna and Virginia, who she knew as Ginny, had been housemates for two or three months. Arianna had initially come to Ireland from her native Vicenza, in northern Italy, to work as an au pair. She stayed on to improve her English. The two young women rented rooms in a house in Dún

Laoghaire, a port on the outskirts of Dublin. They quickly became close; Ginny, who was a year older than Arianna, made no secret of her mother's rough relationship with her partner, Ian Bailey.

On 22nd December 1996, Arianna travelled from Dún Laoghaire to Cork, where she broke her journey, staying at another friend's house: *I only stayed one night as Jenny* [Ginny, a transcription error in the part of the Guard taking the statement] *had gone to Schull a few days earlier.* The following day, 23rd December, Arianna took a bus west to Schull. *I recall while on the bus that it came on the radio about a murder in Schull and I was surprised as I thought of nothing it* [sic] *a peaceful place.*

Arianna told me that she had been thinking about that far-off Christmas on the Mizen, replaying it in her mind, ready to answer my questions. Now, with the sheet of A4 paper in her hands, she saw there were aspects of the statement that were not quite right. There was the minor mistake with Ginny's name. There were a couple of other details, too, that made her think, made her dig deep into her memory. Still, some things were easy to recall. Arianna had had fun nights out in Schull with Ginny and Saffron and their group of friends. Then there was the big swim off the pier in Schull – traditionally held at 12 noon each Christmas Day – when townsfolk hurl themselves whooping and screaming into the chilly waters of Roaringwater Bay. Arianna had seen that.

One strange thing was that the Guards had only asked her for a statement two years after the murder. At that time, Arianna was still in Ireland, working for an airline reservations centre. Why did the Guards approach her so long after the crime? Why had they not contacted her sooner? They knew Arianna had been staying at the cottage at the Prairie for Christmas that year, and that she had been the only houseguest. After all, this was noted by the Guards who asked Bailey and Thomas to fill in questionnaires in the immediate aftermath of the murder. Neither Bailey nor Thomas had hidden the fact of Arianna's visit or been in any way cagey about it.

It was Monday, 23rd December 1996, and Arianna was sitting on a bus heading west from Cork City, aware that a brutal murder had taken place close to her destination. Jules Thomas picked Arianna up from the bus stop in Schull and drove her back to the cottage. It is fair to say that nothing could have prepared her for what came next. Arianna's statement described what she saw:

When I arrived at Jules' house I met Jules' boyfriend Ian. I immediately noticed heavy marks from scratches, on both of his hands. They were numerous on both hands and they were up as far as his forearms and they were fresh.

Arianna looked at the statement again. Something else had caught her eye.

I asked her: "How do you remember the scratches on Ian's arms?"

"I remember the scratches. But I can't say that they were 'heavy'."

"What were they like?"

"There were a lot of scratches. There weren't just one or two. Also, I can't say if they were still fresh or if they had formed scabs." Arianna said they were not fingernail scratches either, because she said you would expect some peripheral redness from that type of scratch, but the scratches on Bailey's hands and forearms had no such redness.

"Did Ian say anything about the scratches?"

"Ian said, or it might have been Jules who said, that they came from cutting down a Christmas tree."

"Does that seem plausible to you, from what you saw of the scratches?"

Arianna said no, it did not seem plausible. What is more, the Christmas tree that had purportedly caused the scratches on Bailey's hands and forearms was in the living room and it was tiny. Someone had hung some foil-wrapped chocolates on it as a decoration, which had stuck in her mind.

"Could Ian's scratches have come from thorns?"

Arianna paused. She said: "Yes, I can confirm they were scratches from a bush."

I asked what kind of bush and Arianna suggested gorse, the one, she said, which has yellow flowers, common in the Italian countryside, common in fact in that very part of Italy we were in. I took my mobile phone and found a random image of a clump of gorse in flower. Arianna, said that yes, this was the kind of thing that could have caused Ian's scratches.

There is gorse on the Mizen, but the bush that Sophie ran through was mainly made of brambles. What gorse and bramble have in common, however, is that their branches are spiked with thorns.

"And Ian's forehead? Your statement says you saw marks there."

Arianna said she had a memory of seeing marks on Bailey's forehead and that someone – although she did not remember who it was – explained to her how they had got there:

"They said it happened to him while they were killing a turkey."

"How likely does that seem?"

"Well, I haven't killed a turkey, but I've" – Arianna put her hands together to indicate the wringing of a bird's neck – "how do you say?"

"Strangled..."

"Yes, I've strangled a chicken. I don't think you get a wound on your forehead from doing that. It's not credible, in my opinion."

I paused to take this in. In the corner of my eye, I saw a group of school students walking along the promenade behind a tour guide. The fascist leader Benito Mussolini chose Salò as the location for his government during the Second World War. The pretty villa that housed his propaganda chiefs was about 100 yards from the café where we were sitting.

I said: "And yet they made a big deal about it. That the scratches were heavy. At the trial, I mean."

"The trial?"

Then the penny dropped. Arianna had no idea that Bailey had been put on trial for Sophie's murder four months earlier, still less that he had been convicted. She was unaware the testimony she

251

gave to a Guard two years after the crime had ended up in the French investigation and formed part of the case against the absent Ian Bailey. I had assumed – wrongly – that she must have found out.

"Was it in Ireland?"

"No, in France. In Paris."

It was a lot for Arianna to take in.

I asked Arianna: "Did the French authorities ever contact you?"

No, she said, the French investigators had never made contact. Had they done so, she naturally would have spoken with them, answered their questions.

Had the French been in contact, Arianna might well have mentioned the clothes she saw soaking in the bathtub. Her statement to the Guards said she saw "dark clothes" in the tub. Arianna told me that at some point when she was in the cottage, she wanted to wash or dry her hair, and she went into the bathroom, and she saw clothes – or something, at any rate – soaking there. She did not get close enough to the bathtub to say what kind of clothes they were, to know what the material was or – now, in 2019 – confidently recall the colour.

I asked Arianna about the general mood in the cottage. She said she had seen empty bottles of hard liquor lying around, and there was some dope smoking. There was also a feeling in the cottage that Ian was already a suspect, even before Christmas Day was out. "Nobody was happy about that," said Arianna. "There was definitely some concern."

Overall, though, Arianna had little contact with Ian Bailey. She observed that Thomas's daughters did not have much interaction with him, either. It was a house where "everyone minded their own business". Bailey had a reputation for being aggressive and Arianna could see that Jules's daughters did not like him. "They were trying to keep their mother safe," Arianna said. The young Italian guest also noted that there was a marked lack of self-esteem among the females living in the cottage.

It was not a surprise, then, that Jules's daughters took every opportunity to keep well away from the place. The *craic* of Schull was fortunately close to hand. "We just didn't want to be in that house. It was eerie, like a ghost house."

For all the laughs and good company in Schull, there was no getting away from what had happened. Sophie's murder was the first in that section of County Cork in living memory. Local people on the Mizen were deeply shocked by its apparent violence and depravity. The story dominated the news and it was an inescapable topic of conversation in bars, in family gatherings, at shops and at Mass.

What impact did the news of Sophie's murder have at the cottage?

"Ian was talking about how he was a journalist, and that he was interested in the case. If it was mentioned, it was spoken of in a sterile way, in that it was an opportunity for him to write articles about it."

Our conversation felt like it was about to end there. Arianna needed to get back to her young children. I looked at her, dressed in jeans and a fashionable sweatshirt, and the expression 'comfortable in her own skin' came to my mind. She told me how she had had the time of her life in Ireland. She was finding herself. At age 19, 20, who wouldn't be? Still, I sensed that her Christmas in 1996 had been a moment of turbulence, lodged permanently in her mind.

She told me, apropos of the murder and the investigation, that she wanted to be "useful", meaning she wanted to be able to clearly remember what she saw when she was under the same roof as Ian Bailey on the Mizen. That wish to help became more profound when she had her own children. Becoming a mother re-focused her perspective.

Arianna's life in Ireland moved on, as all lives must. She kept in vague touch with Ginny, principally via Facebook. Ginny came to visit her in Vicenza some years ago – the Irishwoman happened to be passing through, on the way to or from a wedding or some other event. The murder of Sophie Toscan du Plantier was not discussed.

Arianna needed to leave but was taking her time, and looked pensive. She asked: "Did you see Sophie's parents?"

I told her that I had seen them at the trial.

She paused. I wondered if she was making a calculation, working out how old they must be. If it happened so long ago, and Sophie already had a teenage son at the time, then Sophie's parents would be, well…

Indeed. They were alive but they were very old.

"And you have children yourself?"

"Yes."

"So you understand."

***

In the autumn of 2019, there was news from Dublin: the Irish authorities had received France's request for the extradition of Ian Bailey. It was the third time that France had sought to extradite him. Of course, this time it was different because the French had now convicted Bailey of murder.

"You should call him," Donal MacIntyre told me after I got back from Italy. "He thinks of you as his friend, bizarrely enough."

I didn't need to call Bailey, because he called me.

"Nick! We haven't spoken since the crucifixion!"

It was late on a weekday evening, last week of November. Bailey's voice was slurred. It had taken six months for the "tsunami", as he put it, to arrive, but now it was here. He told me he was having panic attacks. He had never had them before. He would start shaking without warning. The last time it happened had been at the Bantry street market on a Friday, "in the shadow of St Brendan's", and a number of people had come up to him to ask if he was okay. He told them he felt faint.

I sensed Bailey was setting up one of his gags.

"I had to grab hold of a trader's pole."

The extradition request was a clear and present threat and

Bailey said he saw no reason why the judge should not endorse it. In the meantime, Bailey said he was getting constant requests for interviews, all of them rejected. "I tell them where to go. You want to find out about me? Go and read *A John Wayne State of Mind*." Bailey was referring to his second collection of verse, named after the American tough-guy actor, which he had recently published (sample poem titles: *Cell By Date*, *A Thousand Arrows*, *I Remain Calm in the Eye of the Hurricane*). Bailey had placed three copies in the local bookshop in Schull. He said he had gone to check the other day and all three had been sold.

Now the nights were drawing in, Bailey had his wood carving to keep him occupied. He said a number of women visited him in his workshop as they had heard he sold wooden penises: "They want them for their girlfriends!" Bailey was also putting his mind to a fusion of poetry and music that he hoped would find a stage in the bars and arts centres of County Cork. Audiences would see Jesus brought back to contemporary Ireland as a street musician. He already had the title: *The Reluctant Messiah*.

Bailey started speaking about his chances of seeing the latest French extradition request rejected. In the end, it was a complicated topic. Apparently, Ireland's top legal minds were divided as to how it would pan out. He said the country's extradition laws had been amended since the most recent European Arrest Warrant had been served, but how these changes affected his case was anyone's guess. It was a waiting game, at this point.

I reassured Bailey that it was all to play for, and that he had a good legal team. I felt like a fraud for saying that. In recent weeks, I had imagined a grinning Ian Bailey receiving good news from the Dublin court, lording over a press conference, opening a bottle of champagne, the cameras rolling, to toast the denial of extradition. It had made me feel queasy.

Bailey abruptly changed the subject: "I'm going to make sure that if I'm sent away it'll be on a stick for you…"

"How do you mean, a stick?"

Bailey said he meant a memory stick. Another one. There was something he wanted to give me, if he was shipped off to France. A document or documents, plural. This was the thing he would be putting on a memory stick. I asked him what it was, but he either didn't hear me or chose not to answer.

Bailey said, I think by way of explanation: "I'm a northern boy. We both are."

I paused to take this in. What could be on the memory stick? Was it something about the Sophie case?

"Nick, what's your favourite Beatles' song?"

"*Hey Jude*. And yours, Ian?"

"*Let It Be*."

A second later, I heard a muffled goodbye and the line went dead.

In another phone call a week or so later, Bailey invited me to his 63rd birthday party at the Prairie at the end of January. I told him I would be there. Then I weighed up the pros and cons. The party would last long into the night. I initially noted this down as a 'pro', but I quickly changed my mind. It was probably a 'con'. My all-night party days were well behind me. Then again, I would be many hundreds of miles closer to the promised memory stick, which seemed important, so that was a 'pro'. But I tended to get more out of Bailey when I was alone with him, which would not happen at his birthday party. I much preferred talking with Bailey one to one. This was the main reason I did not travel to County Cork in January 2020. I figured I would go in March or April when the weather would be better, and we would be closer to the date of the hearing in Dublin that would rule on France's extradition request.

I didn't get to see Bailey in the spring. Like just about everyone, I didn't go anywhere at all for months, because in 2020 the world changed.

Chapter 21

DEUS EX MACHINA

The coronavirus pandemic altered everything. By mid-March 2020, the spaces outside our confined lives became places fraught with danger and worry. The threat was real — newspapers and television reported a sharply escalating death count — but it also was invisible. Anyone could be carrying the coronavirus, and so everyone was under suspicion. These days, few people walked across the square in front of our apartment block, and those who did invariably wore masks to cover their nose and mouth, making themselves anonymous in the process. Our city locked down, the choices we had made in life — who you had married, your children, if you had any, the home you had chosen — were starkly crystallised. We held our breaths and waited for good news, some light at the distant end of the tunnel.

At least we were safe inside. One day there was an unexpected knock on the door of our apartment. I took a defensive step back as I slowly opened the door. Outside was a neighbour living on the same floor, a woman I barely knew. She handed me a slip of paper with her name and a mobile phone number. "In case you need anything," she said. I immediately sent her a text to give her my phone number so she could reach us, too. I had been paranoid at who might be outside our door, and what they might want. I felt a bit ashamed about it, my fear made me slightly ill at ease. After all, in this altered environment most people seemed keen to lend a hand to strangers where they could.

Across the border in France, the authorities required you to print out an official form with a list of permitted reasons if you left your home. You had to put a cross in a box alongside one of them. A gag that did the rounds showed a photo of the official form with an extra, hand-written reason – *Because my wife is driving me mad*. A sort of gallows humour filled our hours, as did an urge to be busy with jobs once put off for another day. I embarked on a spring-clean of my Sophie papers.

Sean Murray's statement recounting his sighting of the man in the passenger seat of Sophie's hire car at his petrol pump was in the police file. Arianna Boarina's short testimony was there, as well. These two were covered with my underlinings and scribbled notes. There were well over 700 statements in all, but some of these were repeated, which brought the total down slightly. A separate list showed a handful of documents that had been redacted, including what appeared to be psychological appraisals of various individuals no longer considered relevant to the case.

Up to now, my approach to the file had not been completely ordered – I had gone through Bailey's statements, Jules Thomas's statements and the small avalanche of items relating to Marie Farrell. As a lead or a new angle came up, I would look in the file. I essentially dipped in and out of it.

With the world at a standstill, it was time to go through all the statements, one by one.

I started by grouping them together – the witness statements given by neighbours and Schull residents, including people who had seen Bailey in the Galley bar on the evening before the murder, the couple of neighbours who saw a bonfire outside the studio on 26th December 1996, and so on. These were one large set. Then there was Sophie's family and friends – a smaller set. The ruminations of various Guards on things they had seen and heard, formalised as memos to the file, was another group. But one statement appeared all on its own. It belonged nowhere. It had been given by Caroline Mangez, the French journalist working for the magazine *Paris Match*, at Bandon Garda station, and was dated 8th July 1997.

I remembered Caroline Mangez from the trial in Paris. We spoke a couple of times on the steps of the courthouse. Mangez was a friendly, confident woman in middle age, blond hair, of average height. She appeared inquisitive and energetic. We had discussed how fond Gilles Jacob – a great friend of Daniel Toscan du Plantier – had been of Sophie. Eighty-eight years old, Jacob had appeared at Bailey's trial as a witness, as an observer of Daniel in the immediate aftermath of the murder, and as an observer of Sophie, too. We were both charmed by Jacob's evidently disinterested, platonic love for Sophie. Immediately Jacob had recognised Sophie was different. She was unlike any of the other actresses and film-world women who had populated Daniel's life. Jacob had admired her from afar. In the courtroom, I had sensed he had only wanted the best for her.

In his memoir, published in 2009, Jacob had said of Sophie, "I loved her tenderly". And what a life he had led. As a Jewish child in eastern France, Jacob had hidden in a Catholic seminary to evade capture by the Nazis. For many years, he was chairman of the Cannes Film Festival, meeting the great and the good and pretty much every movie star you had ever heard of. Anyway, after we had stopped chatting about Gilles Jacob, Mangez also told me that she was planning to go back to Ireland to interview Bailey again. She had excellent access to Bailey, she said.

In fact, Bailey had mentioned Caroline Mangez a couple of times to me, talking about his life in the aftermath of the murder, and his contacts with the media. Bailey was wary of French journalists in a general sense, but I got the impression from the way Bailey spoke about Mangez that he had taken a particular shine to her.

It struck me that it was a cunning – provocative, even – ploy of the editors of *Paris Match* to send a young journalist – who was undeniably a bit similar in appearance to the murdered Sophie – to doorstep Bailey after the killing.

As I read Mangez's statement, I realised that parts of it were familiar. As I said, I had dipped into the Garda file now and again, skimming various documents, and this was one that I had already read quickly.

I work as a Journalist with Paris Match. *As part of my work, I was asked to travel to West Cork to cover the story of the murder of Sophie Toscan du Plantier. I first arrived on 1/1/97 and stayed until 7/1/97, I returned on 11/1/97 and stayed until 18/1/97... After 11/1/97 I spent a lot of time with Ian Bailey. On 15/1/97 he said Jules Thomas his partner was fed up hearing about the murder and that we should meet at his house, the Studio, and that I should come alone.*

When I arrived there, he told me he wanted to make a book or film based on the murder... He then said he had an idea for the end, that a French journalist would arrive to cover the story and she will be very close to solving it, but will never actually do so. She will fall in love with the country, buy a house here and two years later she too will be murdered in the same circumstances on a moonlit night.

Mangez asked Bailey what the Frenchwoman in his imagination looked like, and if he was talking about her.

Bailey replied: *"Guess!"*

Mangez told the Guard interviewing her that this was not the first time Bailey had made an off-colour joke, but that *I knew that this was different and it made me feel very uncomfortable.*

Bailey told Mangez that he wanted her to stay in the house. Mangez replied she had to be on her way, and she left.

Subsequently, Bailey told the Frenchwoman that he had been the first journalist to arrive at the murder scene and that he had a wound on his forehead and scratches on his arms, but that these were from killing three turkeys and cutting a Christmas tree. He also told Mangez that he could have committed the murder to re-launch his journalistic career.

Like me, Mangez had been subjected to the inconsistencies of

Bailey's account of his journey back home from the Galley bar on the night of 22nd to 23rd December.

He spoke about his alibi for the time of the murder. He told me that Jules and he came home directly from the pub, the Galley, and drove via Hunt's Hill Road and that he didn't get out of the car. I said, you told me previously that you got out of the car at Hunt's Hill for a while to have a walk and that it was a moonlit night, and that you had a powerful feeling and a premonition when you looked at Sophie's house and that it gave you goosebumps on your skin. He denied this completely.

Mangez told the Guards: *He was always talking about Sophie's laptop computer.*

Looking at her statement again, I can see that Mangez did a good job. She was courageous, insistent, and she got to know Bailey from the inside out, so to speak, on his own patch. She also spoke with Jules Thomas, both with Bailey and separately.

On 11/1/97 Jules told me she had taken pills on the night of the murder as she had period pains and she was quite unconscious. She later said: "I'm not really sure, Ian would often get out of bed during the night... I can't believe he's done this. It would mean that for seven weeks now he has deceived me and I am scared for my daughters and I have no protection from the Gardaí".

Bailey told Mangez that he had special powers, and that sometimes when he was meditating *he is neither a man nor a woman, and that at these times of great powers and energy... he likes to dance in the night in his underwear.*

It seemed Bailey could not take no for an answer: *He constantly asks me to sleep in his house and told me he had prepared Fenella's room for me. I always refused as I was very apprehensive about staying there... Jules told me she can't bear to be separated from Ian for more than a few days, and that they have a very strong link between them.*

Rather like Arianna Boarina a few weeks earlier, Caroline Mangez was in a position to see for herself the peculiar dynamic of Bailey and Thomas's household.

I was speaking to Ian and he told me I was a very special person, that everybody who met me was very impressed by me. I was scared and I didn't want to enter into this kind of conversation with him. I was uneasy. Any time that Jules came near the kitchen where we were talking, Ian would tell her to go away.

The square outside my apartment block was deserted. It was dark now, and silent. The streetlamps illuminated the Dutch-style gables on the tops of the townhouses opposite my window.

Mangez said in her statement that Bailey had said to her:

"I've got visions, I've got intuitions and premonitions… ask me whatever you want and I will tell you the truth."

Bailey also said that his solicitor *had told him to shut his mouth, but that he's always dreaming about being famous.*

When I read that line, I half-smiled. Bailey had wanted to be famous his whole life, and he had succeeded.

I looked back at Mangez's statement and saw:

He said that in 1997 the world was entering the year of Kali, an Indian Goddess of destruction.

Had I really read that?

I stared at my computer screen. I checked the name of the document again. Yes, it was the statement given to the Guards by Caroline Mangez, the French journalist working for the magazine *Paris Match* on 8th July 1997, referring to interviews with Bailey in January 1997. I had not mixed up the files. This was Mangez's sworn testimony, and she had told the Guard who took it down that Ian Bailey spoke to her about the Indian goddess Kali.

The same Kali that had so fascinated Sophie.

It was night, but I felt suddenly alert; my brain raced ahead, drawing conclusions, calculating the odds – the odds of this mention of Kali somehow being a coincidence. If it was a coincidence, then this meant that Bailey had *not* heard Sophie talk about Kali, and that Bailey – addressing a Frenchwoman who resembled the murdered Sophie – had plucked this random reference to an Indian goddess and her place in the cosmos out of thin air. This hypothesis seemed very unlikely.

Reading this, in my heart, I felt I knew: Bailey had known Sophie and they had talked, somehow *really* talked. I cast my mind back. Bailey had never mentioned eastern religions to me before, and I had not seen any reference to Indian gods or goddesses in any of his writings. At the civil case in Dublin, there had been a brief quotation from Bailey's diaries about him potentially looking into Buddhism to calm him down or to see his life from a different perspective. As far as I was aware, he had not acted on this. Also, and as far as I was aware, he had not been to Asia.

Bailey's mention of Kali, unprompted, seemed to me to be firm evidence that Bailey had known Sophie. Emotionally, I felt that this was it – the scrap of information changed everything, like a litmus paper changing from pink to blue – but, again, the cogs in my brain had to whirr in parallel to process this information intellectually.

What did it mean? Precisely what conclusion could I draw? It was not the kind of physical link between them that you would have if, for instance, the Guards had found a shop receipt belonging to Sophie in Bailey's trouser pocket. This was a psychological connection, and it made powerful sense. Sophie was not a woman for small talk; if she was going to enter into a conversation with a man on the Mizen – even a good-looking man of her own age – it had to be about a subject she considered valuable. It needed to be something important. It was in her character.

I woke up my wife. I told her what I thought: Bailey knew Sophie. This is it. After all this time. The signs had been there under my nose, there in Sophie's travel journal, and here in the police file. They had been in plain sight.

I thought again of the time Ian Bailey had taken me to see Sean Murray. I thought of my return visit to Ireland – a trip predicated on the question I urgently needed to ask Bailey. Could he account for his whereabouts at the time Sophie was driving west from Cork Airport, when she stopped for fuel at Hurley's Garage? I thought of his reply, and the seed of doubt that took root there and then. The voluntary, unbidden, mention of Kali to a French journalist made that seed of doubt grow. In 1989, Sophie had holidayed in India. In Calcutta, she had seen the Indians bathing in the river. She saw flowers passed from one human hand to the next, given as gifts. Sophie had been mesmerised. She imagined a woman in a white robe. She wrote in her journal: *It was difficult to accept, to die dressed in white under a ton of petals.* Life was about survival but it was also a preparation for dying, an apprenticeship played out on the stage that was this teeming Indian city.

Down at the riverbank in Calcutta, once a year, effigies of Kali, the goddess of death, are sent bobbing away into the inky night. Sophie was there to see it. The effigies are made of papier-mâché and sink in the tepid water. They do not stand a chance. Sophie wrote: *What if you took one of those figures in the river by her hand? What if you got carried away by the current with her, and drowned with her?*

I looked at the word Kali in Sophie's handwriting on the pages of her journal.

The people see Kali drown, wrote Sophie.

And they take pleasure from it.

***

The Kali discovery told me that Bailey *had* known Sophie. It was a core aspect of the case. I now had no doubt about this. Of all the things that could have connected them, Kali stood out, and it was sinister. Not only that, the importance of Kali to Sophie or, rather, the importance of the 1989 trip to India, was underscored by the fact that the Justice Committee had only made public two documents authored by Sophie. One of these was her brief, impressionistic journal describing what she saw on the India journey.

Now what to do with the information?

I called an English barrister friend who had worked on criminal cases, familiar with Ireland. I set out the facts: Bailey had been found guilty in France. In Ireland, the murder file was still open, at least technically. Did I need to pay a visit to the Guards to tell them about my discovery? My barrister friend said no, he thought not. I had not proved that Bailey had killed Sophie, and that was what counted. I decided the Kali connection would stay under lock and key. I only really trusted myself with the information. One day I would put my cards on the table and see Bailey's reaction, and Kali was the strongest card in my hand.

I would get my chance to confront Ian Bailey in Ireland, if the courts denied France's extradition request, or in France, if Ireland endorsed the request and Bailey was bundled onto a plane bound for Paris. The coronavirus crisis had understandably delayed the Irish courts system – many judges were older men, precisely the demographic most at risk in the pandemic. They would presumably not be keen to rush back to work. The High Court hearing to rule on the extradition, scheduled for May, had been put back to July at the earliest. Still, even with a possible appeal to Ireland's Supreme Court, this meant that Bailey would likely know his fate by the end of 2020.

Then I would ask him about Kali. I would drop my mask.

***

Two days later, my phone rang. 'Bailey' appeared on the screen. It was the week before the anniversary of the murder trial in Paris. I had heard that he was becoming increasingly nervous. "It's like I'm riding a horse and I've come to a crossroads," said Bailey. At the fork in the road, there were two signposts, he told me: "One says 'Glory', the other says 'Shitsville'." Bailey had taken up meditation. When he adopted the lotus position, he closed his eyes and saw butterflies flying past, and all was calm. When he opened his eyes, his predicament was the same as ever.

Would the agony ever truly end?

"No, not unless somebody confesses!"

Bailey's news for me that day was that he had started writing. Not poems or poetry set to music, or riffs on Jesus Christ and his final days on earth. Bailey was writing about the time of Sophie's murder, the run-up to Christmas 1996.

Bailey said: "I wrote a scene from the perspective of a drone. A crow's view of an isolated cottage on a hillside. The views are magnificent. There are two men hacking through gorse. They are in uniform and they start to shout, and then other men come and they are hacking through the gorse, too, and suddenly they all start looking to the east and they see a car approaching along the *boreen*. The driver is tall and dark-haired and next to him there is a lady. She has a long-lens camera."

"Who are they, Ian, these two people?"

"I'm the driver and Jules is the lady with the camera. I had forgotten about it for a long time, but then it just came back to me. I was wondering why it's coming back now…"

Bailey's voice became indistinct. I guessed he was holding the phone away from his face. There was some background noise. He was probably out in the yard. He would usually step out of the house to talk to me, unless the weather was bad. What I heard next was: "I didn't want to think about it". I think Bailey meant that, until now, he had not wanted to think about driving up to Sophie's house in his car. He had not wanted to replay the episode in his mind.

I had never heard him talk this way before, recounting his own experience in the third person. It was as if he was outside his body and observing himself from a distance.

Bailey snapped out of his reverie. He returned to the familiar theme of the people trying to make contact with him, trying to get close. Writers, reporters, people with media projects. These days, he gave them short shrift. "They are flaky, wobbly, or whatever," said Bailey.

Another pause. Some more background noise. The wind off the Atlantic sweeping through the yard.

"But I trust you."

Chapter 22

THE MAN WHO KNEW TOO MUCH?

In the autumn of 2019, I had mailed the press officer of the French court to see if there was a transcript of Bailey's trial available. He replied that there wasn't. I had not seen a stenographer in the courtroom but I had presumed there was a tape of the proceedings and that a transcript would be typed up from the recording. I was wrong.

A transcript would have been useful. I was digging deeper into the testimony of Bill Fuller, one of the two witnesses who had travelled from Ireland to France to give evidence. I had three sheets of paper on my desk, marked *Fuller evidence to Guards*, *Fuller in Paris*, and *Fuller at Cork libel action*.

Now I have to rewind the story a bit, and recap.

Bill Fuller cropped up in the Sophie investigation on several occasions. Firstly, he reported to the Guards that he had seen Jules Thomas driving alone on the Kealfadda Road on the morning of the murder – the road that has a turn-off leading to Sophie's house in Toormore. At 11 or 11:30am on 23rd December, Fuller said he was driving behind Thomas's white Ford Fiesta. Fuller turned left where the Kealfadda Road met the main Schull to Crookhaven road – close to Kealfadda Bridge. He reported seeing Thomas turn in the opposite direction, towards Goleen. This was significant because James Camier, the fruit and vegetable seller, testified to the Guards that Thomas had approached his stall in Goleen on the same morning, at approximately 11:30, and told him about the murder of a Frenchwoman nearby, adding that Bailey was investigating it as a journalist. This was more than two hours before Bailey received the call from Eddie Cassidy of the *Examiner* alerting Bailey to the death of a woman in the vicinity, so how could Thomas have known about it at 11:30?

As we know, Thomas flatly denied being in Goleen that morning. She said she was at home the whole time.

In 2014, Marie Farrell said at the High Court in Dublin that much of her evidence, given in signed statements and under oath at the civil case that Bailey brought against the newspapers in Cork in 2003, was untrue. It was the result – she said – of undue pressure from certain Guards. Following her switch to Bailey's side, Farrell had claimed that on the late morning of 23rd December 1996 she had spoken with Bill Fuller outside her shop on Schull Main Street and given him permission to sell his last Christmas trees there, which is what Farrell said he did. Nobody can be in two places at the same time – and Fuller was adamant that he had not had any such conversation with Farrell.

In the Dublin courtroom, the barrister for the State remarked that the only reason Farrell would make any such claim would be to attempt to undermine Fuller's testimony that he saw Thomas in her car at 11 or 11:30 am on 23rd December, and also to cast doubt on James Camier's assertion that Jules Thomas had told him about the murder the same morning. (By the time of the Dublin court case, James Camier had passed away.)

Secondly, Bill Fuller had reported to the Guards that on 6th February 1997 Bailey had told him how he had gone up to Sophie's house after seeing her in Brosnan's supermarket, and had killed her. It was in this connection that a transcript of the Paris trial would have been useful. Ian Bailey, of course, denied he had said any such thing to Bill Fuller.

The indictment setting out the case against Bailey had been drawn up by the office of the investigating magistrate, Nathalie Turquey. The document contained 43 pages of dense text, starting with an introduction to the crime scene. Among other things, the indictment listed the witnesses in the Galley bar who said Bailey visibly had no scratches on his hands or arms, and no cut on his forehead, with just one customer saying that Bailey *might* have had a scratch or two on one of his hands. This was a key plank of the case against Bailey, and the public prosecutor in the courtroom explained the argument regarding the scratches precisely as it was set out in the indictment order. So far, so good.

However, the last page of the indictment contained a surprise. My first reaction was: how is it possible I had not spotted this earlier?

The only version of the indictment I had was in English, and the translation from the French was not brilliant. It read: *In many occasions and in front of different people, Ian Bailey either admitted to the crime or rendered speeches in which he indirectly confessed to it.* The indictment briefly mentioned Helen Callanan, Malachi Reed and the Shelleys. Then it said: *More attention must be paid on Bill Fuller's testimony.* What this meant was, those other alleged confessions are interesting, but we think this one is special and different.

When Bill Fuller had approached the witness box in Paris, I thought he appeared slightly nervous, as most people do when they are witnesses in court. He was wearing a neat dark grey suit and to my eye looked – and I mention this because had I been in his position I would no doubt have been the same – very slightly self-conscious in his smart attire, as if he did not wear a suit every day. The judge, Frédérique Aline, asked Fuller to give his evidence to the court, which he did, in English via an interpreter.

Fuller told the judge he was a chef, and had previously been a gardener, giving Bailey a few gardening jobs during the course of 1996. He gave his age and I worked out he was 15 years younger than Bailey. It struck me as unusual that a man in his 40th year had been casually employed by another man in his mid-20s. In fact, Bill Fuller would have been 25 when the murder took place, married with a small child.

In Paris, Fuller recounted where he had seen Jules Thomas in her white Ford Fiesta and at what time on the morning of 23rd December 1996. Next, he mentioned calling on Bailey at his cottage at the Prairie in late January 1997, when Bailey – flush with money earned from his newspaper articles and 'fixer' gigs for French journalists – was cooking a large pot of chilli. Fuller said Bailey had told him that the chilli was intended for a "post-murder" party for a "select group" of around 50 guests. Bailey was wearing a black skirt at the time. He told Fuller it was comfortable and said it was a kilt. Fuller was incredulous, and asked Bailey: "Why are you wearing a kilt if you aren't even Scottish?" In that period, Bailey phoned Fuller from time to time to find out from his friend what people on the Mizen were saying about him.

Fuller described to Judge Aline what happened when, in early February 1997, he paid another visit to the Bailey-Thomas residence. Fuller repeated to Judge Aline, more or less word for word, as far as I could tell, what he had told the Guards on 20th February. Inside the cottage, Bailey had said to him, according to his statement:

"You saw her in the Spar and she turned you on walking up the aisle with her tight arse. So you went there to see what you could get, but she was not interested, so you attacked her and she got away, and so you chased her and stove something into the back of her head and went a lot further than you meant to."

Fuller said he replied to Bailey that this was "the sort of thing you would do". Bailey then responded: "That's how I got to meet Jules. I saw her tight arse, but she let me in."

Judge Aline asked Fuller if he thought that Bailey had meant it as a confession, despite the way that Bailey had spoken in the second person ("You fancied her, you went up there..."). The confession aspect was no doubt important, but the indictment made the key part of Fuller's testimony the five short words: *the back of her head*. Did Judge Aline, the prosecutor for the Republic or one of the barristers representing the Bouniol family or the Justice Committee make a specific reference to those five words while Bill Fuller was taking the stand? For instance, did they ask Fuller if he was sure that Bailey had said exactly that? I don't think that they did. I looked over my notes, but I did not see any specific note or comment about *the back of her head* – and this despite the fact the indictment had flagged Fuller quite deliberately (*More attention must be paid on Bill Fuller's testimony*). The judges and the barristers (for the prosecution, Bailey was of course not represented) were free to work with the witnesses and the indictment as they wished. None of them was duty-bound to focus on the words *the back of her head* – and I was fairly sure they did not. A transcript would have proved it one way or the other.

In any event, this was an intriguing piece of police work. The French detectives working under the investigating magistrate had spelled it out in the indictment:

Only the author and first-hand witnesses of the crime could have known that Sophie Bouniol had been hit from behind, and more, with the means of an object.

There was indeed a hole in the back of Sophie's head, in her skull in an area above the back of the right temporal lobe. That Sophie was attacked from behind was demonstrated by Professor Harbison, the State pathologist, who noted multiple lesions on the victim's back caused by a number of oblique blows caused by an implement.

This was therefore not a wholly frontal attack. The French detectives were advancing the argument that there was no way that Bailey could have known this, unless he had had intimate knowledge of the murder. But there was a serious problem with their thesis. In the days following the killing, many regional and national newspapers in Ireland were publishing stories about the murder. They informed their readers that Sophie fled her attacker downhill.

A number of these stories – including one penned by Eddie Cassidy of the *Examiner* – mentioned that Sophie was struck with a blunt instrument from behind (some journalists speculated that it had been a poker from Sophie's hearth). These details would therefore have been known to a large number of people on the Mizen. It was far from being the 'slam dunk' the French cops might have thought they had.

I looked again at Bill Fuller's contested testimony. I read it as slowly as I could. I must have read those brief sentences 20 or more times, over the years. Each time, I had the same reaction. You look at what Bailey is alleged to have said and what do you see? Specifically, as a *native* English speaker what do you see? If you are like me, it is the lewdness of the language Bailey is claimed to have used. Then there is the insane logic: a man sees a pretty woman and, when things do not go as planned, it apparently has to lead to the most extreme act of violence. The "to see what you could get" also floats around in the imagination, since it is so brazen: here is someone turning up late at night on a woman's doorstep in the middle of the countryside, and yet there is an implication that he thinks there is a potential sexual bonanza in store for him. After reading Fuller's report of the snippet of conversation a few times, I also started to see some irony in the phrase "to see what you could get". Rather than a late-night sexual encounter, what Bailey ultimately got was a date in a courtroom in Paris with the strong likelihood of a conviction.

These were thoughts I found difficult to suppress. If you are researching a book about a puzzling murder case, it is as well to keep your mind open, so I suppose there was nothing wrong on that level. The problem was that reading too much into this or the other phrase could obstruct the real value of the evidence. To put it another way, I risked not seeing the wood for the trees, since – had the French detectives been right – the words that really counted were *the back of her head*, and I had not even noticed them, even after reading the statement multiple times. I think the French saw this more clearly because – and here I'm guessing – they looked at the meaning of each word, translating them individually into French. They were not distracted as I was, rushing to join up the dots. For once, working in a foreign language was not a handicap – it was an advantage – even if ultimately this specific argument in the indictment did not stand up to scrutiny.

I do not know how the Guards framed Bill Fuller's testimony in their submission to the Director of Public Prosecutions, since this document has never been made public. What can be checked, however, is the DPP's position paper from 2001 justifying its decision not to prosecute Ian Bailey. The DPP paper made no reference whatsoever to Bill Fuller's testimony about Bailey's alleged confession in February 1997.

When Bailey sued the newspapers for libel in 2003, the defence barrister cross-examined him in the Cork courtroom about his alleged confession to Bill Fuller. Bailey did not say that Fuller had misunderstood him, and that he (Bailey) had only been repeating what other people had said about him – the line he generally took with regard to his confessions to Malachi Reed, Helen Callanan and the Shelleys. When it came to the second-person confession to Bill Fuller, he told the Cork court that none of what Fuller had told the Guards and signed in a sworn statement was true. In short, Bailey claimed Bill Fuller was telling a pack of lies.

Bailey also complained to the judge in the Cork libel case that Fuller and another man, Julian Bielecki, another of Bailey's former friends, had been staring at him during the lunch recess, and that Fuller had mouthed to him the words "we've got you now". As a result, the presiding judge, Patrick Moran, took the unusual step of expelling Fuller and Bielecki from the courtroom until such time they would be called to take the stand. (Julian Bielecki had taken Jules Thomas to hospital after Bailey's attack on Thomas in May 1996, and stayed at the Prairie to protect Thomas after she had received medical treatment, keeping a hammer next to him while he slept, so fearful was he of Bailey.)

At any event, when Fuller took the stand, Bailey's barrister questioned him about what he had said to his client and Bill Fuller claimed that what he in fact had mouthed to Bailey was not "we've got you now", but "you have sweat on your brow". Whatever the truth, it looked like Bailey had succeeded in undermining Fuller, making him appear unreliable, and Judge Moran had sent a powerful, although unintentional, message in banning Fuller from observing proceedings in the courtroom.

In Paris, my view was that Bill Fuller was a credible witness. I had the feeling he was there to do his duty, just as Sophie's son had implored the Ireland-based witnesses to do so outside the church at Goleen a week before the trial.

It is also clear that Fuller had approached the Guards promptly after going to Bailey's cottage and hearing him utter those alarming words. Moreover, if the whole confession episode was invented, as Bailey claimed, it did seem odd to me that Bill Fuller would have included such extraneous detail – the blow with an implement *and* to the back of the head. In the weeks following the murder, there had been plenty of gossip swirling around the Mizen about the violence of the attack, the amount of blood on the ground and the victim's body and, most of all, the horrific injuries sustained to Sophie's face. If Fuller's testimony was true, and recalled precisely, Bailey's hotly contested confession told us how the murder happened.

You get some more context from a short statement given to the Guards on 18th May 1997 by Dr Larry O'Connor, who had been the medic called out from Schull on the morning of 23rd December. He confirmed to the Gardaí that the first time he spoke with Ian Bailey was in the late afternoon of 31st March 1997 – Easter Monday – when the doctor was in the Galley bar. O'Connor was enjoying a quiet drink on a holiday weekend. As a general practitioner with three decades of experience, he was a mature man and had some standing in his community. O'Connor reported how Bailey approached him in the bar, and remarked that the doctor's involvement in the case must have been "very traumatic". O'Connor: *He then proceeded to enquire about the wounds sustained by the deceased. I told him a whole concoction including that she had lacerations on the left side of forehead and face where she had nothing at all and also that she had lacerations on the neck when in fact she had no injuries in that area, never mentioning at any stage any actual wounds sustained by the deceased Sophie Toscan du Plantier. I felt at that stage he realised that I was trying to mislead him...*

O'Connor certainly was misleading Bailey since the main injuries to the victim were on the right side of the skull (Sophie's head was found tilted slightly to the left).

...and I stated that there is a maniac with a hatchet around West Cork and the sooner he is caught the better. We then went our separate ways.

At the end of March 1997, Ian Bailey was essentially unemployable as a reporter or a media 'fixer'. His career as a journalist was over. So why was he quizzing O'Connor about the specific nature of Sophie's wounds?

***

Later I dug out Bill Fuller's complete statement to the Guards – the one that contained the alleged confession that Bailey said Fuller had invented. Fuller told the Guards he was born in Essex but had grown up in Devon. He came to the western section of County Cork in 1991, when he would have been about 20. As a boss, his view of Ian Bailey's gardening skills was mixed, to say the least: *he was no good with machinery and I just let him do manual work.* It was an echo of the view of John Montague who wrote in *The New Yorker* to the effect that Bailey seemed rather clumsy around tools in the garden. *We became more friendly, and I would visit him and Jules at their home.*

On the morning of 23rd December: *I remember the Monday because it was my last day for selling Christmas trees... I did most of the boreens.* Fuller mentioned the names of a few people living near the Kealfadda Road he called on to see if they needed a tree, although he did not drive up the valley to Toormore to try his luck with Alfie Lyons. *I drove down the road towards Kealfadda Bridge* [and] *saw a white*

Fiesta in front of me, I knew it straight away as Jules' car and I knew that it was Jules driving it. It was about 11am at this stage. I followed her, I was in my Jeep, all the way to the main Schull-Goleen Road... I must say that shortly after I saw her, she put out her left hand across to the passenger side as if to stop something from falling over. When she entered the Causeway [i.e. Kealfadda Bridge] *I just carried on towards Schull. She was alone in the car at all times.*

Fuller was in quite close contact with Bailey after Sophie's killing: *Some days after the murder he rang several times, asking about whether we knew anything about the murder or what was being said about it. His main words were that it was someone from France that did it.*

On the day of the alleged confession in February, Fuller said that Bailey *was agitated and also on a "high". He said he had just cashed a cheque for £900 and there was plenty of food and drink there. He gave me cider to drink. It was about 5.30pm.* The conversation moved from one topic to another, according to Fuller: *You can't even give someone a lift these days,* said Bailey. *I gave Malachi Reed a lift home the other day from school and they* [the Guards] *questioned him about what I had said. I* [Fuller] *said, "What did you say" and he replied, "Nothing, I gave the guy a lift home because it was getting dark". The conversation died down and Ian sat back pondering something, then he started looking for photographs and after a while found some. He passed remarks about Jenny* [Ginny] *and her Italian friend... He pointed to people in the photographs* [of the Christmas Day swim at Schull pier] *saying "it could be him or it could be him". Anyway, the conversation died again and then he said out of the blue to me "You did it, didn't you!" I said, do not joke about it because it is serious, and he carried on: "Yes you did it, didn't you, you saw her in the Spar and she turned you on, walking up the aisle with her tight arse. So you went there to see what you could get, but she was not interested, so you attacked her and she got away, and so you chased her and stove something into the back of her head and went a lot further than you meant to."*

I said, "That is like the sort of thing you would do". He laughed and shrugged it off. I got a bit afraid of him. He was going from highs to lows and then he said, "Actually that is how I got to meet Jules, I saw her tight

arse and wanted her". I finished my drink and left the house and I was
shaking. I decided not to go to see him again for a good while.

Since the day Ian was arrested, I have been seriously thinking that it
could have been that he murdered Sophie.

***

Ian Bailey's hearing to protest the application from France to
extradite him following his guilty conviction took place over three
days in July 2020 at Dublin's High Court. Bailey arrived at the
proceedings wearing a bright green bandana over his nose and
mouth – an idiosyncratic precaution against coronavirus, its colour
a nod to his country of refuge. In a matter of months, we would find
out if Ireland would extend that refuge to Bailey definitively.

For someone who had pretty much no assets to his name, Bailey
had blazed an expensive trail through Ireland's civil courts system
– first a mainly unsuccessful libel trial before a circuit judge in
2003, then in 2014 and 2015 a months-long case against the Irish
state, which he lost. He succeeded in deflecting France's attempts
to use the European Arrest Warrant to force him off the Mizen,
taking his case to the Supreme Court on two occasions. There had
also been court appearances for assaulting Jules Thomas and for
drink-driving.

This would be his final throw of the dice.

I had little inclination to speak with Bailey. I had been thinking
of Paris. I pictured Sophie's friends and family at their meetings of
the Justice Committee, month after month, year after year, crowded
into Jean-Antoine Bloc's neat sitting room, their hopes dashed
repeatedly until – finally – the date of Bailey's murder trial was
announced. I had been thinking of Jean-Antoine Bloc himself, of his
selfless dedication to searching out the murderer of the daughter of
a family friend. I thought of Pierre-Louis addressing the journalists
outside the courthouse after Bailey's guilty verdict had been handed
down. Ian Bailey had murdered his mother, Pierre-Louis had said,

and Bailey was a "monster". I remembered how he spat out that word.

I had heard from a couple of contacts present in the courtroom that the case looked like it might well go in Bailey's favour when the judge delivered his ruling in October.

My phone rang. The name 'Bailey' appeared on the screen.

Bailey's voice was perky, happy. That alone told me how the hearing must have gone. I asked him about the trial.

"I've decided not to think about it. Whatever happens, happens. Where are you, by the way?"

"In France. We're on holiday. On a boat, moored on a river."

"So I'll say *bonsoir*," said Bailey. "I'm assuming there is a decent hostelry nearby you can retire to?"

We spoke for a couple more minutes. Bailey wondered how my book was going. I told him it was going fine, and thanked him for asking. I added that he had been in my thoughts, the last few weeks. I suggested a trip to Ireland – the pandemic permitting – in November. I said I wanted to ask him a question or two to round off my research. Bailey replied that I would be very welcome.

Chapter 23

MARTHA

Sophie Bouniol knew that every good story had a beginning, a middle and an end. Good stories were all around her. It was inevitable: Sophie's husband was Daniel Toscan du Plantier, the most powerful man in French cinema, former chairman of the Gaumont film company, latterly the boss of UniFrance, France's film promotion board, as well as being a celebrated producer in his own right.

It was the early 1990s. Sophie had a story in mind. Sophie's story was about the village in Lozère where her paternal grandparents had come from. The village was a real place, she knew people there. Sophie was a writer, and she had confidence in her abilities. Hadn't her mother always said how beautifully she wrote?

As a child, Sophie had taken countless trips with her parents and brother Bertrand to their holiday home in the Lozère (Sophie was already in her mid-teens when Stéphane, her younger brother, was born). The Lozère was a place you came to if you set off in your car from Paris in the direction of the beaches of the South of France and, a couple of hours' drive short of the sparkle of the Mediterranean Sea, you took an abrupt turn to the right and went upcountry. You would drive along empty winding roads until you finally got there, to a windswept plateau and the straggle of stone houses lining three sinewy streets that comprise the village of Combret. One of these old stone dwellings belonged to the Bouniol family. It was a permanent, physical reminder of where they were from, who they really were.

Sophie brought her story to life in longhand, in one of her notebooks. In her mind's eye, Sophie saw Combret in the middle of the night, at the tail end of August. A slight chill hovering in the dry air was the first sign of the arrival of autumn. In the village square, the street lamps had been switched off; the water in the gurgling fountain stood still. Stars punctured a dark sky. The scene was set. It was time to introduce the main character in the story.

The woman's name was Martha.

In Sophie's story, Martha walked through the deserted village, hobbling. One of her feet was strong, but the other was broken, helpless, done in at the heel. A permanent limp. Nonetheless, slowly, steadily, one good foot, one bad foot, she climbed up to the fields, unnoticed. All this time Combret slept, undisturbed.

In the Lozère, the menfolk tilled the land, worked the harvest. The men loved the land because it was all they had. But they hated it, too, for the same reason. The land trapped them. Sophie wrote: *It's a sort of hateful love. They are attracted and repelled at the same time.*

Meanwhile, the open fields were the domain of the women of the village. It was the women and the girls who had the job of herding the cows and drawing milk from their udders. Cattle reared for their meat roamed at will on the high pastures and built up muscle until the day they were sent to the slaughterhouse, where they were stunned and sent on their way. The women wore no makeup, their skin was burned olive-brown by the sun. They worked together, often with a radio playing in the background. In the real-life Lozère, you never saw any of the women reading a book.

The women were suspicious of the bulls. Of course, the bulls had to be there – how else would new calves be born, how else would the cycle continue? But the problem was that the bulls were unpredictable. One moment they were peaceful, docile, doing nothing and the next, all hell would break loose. That was why bulls known to be temperamental were fitted with a ring through their nose. A tug on the bull's ring would usually help bring the animal into submission. But you could never entirely eliminate the risk.

One day Marie, Martha's mother, was working the fields and a bull got worked up over something or other and gored her. Marie was taken down to the village for treatment, and it looked like the doctor had Marie set on the road to recovery. But suddenly Marie's condition worsened and she died. Martha found herself living alone in the stone house.

To add insult to injury, it wasn't even their own bull. Marie and Martha didn't have any cattle to their name. They looked after other people's cows. The bull that attacked Marie belonged to a family that had moved away, packed up and gone to Paris.

Martha's brother Fortuné was a mason – not a very imaginative one, wrote Sophie, but the bar is set low in the Lozère, in such a depopulated region if you're the village mason you're not likely to face stiff competition. Fortuné had built himself a nice new stone house on the outskirts of the village. Martha rarely saw Fortuné but, with their mother dead and buried, each week he placed packages of food and hearty casseroles on her doorstep. Martha was his family, after all. It was the way things were in the Lozère. When Fortuné came calling on Martha, he would shout out, to let her know he had passed by.

As for Martha's sister, she married and moved to another village further down the valley. She had a family of her own by now. Martha almost never saw the sister, who might as well have been living on the dark side of the moon. The village in question was about four miles from Combret.

Marie, the mother, had been widowed young and her plan was to keep one of her daughters at home, to look after her in an old age that never did materialise. There was no possibility that the son would look after the mother, this was a job for a girl, not a man, and anyway, his relative good luck had been chiselled into the name with which he was baptised: Fortuné.

That left Martha and her sister. Only one would get wed and start her own family. Martha was the eldest, the closest in age to her mother.

Sophie wrote: *Marie decided to sacrifice Martha.*

With Marie dead, Sophie remarked that Martha became a sort of widow – a widow to her mother's defunct demands and obligations – and she dressed the part, too: black blouse, black skirt, a woollen cape for warmth. But this didn't stop Martha keeping her parents' bedroom clean and dusted, a bedspread folded neatly on the mattress, as if one day they might return. In the scullery, Martha pinned a handful of postcards to the wall: fading images of Nice, Normandy, Brittany, Paris. Places Martha had never been, places that occupied her imagination, nourished her fantasies, giving her an illusion of a lived life; a collection of almost-memories for an almost-widow.

In fact, Martha never once left the Lozère.

This is when things changed in Martha's life. With her mother gone, Martha began to take long hikes across open country, through the upland meadows, higher and higher. In every season, but always at night. When the heat of the summer drained away and the storms arrived, Martha would leave the village, unnoticed. She was fascinated by thunder, fascinated by the jagged bolts of lightning that for a split second gave a pleasing shape to the clouds and the horizon. An occasional shepherd, troubled, would report seeing the ghostly long shadow of a woman coming down from the uplands at first light.

The shadow was Martha.

One day, Fortuné, Martha's brother, left a casserole on her step and called out to her. There was no reply, which was unusual. It transpired that none of her neighbours knew where she was. The day was closing in and cold rain was lashing Combret and its tight valley. Fortuné organised a search party. The men marched out of the village and up to the fields. They climbed beyond the pastures where, in a different season, the womenfolk would take the cows to fatten them up. They found Martha in a shepherd's hut, staring at the storm.

Fortuné asked his sister to stop wandering about the countryside after dark.

In Sophie's story, Martha was unable to stop her midnight wandering. Why was she unable to? What are these patterns that we lock ourselves into? What is it about our past that so strongly informs and guides our future?

The nights grew longer and colder. It was now midwinter. Again, Fortuné dropped off some provisions at Martha's house and called out. There was no reply. But it was late in the day; there wasn't time to drum up a search party. On this occasion, it would just be Fortuné and Odilon, another villager, who would go out looking for Martha. The two men took Fortuné's car and drove out of the village up a rough track. Fortuné had an idea where his sister might be – in the same hut as the first time she went missing. The higher the men went, the colder it got. It started to snow. They found the shepherd's hut empty. There were other makeshift refuges the men knew about, but they were further away, and the men could not reach them safely in the blizzard. Fortuné and Odilon returned to the car, but the engine would not start. They were snowed in. They now had little choice: they would have to wait out the blizzard and huddle together in the car for warmth. They would go back to Combret at sunrise.

The next morning another group of men set out from the village. This new search party was looking for Fortuné and Odilon. They found them in the car: Fortuné had died of exposure and Odilon was barely clinging to life.

The villagers went to Martha's house. A plume of smoke rose from the chimney. She was at home. Martha had made her way down from the mountains just as Fortuné and Odilon were driving up. There had been no need to search for Martha after all.

Combret buried its son Fortuné. But the villagers noticed that Martha showed little grief at his funeral. She was resigned, but she was spirited, too. In fact, she appeared light-headed. Her attitude was indefensible. In Martha's mind, her parents were gone, and now her brother was gone, but they were all present in her thoughts, so in a way they lived on.

This was what started it, Sophie explained. This was when the people of Combret started to hate the woman who wandered the fields after dark.

A new group of men formed. Their wives and mothers gave them encouragement: "It has to be done, it's for her own good." The village vet was summoned. The men went to Martha's door. This time, no soft words. The men dragged Martha out of her home.

Country folk know very well: when an animal does not stay still, when she runs off, when she goes where she should not go, the remedy is straightforward. A simple cut with a knife produces a limp. A lateral incision through the tendons of the heel of the beast. The vet took hold of his veterinary knife. Martha was held down. The vet made a cut through the tendons of Martha's heel, the same cut that farmers had asked him to make a dozen times.

In time, the wound closed. Martha was left hobbling in the way the villagers intended. A couple of women neighbours began to leave food on Martha's doorstep, as Fortuné had done. Martha was not bitter, wrote Sophie. Over the years, her blue eyes paled; her hair greyed. She aged, slowly. Limping, Martha still walked the fields at night.

***

Sophie's story had not quite reached its conclusion. There was to be a final twist.

One day there was a knock on Martha's door. Martha paid no attention. By now, she had turned her back on the rest of the village;

she had no reason to open the door. But the knocking didn't stop. It was loud and urgent. Martha approached the door and listened to the voice on the other side.

"Come on Martha, it's Georges! Open the door, just for a moment."

"I can't. I'm in no fit state."

There was a pause. Martha continued: "How are you? How are the children?"

"They're fine. But what about you? That's what interests me. How are you? Open the door, I promise I won't say anything to anyone."

"But Georges, I don't see people any more…"

The conversation continued in this vein for some time. Martha said that she couldn't open the door because she wasn't dressed to receive visitors, and anyway she was too old. Georges countered that none of that was a reason to lock herself away. Then Georges said that the conversation through Martha's door was making him hungry and thirsty. This was always going to be a winning argument in the French countryside.

Martha opened the door. Sophie wrote: *When Martha finally gave in, it was out of a certain respect for the man on the other side of the door, and also because the man intimidated her.*

Georges was Martha's friend. They had played together as children. Georges had been sent from Paris to Combret during the War. His parents had hoped he would be safe there, miles from anywhere, miles from the guns of any German soldiers. As an adult, he had built a life and a profession from next to nothing. He had sent his children off confidently into the world. He was a grandfather.

And now, Georges just wanted to see Martha's face. The proof that she was still alive. Sophie wrote:

It was an act of one survivor towards another survivor.

More years passed. Each time Georges came to Combret, he knocked on Martha's door. Martha still walked the fields at night, one good foot, one bad foot. The life and traditions of Combret stayed mostly the same, *only at night things were stranger, more ironic, and somehow more exotic.*

On one such night, the quiet of the village was shaken by a woman's cry, long and shrill, turning into an anguished moan. Just as it was about to fade, just as the owner of the voice was about to expire, the voice became a laugh. The woman had found a final reserve of strength. Her final act was a deep, vigorous laugh that filled the air.

It was Martha's voice, wrote Sophie.

Martha had died.

***

In the early 1990s, Sophie sat down and wrote a story about a woman living alone in a house in an isolated village. In Sophie's story, a man knocks on the woman's door, he is insistent, he keeps knocking and he calls out repeatedly. Finally, the woman opens the door. Georges – the man at the door – wanted Martha no harm, he only wanted to see her face, to see that she was still alive.

Several years later, in a remote corner of Ireland, a couple of days before Christmas, 1996, Sophie Toscan du Plantier was alone in her house in the middle of the night. There was a knock at her door. Sophie opened it. Her visitor was someone she did not fear. In Ireland, just as in the Combret described in Sophie's story, the still land was disturbed by a scream. Later, interviewed by the Guards, a farmer living a mile away from Sophie reported that he had heard a strange noise in the middle of the night, but thought it must have been the bark of a dog or the cry of a wild animal. It was only when he heard about the Frenchwoman's murder that the farmer put two and two together, and wondered if the scream might have come from the track outside the whitewashed house at Toormore.

After Sophie's murder, Marguerite Bouniol kept Sophie's stories and journals in an old filing cabinet. Occasionally Marguerite showed the stories to journalists. Members of the Justice Committee enjoyed seeing them and reading them – they were a tangible reminder of Sophie's talent, her spirit. The filing cabinet contained the journal from Sophie's 1989 trip to India, the journey where she saw the effigies of Kali, the Indian goddess of death, float away on the dark river in Calcutta. It also contained a story entitled *Love of the Land*, set in Ireland, which describes a fox that comes out at night to hunt a flock of sheep. In this story, the fox bides his time. He sees the lambs and checks them out one by one to figure out which are the weakest. At no point do the sheep see the fox; at no point do they smell him. The moon is almost full, illuminating the animals in the field. Sophie was an observer, but the fox drew her in, forcing her to become his companion in the hunt. Later, Sophie watched as a ewe attempted to revive a lamb which had been set upon. But it was too late, the fox's attack had been too fierce. The lamb did not have the strength to get up.

Sophie was a young woman in the prime of her life, and yet she wrote about death. She told the women she was closest to that she would die young. On one level, Sophie's Martha story contains a well-worn cliché of horror fiction: the vulnerable young woman alone in an isolated house and the scary knock on the door. The viewer, or the reader, knows who is knocking on the door, but the woman does not. When you know what happened to the writer, you read the Martha story differently. The tale is not merely poignant – it is spooky.

***

Many people will have surely read about the murder of Sophie Toscan du Plantier and wondered from time to time: what if? Of course, it would have been much better for Sophie's family and her grieving husband if the assailant's DNA had been harvested from the scene of the crime. This would not have brought Sophie back, but it would have saved her loved ones from the nightmare of their long and painful quest for justice. As things stand, our contemporary interest in forensics and 'CSI' TV shows risks us – as observers, and perhaps one day as members of a jury – demanding that usable DNA evidence is required in every case of a violent physical attack. Some prosecutors call this the 'CSI effect', an insistence on the value of forensics, above all other types of evidence. 'Every contact leaves a trace' is a maxim of forensic science. But whatever trace had been left at the crime scene in Toormore, it was not detected.

In Ireland in 1996, the science of DNA harvesting was in its infancy. The Guards were poorly prepared to deal with a complicated murder. For some individual officers, it was the first murder they had investigated. Some aspects of the investigation were botched. At the outset, the crime scene was not perfectly secured. The Gardaí lost witness statements and – as I have mentioned – they also lost the blood-spattered gate near where Sophie's body was found. For such a large and important piece of evidence to become mislaid in a Garda storage facility is frankly mind-boggling. Meanwhile, the Guards took away some of Bailey's items of clothing and footwear for analysis as late as 10th February 1996, the day of Bailey's first arrest. Surely this could have been done sooner? Also, the brambles and briars which Sophie and her killer ran through were not adequately analysed. Remarkably, TV news bulletins from 1996 show them being hacked down almost indiscriminately. Anyone probing the mystery needed to accept this situation and move on.

Meanwhile, the people who approached the Guards in good faith with evidence about Bailey's confessions, and about what Bailey said to them, did their duty. In some cases, they deserved better from the Irish Office of the Director of Public Prosecutions. Some deserved better than to have the DPP implicitly criticise the good faith of their own testimony, albeit in a position paper that was supposed to be confidential, and which had surely been authored under that assumption.

Where does this leave us? Who murdered Sophie Toscan du Plantier? I offer no proof, no evidence beyond reasonable doubt. But I have a deep-seated conviction – an *intime conviction*.

Bailey's assertion that he did not know Sophie appears to me to be contradicted by the Kali connection. I cannot believe that Bailey's reference to Kali when he was talking to French journalist Caroline Mangez came from anyone but Sophie – the odds of a strange coincidence are remote.

If you were going to make a case against Bailey, it might look like this. First of all, there is no motive as such. But I do believe Bailey knew Sophie, and that would have given him a pretext to knock on her door that winter's night. He also had opportunity – no alibi for much of the night of the murder. As demonstrated at the trial in Paris, his phone calls in the late morning and early afternoon after the crime appear to show he was already aware of the murder, and did not need Eddie Cassidy of the *Examiner* to bring him up to speed on it. His confessions to Malachi Reed, the Shelleys and Bill Fuller seem to me to be precisely this – the confessions of a man who has brutally murdered a woman. There is ample evidence that Bailey had no significant marks on his hands and forearms, and on his forehead, on the evening before the crime – but he had all of these after the murder was committed. There is thus perhaps a case against Bailey without recourse to the tarnished testimony of Marie Farrell.

Then again, were Bailey's alleged confessions the rants of a man under intolerable stress? Did he get caught up in his own exaggerations and his desire to be in the limelight? And, assuming Bailey was the murderer, how did he get briar marks on his forearms if he was wearing an overcoat that night? He might have driven to Toormore and left his coat in the car, in spite of the cold – this was always a possibility. Finally, a key plank of any defence argument was that there was no forensic evidence connecting Bailey to the crime scene.

Ian Bailey has strenuously and repeatedly denied knowing Sophie Toscan du Plantier, just as he has always said he had nothing at all to do with her murder. He also firmly denies that he was the mystery man in Sophie's car.

But if Bailey was the very tall man in the passenger seat of Sophie's hire car recalled by Sean Murray at his petrol station in Skibbereen, it follows that Bailey had a conversation with her. It might have been on that final drive to her holiday home that Sophie mentioned Kali to Bailey. Guy Girard flagged Bailey as being a man interested in the "theme of violence". Given that Sophie had mentioned Bailey's interest in violence to Girard shortly before she left for Ireland, the topic could have been a natural discussion subject for them. The logistics of the meeting could have been straightforward: Bailey could have found out when Sophie was arriving in Ireland – possibly from Sophie herself – and worked out which flight she was taking. He could have gone to the airport on Friday, 20th December, introduced himself well away from the only CCTV camera that caught Sophie's image, and asked her for a ride back to the Mizen. Otherwise, he might have arranged by phone to have her pick him up in Skibbereen town centre, for instance.

In this scenario, the name of the Indian goddess of death stuck in Bailey's mind to the extent that, when he met another young Frenchwoman a few weeks after the murder, *Paris Match* journalist Caroline Mangez, who resembled Sophie somewhat, the name Kali – the Indian goddess of "destruction", as Bailey put it – slipped out in conversation with her. Meanwhile, Sophie's strange state of mind in the period directly before her death was revealed by her friend Yvonne Ungerer, who told the Guards (and Bailey, for that matter) that when Sophie passed by her house at Three Castle Head on the day before she was killed, she appeared anxious and troubled. On top of all of this, we have the unusual way she took leave of her mother before she flew to Cork (saying to her *"adieu,"* farewell) and the creepy discussion of her short life-line with her mother and her aunt a number of weeks before that last journey.

After years digging into this often baffling case, I am approaching the end of my amateur investigation. I hope that one day the person or people withholding information on Sophie's killer, should they exist, will find the courage to come forward and tell the authorities what they know. For Sophie's long-suffering parents, time is surely running out.

One puzzle remains. Why did Sophie leave the anthology of poetry in her kitchen open at the page of W.B. Yeats' *A Dream of Death*? Again, let us rewind a bit. I can understand a kind of continuum: an interest in death that began by being not especially morbid, but was rather – and I hesitate to use this word – *sensuous*. It appeared to have been triggered by Sophie's trip to India and the sense there that mortality, *our* mortality, can be seen differently. In India, death generally is not swept under the carpet or rendered a taboo; it is a part, so to speak, of life, part of our common existence. The hundreds of effigies of Kali which Sophie saw bobbing away on the inky tropical water in Calcutta are evidence of this.

India has long had a particular impact on western travellers, especially young ones. For a period in the 1980s and 1990s, France had a diplomat stationed in the country tasked with helping French visitors exhibiting 'India syndrome'. This refers to how some westerners come to India and embark on a journey of spiritual self-discovery. You could argue that setting aside a time and space for reflection – looking inwards, rather than outwards – is no bad thing. In some rare cases, though, this self-discovery can cause a seismic change in their personality and worldview. Often, 'India syndrome' disappears when the person gets on a plane and goes home. Sometimes, it lingers, as may have been the case with Sophie. (Not so Sophie's friend and mentor, Catherine Clément, who hosted Sophie in India in 1989. Clément wrote that you could not avoid seeing people with open sores, people who were deformed; there was disease, dirt, even corpses floating on the rivers. However, none of this ever made Clément fearful.)

The page left open at the W.B. Yeats poem *A Dream of Death* does not feel like a coincidence. Its account of a young woman dying in a foreign country *by no accustomed hand* is startling when you know what happened to Sophie, hours or perhaps even a matter of minutes later.

But the poem also does not feel like a message. Sophie fought hard and fought bravely when her assailant came calling. She fought to the last. She did everything to avoid dying a stranger in a foreign land. Why she marked her anthology of poetry at that particular poem, we will probably never know for sure. Whether coincidence or not, the poem seemed to have been eerily prescient.

***

For much of that long, hot, unique summer of 2020, Ian Bailey worked the farmers' market in Schull, selling his baked goods and a few kitchen utensils carved from wood. Thomas had a selection of small paintings on the stall – her blustery, foamy seascapes. Far from retiring to the Prairie and closing the curtains and keeping a low profile, Bailey and Thomas's market stall now prominently featured a board with a large photo of Bailey on both sides. It was the same image he used for the cover of his latest poetry collection – a close-up of Bailey's face, his lips making a half-smile, wearing a cowboy hat. Tourists and the curious approached the stall, and had a bit of a chat. Not even the pandemic kept them away. Some locals looked on, appalled.

There was the beginning of a chill in the air. On the other side of the square from my apartment block a three-quarters moon hung in the black emptiness. Five weeks to the extradition ruling. A sort of ending was looming.

I thought of the two of them on their stall, white clouds scuttling over a wide Atlantic sky, the constant screech of seabirds down at the harbour, where they met, when Bailey was working at the fish factory. I thought of them loading up the stall. Packing, unpacking. Putting the little price tags on all the stuff. Counting the takings. Then the ride back to the Prairie over well-worn roads, known roads.

What do they talk about in the car together? In the silences, what goes through their minds? What is it they choose not to say to each other?

The unnamed detective who came out from Cork City on Christmas Eve 1996 and saw Sophie's body on the track, said that her killer was a *fucking headcase*. He wondered why the killer used so much violence when he could have strangled her and it would have been over in seconds. The woman's face, destroyed. *She was a human being*, he lamented, *You wouldn't do that to a dog*. Over time, Bailey became the detective's prime suspect.

The detective also had a theory, at least early on in the investigation. He thought that Bailey had blanked the murder perfectly from his mind. The detective had an idea that Bailey simply could not remember he had killed the young woman with blond hair and freckles and the glamorous life and the money and the promising career in the film world. Apparently, this type of amnesia sometimes strikes murderers who carry out their crimes with extraordinary violence. On the other hand, maybe the detective got it wrong. If Bailey was the murderer, maybe he kept his crime front and centre. Maybe he was unable to forget it or keep it conveniently in some deep recess of his mind. Maybe he did not blank it out at all.

Chapter 24

THE UNRAVELLING

On 12th October 2020 at the High Court in Dublin, Mr Justice Paul Burns delivered his 64-page ruling on France's third attempt at getting Ireland to turn over Ian Bailey to the French authorities. I had heard fresh rumours that things were likely to go Bailey's way. Still, I couldn't help but feel deflated when the result flashed up on the screen of my mobile phone: *JUDGE DENIES EXTRADITION*.

"The background history to this application is long and complex," Justice Burns noted. It certainly was – in fact, the judge's observation felt like the understatement of the year. However, to the dismay of Sophie's family and friends, Justice Burns went on to say: "It must be remembered that the guilt or innocence of the respondent in respect of the murder of Madame Toscan du Plantier is not an issue in these proceedings." This meant, in effect, that the conviction of Ian Bailey in the Paris courthouse in May 2019 was not going to weigh on his decision.

Pierre-Louis and the members of the Sophie Justice Committee had hoped – perhaps even expected – that the outcome of the murder trial would be a deciding factor. After all, France was a fellow member of the European Union. Ireland had signed up to the European Arrest Warrant scheme, just as France had done. How could the Irish courts throw out France's application for the surrender of Ian Bailey on this third occasion, when Bailey's conviction was a game-changer? I knew the French side would be bitter – it was as if the Paris trial and the guilty verdict had counted for absolutely nothing.

What was at stake, Justice Burns pointed out, was whether the Irish state, represented by the Minister for Justice, was entitled to execute an order for the surrender of Ian Bailey to France. One of the barristers for the Irish state had argued that there was a "strong public interest" in shipping Bailey to France. But the key point appeared to be the principle of reciprocity. Following an amendment, Irish law now provided for some degree of "extraterritorial jurisdiction", but only when the alleged perpetrator was Irish or was resident in Ireland. In plain English, this meant that an Irish court could try an Irish national, or an Irish resident, for a serious crime committed overseas. The judge flagged this aspect in his ruling, but it was not a winning argument. "One may look at it another way by reversing the circumstances," said Mr Justice Burns. "If an Irish citizen was murdered in France by a UK national, who was ordinarily resident in France, Ireland would not exercise extraterritorial jurisdiction or seek the extradition of the offender. Thus, the requisite reciprocity does not exist."

Ian Bailey's legal team had scored a significant victory. Outside the High Court in Dublin, Bailey's solicitor said that his client was "extremely relieved" at the outcome, adding that "he always expresses his sadness and his sympathy for the late Madame Toscan du Plantier while at the same time maintaining his innocence in relation to any connection to that dreadful crime". Ian Bailey now, his solicitor said, intended to return to West Cork and try to get on with the rest of his life.

Bailey later told the Irish press that "I have been fighting for justice for almost 24 years [and] people tend to forget that".

On that windy Dublin afternoon, there was one immediate

unknown. Would the Irish state appeal Justice Burns' ruling and take the matter to the Supreme Court? Two weeks later, we found out: no, the Irish state decided not to lodge an appeal. France's options at getting Bailey surrendered to France now appeared exhausted, short of taking the matter to the institutions of the European Union, and lobbying there. The Sophie Justice Committee was, of course, aghast that there was to be no appeal. As for the argument of a lack of reciprocity, which had been a main plank of the ruling, the Justice Committee released a statement saying that while the reciprocity argument might at first sight appear uncontroversial, in the circumstances it was "totally spurious".

I had not called Bailey after the ruling was handed down on 12th October, but when the news broke that the State was not going to lodge an appeal, I could not hold off any longer. He would be expecting me to phone him, and I wanted him to keep believing that I was one of his "supporters", at least for a little while longer.

As I selected his name in the contacts list on my mobile phone, I thought of something he had said at the Dublin courthouse in 2014. He told the court that he had hoped that a "cavalry" of journalists would gather to defend him, and ride to his rescue. When I first read the reference to a cavalry, I thought it was a colourful image – and an amusing one, thinking of some desk-bound journalists I had known – but nothing more. Now I wondered: had Bailey really meant it? Had he persuaded himself that his case was so solid that fellow newspaper writers were bound to sign up for his cause?

He certainly could provide a useful soundbite. Over the years, that ability had not changed. In late October, Bailey told an Irish radio journalist that the reason that the murder of Sophie Toscan du Plantier was still unsolved was that there were people with information on the killing who were prevented from coming forward for reasons of "omertà". Bailey was referencing the southern Italian code of silence about criminal activity. This was not exactly Bailey's longstanding claim that there was a "French connection" to Sophie's murder, but the use of the foreign word seemed to point a finger to the European continent.

I dialled his number.

Bailey picked up.

"You must be delighted, Ian," I said.

I was a bit surprised that Bailey did not seem as upbeat as I had imagined he would be. "I thought I would be more relieved," he said to me. "I'm in a kind of vacuum here."

Bailey had recently been stopped by the Guards on the Mizen and subsequently charged with driving under the influence of drugs. It was "a certain green weed," said Bailey by way of explanation. He had made an appearance in court in Bantry a few days previously. Bailey was surprised when I did not know the full details of the drug-driving charge. After all, it had been reported in the press. Not for the first time, he suggested that I should put an alert in my internet search engine so I did not miss news of his life and exploits.

"Anyway," Bailey said, wrapping up our call, "it's always nice to hear a Scouse voice."

Bailey said the words "Scouse voice" with an approximate Scouse pronunciation.

"I think of the Beatles," he said, "I think of John Lennon."

"So do I," I replied, for no particular reason. Force of habit, I suppose. Sitting at his old wooden dining table in his Irish kitchen, or speaking on the phone, Bailey would say something about the Beatles or their songs, and I would say something along the same lines back to him. It was a rut I had fallen into – and one I needed to get myself out of.

***

The day after Justice Burns handed down his ruling, Pierre-Louis Baudey-Vignaud, Sophie's son, gave an interview to the French radio station RTL. In his introduction, the presenter told listeners that the crime was so barbaric and violent that Sophie's own mother barely recognised her daughter's face in the morgue in Cork City. *We're going to discuss the Sophie Toscan du Plantier case, or should I say the Ian Bailey case*, said the presenter, and it was at that moment that I felt a pang of pain for Pierre-Louis. It might have been a slip of the tongue on the part of the presenter – after all, Bailey was in the news both in Ireland and in France following the Dublin court ruling – but it showed just how far Sophie the adored mother, the cherished daughter, had been pushed into the background of the story.

The RTL presenter's questions were pertinent, and he put them kindly and respectfully to Pierre-Louis, but listening to the interview I remembered something that Daniel Toscan du Plantier had said. Daniel remarked that Bailey had made a kind of career out of the notoriety of his connection with the case, and Daniel was sometimes asked for news about Bailey when he was out and about in Paris. This had unsettled Daniel, to say the least. The sadness I felt for Pierre-Louis was compounded by the feeling that the same thing was now happening to him, two decades after it had happened to his late stepfather. Pierre-Louis was the expert on the case by virtue of the fact that it was his mother who had been murdered. But it also meant that he was taken to be someone who could explain Ian Bailey to a French audience. How much it must have disgusted him to do so, I thought.

I played over a sequence of the RTL recording several times. The pain in Pierre-Louis's voice was palpable.

Presenter: *Who is this strange Ian Bailey?*

Pierre-Louis: *Ian Bailey is a failure, socially, professionally, in terms of a family life. He's a drug taker, a drinker, he wrote in his private diaries that he wanted to kill his partner... He beat her up, twice to the point she ended up in hospital... He's a kind of stray dog going from bar to bar trying to find a meaning to his life.*

Pierre-Louis said that Irish justice has been a "shambles" from the beginning, although this was not necessarily true when it came to the Irish state, which had duly processed the European Arrest

Warrants on all three occasions. Meanwhile, the main aim of the Irish Director of Public Prosecutions was to avoid taking risks. As for the judge who had dealt with the latest attempt at extradition, Pierre-Louis regretted that – in his view – he had not found the required courage to look into the case in detail.

The presenter read out a brisk history of the case, including excerpts from the testimony of Malachi Reed, in which the teenager related that Bailey had told him that he had "smashed [Sophie's] brains in with a rock", and the evidence of Bill Fuller, who said that Bailey had told him that "you went too far and you had to finish her off". The details were maybe necessary for the radio programme, but how much it must have hurt Pierre-Louis, who had to listen to them all over again.

The presenter asked Pierre-Louis if he had ever seen Bailey. I knew he had, of course, and more than once. I knew it had been a severe shock to his system each time.

The last time Pierre-Louis had seen Bailey was when he was walking in Schull with his two children.

I was just a few yards away. He looked at me with a kind of arrogance.
Did he know who you were?
Of course he did.

***

I was now at the end of the road. I had packed away my notebooks and witness statements and press clippings in boxes, ready for storage. Six years of digging around, six years of trying to join the dots. I was ready to let go – almost. Before I did, there were a couple of things left for me to do. The first was to write a letter.

Dear Jules, it began, *I hope you and your daughters and grandchildren are well.*

I am writing to you to let you know that in the spring of 2021, I will be publishing a book on the murder of Sophie Toscan du Plantier. In the book, I set out strong evidence that Ian knew Sophie Toscan du Plantier. I also believe that this evidence, which is entirely new, shows that Ian and Sophie spoke about things that were profound and philosophical.

I printed the letter and signed it. I left it on my desk. I would send the letter to Jules in the New Year, towards the end of January or in February. For the moment, the letter could wait.

One thing that could not wait was a phone call. I had known for some time that this moment would come. My suspicions of Bailey were raised at the beginning of 2016 when he calmly asserted to me that Sean Murray had told us that he was not the passenger in Sophie's hire car on the afternoon of Friday, 20th December 1996, even though Murray had said nothing of the sort. On top of that, Bailey had flatly refused to cast his mind back to what he was doing on that Friday afternoon – to construct an alibi, in other words.

Then there was the evidence – which was "overwhelming", according to the French prosecutor at Bailey's murder trial – that Bailey had killed Sophie. The more I studied that evidence, the deeper I delved into the Garda file, the more I spoke with witnesses, the clearer things became in my mind. Before that, though, I had hoped that Bailey was innocent, and that I could help him prove it. After all, who wants to share meals in a country kitchen and drives in the countryside and pints in the pub with a man who killed a young mother with such appalling violence?

Finally, there was the Kali connection. Why Bailey had given himself away with the unbidden mention of the Indian goddess was a mystery. Was it some sort of game, perhaps? Did Bailey enjoy taking risks? Not so much the stooping, greying Bailey I had got to know, but the younger Ian Bailey. In January 1997, he was a confident, eloquent man approaching his 40th birthday. Had that younger Bailey treated the aftermath of the murder at the whitewashed house at Toormore as a sort of chase, always keeping a few steps ahead of his pursuers?

Of course, I would have liked to have put all this to Bailey in person, face to face. However, longstanding coronavirus restrictions in Ireland meant that meeting people in their homes was out of the question. A partial loosening of the rules at the beginning of December 2020 still meant a long quarantine for travellers entering Ireland from overseas. My manuscript was due at the publishers in the middle of the same month. Quite simply, I was out of time. The previous summer, I had told Bailey that I would fly to Ireland in the autumn to ask him a few more questions. I was also hoping to get my hands on the memory stick or bunch of documents that I thought Bailey would have given me if the extradition ruling had gone the other way, had he been bundled on a plane to Paris. With Bailey now seemingly safe from the long arm of French justice, there would be no need for him to give me any files for safekeeping.

The upshot was that Bailey would have to find out that I had ceased being his "supporter" over a phone line.

I thought of Daniel Toscan du Plantier, Sophie's second husband. *I was tempted to go to see him*, Daniel told an interviewer a couple of years after his wife's murder. The interview took place in an opulent reception room, beside a blazing fire. Daniel sat in a magnificent armchair, intricately carved wood, richly upholstered. Of course, there was no way to challenge Bailey discreetly, and Daniel knew this. He never did walk up the drive of Bailey's Prairie cottage on the Mizen.

But supposing he had done?

I would have said to him, "You were the last person, she and I had just hung up. So, you tell me…" Daniel did not finish his sentence; he did not need to. It's the *why*. The depravity of the crime makes it unfathomable, and the same depravity is part of the reason why solving the murder is no less urgent than it was at the very beginning, even though nearly 24 years have now passed since Sophie was killed.

He killed her, and he's slowly dying from it, Daniel said. *I pity him. Hand me a gun, put me in front of him, I'll put the gun down on the table. I'm against the death penalty, even in this personal case.*

I dialled Bailey's mobile phone. A weekday evening, first week of December 2020, close to nine o'clock, Irish time, an hour later in Brussels, where I was. I was sitting at my desk, a sheet of paper in my hand, questions written out. After 10 seconds, Bailey picked up. I asked him if he could hear me. "I can hear you," he boomed, "can you hear me?"

I told him that I could hear him loud and clear. I asked after Jules. Bailey replied that she was well.

"Ian, this is not an easy call to make, so I'm going to cut to the chase, if that's okay with you."

I paused. Bailey was waiting for what I had to say.

"So, Ian, tell me what happened on the night you went up there."

"What?" Bailey replied, incredulous. "What are you going on about?"

"The night you killed Sophie. What did she do to wind you up? What did she do to make you lash out? What made you so angry? Did she hit you first?"

"You've got the wrong man, Nick. You've got the wrong man."

I was speeding up now, trying to pronounce each word clearly, but doing my best to ensure Bailey heard me out: "You figured she would be happy to see you, but she wasn't. She wasn't calling you 'Ian' anymore, now it was *Monsieur, Monsieur* and she was furious…"

Bailey said it again: "You've got the wrong man."

Then I said to him: "Ian, you left a clue after the murder. Evidence that you knew Sophie. I don't know if you left that clue on purpose…

Again, I was talking quickly. I wanted to get to the end of my list of questions. I wanted to finish my script for the call.

"…Why did you leave that clue? Why did you do it?"

Once again, there was a pause. I thought I heard the sound of Bailey breathing heavily at the other end of the line.

This time, Bailey said nothing more. The line went dead. He had hung up.

302

ACKNOWLEDGEMENTS

I would like to thank, in particular, Steve Langridge, Jack O'Driscoll and Michael Sheridan. This book would have been difficult to write without their great help and support. Thanks also to Jack O'Driscoll for drawing the maps of County Cork, the Mizen peninsula, and the crime scene.

I would also like to thank Mary Foster, Katiana Velazco, John McGartoll, Paul O'Driscoll, Andrew Forde, Arianna Boarina, Sophie Rieu, Olivier Proust, Bill Hogan, Viv Hargreaves, John Hawkins, Martin Westlake, Colm Quinn, Frank Ledwidge, Ligia Mora, Jonathan O'Sullivan, Donal Macdougald, Jan Robberecht, Peter Eade and Stewart Reynolds, together with, of course, the members of the Sophie Justice Committee (*L'Association pour la vérité sur l'assassinat de Sophie Toscan du Plantier née Bouniol*), especially Jean-Antoine Bloc.

My gratitude, too, to my agent Ben Clark of the Soho Agency, for his hard work and steadfast belief in this project. A big thank you, as well, to Jo Sollis, Chris Brereton and Simon Monk, my editors at Mirror Books, and their team.

I would also like to pay tribute to the fine reporting on this case by Barry Roche, Southern Correspondent for the *Irish Times*, which I have frequently used for fact-checking. The following books provided useful background: *Sophie Toscan du Plantier: Un déni de justice*, by Jean-Antoine Bloc and Julien Cros (Éditions Max Milo); *Mémoire*, by Catherine Clément (Champs); *La vie passera comme un rêve*, by Gilles

Jacob (Robert Laffont); *A History of the Fastnet Lighthouse*, by James Morrissey (Crannóg Books); and *A Dream of Death*, by Ralph Riegel (Gill Books), particularly its account of the Irish media coverage of the Sophie Toscan du Plantier story over the years. The archives of the film and TV section of the Bibliothèque nationale de France were also a big help in researching this book.

CONTENTS

THE BRITISH
TOMMY IN THE
GREAT WAR

THE purpose of this book is to act as a guide to the life of the average soldier of the 'poor bloody infantry' in the Great War from joining to demobilisation. Among other topics, it will examine what he ate, where he slept, what he wore, how he fought and what he endured. Most families have someone who served in the First World War; this book might help interpret the fragments of memory passed down to them.

The Great War was truly a world war, with campaigns fought by British troops on three continents – Europe, Asia and Africa. For the most part, the Western Front (situated in Western Europe) was both to demand most attention and to consume, in ever increasing numbers, men and materiel. This front became a continuous line of trenches stretching from Switzerland to the North Sea, 475 miles across varied terrain. British and Commonwealth troops were to occupy 120 miles of the front, in the strategically significant zone straddling the Belgo-French border, extending south deep into Picardy. Engaged from August 1914 at the Battle of Mons, the British Expeditionary Force (BEF) was to grow in size and stature to become the backbone of the Allied effort in the closing months of 1918, in campaigns that defeated Imperial Germany – with 5,399,563 troops from across the British Empire employed on the Western Front alone, the vast majority from the United Kingdom. At Mons (1914), First and Second Ypres (1914), Loos (1915), the Somme (1916), Arras, Messines, Third Ypres and Cambrai (1917), the German offensives and Allied advance of 1918 were all to take their toll of casualties on the BEF. Elsewhere, British troops were among Allied forces engaged in the costly gamble at Gallipoli in 1915, and in other campaigns against the Ottoman Empire in Mesopotamia and Palestine from 1916. They would face the Bulgarians in Salonika, the Austrians in Italy and the Germans in East Africa. In all, the United Kingdom would suffer 3,058,985 casualties out of 5,704,416 soldiers enlisted, comprising: 724,407 killed; 2,064,451 wounded; and 270,117 missing or prisoners of war.

Battles in all cases would be bloody and give rise to the widely accepted view that the Great War was one of unending horror – but the truth is more

Opposite: One of the iconic photographs of the Great War: British soldiers silhouetted against the skyline on the Broodseinde Ridge, near Ypres, October 1917. [IWM Q.2978]

5

rounded, with long periods in which the British soldier would not be directly engaged with his enemy. Lieutenant Charles Carrington of the Royal Warwickshire Regiment described a typical year in 1916: 101 days in the front and support lines; 120 days in reserve; seventy-three days out on rest; and seventy-two days travelling, at the base being trained and on leave – in total 28 per cent of the time under direct fire. Although an officer's experience (that of the ordinary 'Tommy' being perhaps more arduous), this would be by no means untypical. This book follows the same cycle.

One image of the British soldier in the trenches has attained an iconic status above all others. This photograph (reproduced in part on page 4) famously depicts soldiers silhouetted on the Broodseinde Ridge in Belgium, burdened with their equipment, bent under their distinctive steel helmets, and carrying their snub-nosed rifles. This image from the Ypres Salient has

At the end of the line: a soldier of the 4th Battalion East Lancashire Regiment on duty at the Belgian coast in September 1917. [IWM Q.2875]

A late-war Service Dress tunic of a corporal in the Honourable Artillery Company, an elite London Territorial battalion, together with a set of 1908 pattern webbing equipment.

become one of a handful that is taken to epitomise the British soldier of the First World War. Although the infantrymen portrayed seem archaic compared with today's laden and camouflaged soldier, the uniforms and equipment of the British Tommy were actually advanced for their time, perhaps more so than those of his fellow combatants. In order to gain the best possible understanding of the life of the British soldier in the trenches, it is important to resolve those silhouettes into an image of a fighting soldier at war.

The khaki (Hindi-Urdu for dust) uniform worn by the troops was first developed in 1902 as a replacement for the traditional centuries-old red coat of the British infantryman. Known as Service Dress, its tunic was characteristically loose fitting, with a turned-down collar, patches at the shoulder to bear the extra wear from the position of the rifle butt in action, and four pockets with button-down flaps. Shoulder straps bore regimental insignia

Top left: Soldier of the Duke of Wellington's Regiment (West Riding) with sleeve trade (proficiency) badges for Machine Gunner (MG) and Range Taker (R). Such badges marked out specialists who gained status and extra pay.

Top right: Veteran soldiers of the Essex Regiment, c.1917, 'somewhere in France'. The soldier on the left is wearing a simplified 'economy' version of the standard Service Dress. Good-conduct stripes and various divisional and battalion insignia may be seen. The man in the centre has been awarded the Military Medal, and bears a wound stripe.

Right: The stiff-brimmed 1905 Service Dress cap of 1914 (with Royal Engineers cap badge), compared with the 1917 pattern soft 'trench cap' (West Yorkshire Regiment). The trench cap was adopted when the steel helmet became the standard headgear in the frontline trenches.

in the form of brass shoulder titles. Throughout the war, insignia were added to the sleeves of the ordinary soldiers — the non-officer 'other ranks' — including rank badges and specialist 'trade' badges (such as those for machine gunners, scouts and so on); divisional insignia would be added late war. 'Old sweats' — soldiers with a long service — could be identified by a series of inverted chevrons on their lower left sleeve, one for every two years served with a clean record of service. Wound stripes — worn from 1916 denoting the receipt of a wound in action — would be worn beneath to complete the effect. From January 1918, smaller coloured chevrons were worn on the lower sleeve of the right arm — one for each year's service overseas.

British soldiers went to war in an awkward khaki peaked cap with stiffened rim; in late 1914 a softer winter 'trench cap' was issued, known universally as the 'gor' blimey', with flaps that could be fastened under the chin for extra warmth. Unloved by Sergeant Majors, it would be replaced by the issue of a simpler soft cap, a stitched peak being its only concession to smartness.

Service Dress trousers had a narrow leg to be worn with puttees, a military fashion derived, like the khaki Service Dress, from the British experience in India, 'puttee' coming from the Hindi word for bandage. Puttees were meant to provide a covering for the lower leg that would give greater support and protection. In fact, tying the puttee too tight was to exacerbate the problem of 'trench foot', a condition akin to frostbite resulting from restricted blood circulation and prolonged water immersion. Puttees and wool socks were worn with the 'regulation' field boot, which was roughly square-toed, produced in thick hide with the rough side out, heavily dubbined. Soles were cleated with metal studs – hard on the feet while marching on the stone-block pavé roads of France.

Officers' Service Dress consisted of a tunic with open step-down collars that was worn with shirt and tie (of all shades of khaki, according to taste), finished with a brown-leather Sam Browne belt. Distinct from their men, officers were easily identified by snipers, particularly when rank stars and crowns were borne in plain sight on the cuff. Some took it upon themselves to move these badges to the shoulder straps, or wear 'Tommy tunics' in battle. Breeches of Bedford cord, a peaked cap and a variety of footwear – from polished riding top-boots and high-laced 'trench boots' to simple brown ankle boots and puttees – finished the ensemble.

A well turned-out soldier of the Welsh Regiment, c.1915, with fancy puttee patterns, and full webbing equipment.

Service Dress tunic belonging to an unknown Captain of the Loyal North Lancashire Regiment, pictured with typical Sam Browne belt, holster and ammunition pouch. The shirt and tie, Sam Browne and cuff rank insignia would provide a target for enemy marksmen.

Left: A typical Highland soldier of a Kitchener battalion, complete with glengarry, swagger stick, kilt and khaki apron.

Below: The Tam o'Shanter: the standard headgear of most Highland soldiers by the end of the war.

Many Scottish regiments were kilted: the kilt was warm to wear with its many folds of woollen tartan; the disadvantage of the folds was their propensity to harbour lice, as well as their ability to soak up vast amounts of water. From late 1914 it was usual to wear it covered by a simple apron of khaki cloth. The Highland soldier wore a range of caps and bonnets, early war the commonest being the glengarry, but also the beret-like Balmoral bonnet and larger Tam o'Shanter in a variety of patterns with diced borders, coloured pompoms and tartan backing for the usually flamboyant Scottish cap badge.

Surviving in the open in all weathers meant warm clothing was a must. The issue greatcoat was cumbersome; more often than not it would be left in the transport lines. Instead, an outlandish, often multi-coloured goatskin sleeveless jerkin was issued in late 1914, mostly replaced from 1915 with a hard-wearing brown-leather version. Protection from the wet weather of

Flanders was through an issue groundsheet, later redesigned as a rain cape. At the other extreme, a cotton version of the Service Dress, Khaki Drill (KD), was the standard uniform issued for warm climates. Trousers were issued, but often shorts were worn with socks and puttees – these were also adopted in the summer months on the Western Front. KDs were usually worn with the 'Wolseley Pattern' cork sun helmet, which provided protection only from the sun (and not from bullets).

The steel helmet was an innovation that was born out of the necessity of modern war, and it stands out in all images of the soldier in the trenches from 1916 onwards. Before then, soft caps were worn in the front line; as a consequence, head wounds were common. The British helmet was invented by John Brodie and was pressed from non-magnetic steel, its dish-like form and wide brim intended to supply protection from shrapnel bursts above the lines. The original War Office Pattern, first introduced in 1915, had a sharp, unprotected rim; a steel rim was later added.

Below left: Early war portrait of a soldier of the King's (Liverpool) Regiment, in stiff cap and greatcoat.

Below right: Private Robert Wheatley of the Yorkshire Regiment in Khaki Drill, Wolseley helmet and 1903 pattern bandolier at Mudros harbour; he would be killed at Gallipoli in 1915.

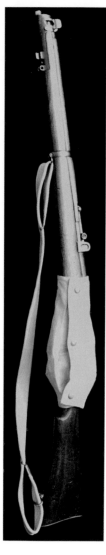

Right: A Mark I 'Brodie' helmet, the standard British steel helmet of the Great War.

Below: The Mills Grenade. Introduced in 1915, it was to become one of the most effective weapons of trench warfare. This one dates from March 1916.

Below: Partial set of 1914 leather equipment. Produced when webbing was in short supply, it nevertheless gave good service, mostly for the men of Kitchener's Army.

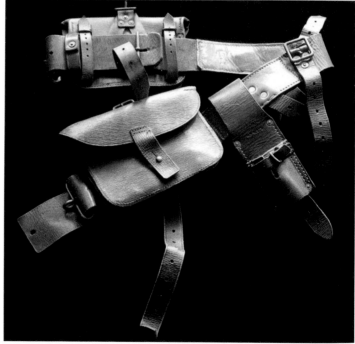

Above: The Short, Magazine, Lee Enfield rifle (SMLE), the standard weapon of the British army. Carried by a webbing sling, its breech cover was developed to prevent fouling from the mud of the trenches.

The 'snub-nosed' weapon of the Broodseinde Ridge photograph was the Short, Magazine, Lee Enfield rifle (SMLE), the principal weapon of the British soldier from 1902. Its ammunition clips or 'chargers' held five Mark VII .303 calibre bullets, the rifle magazine holding ten altogether. With the development of this short rifle came the need for a longer bayonet – 17 inches long; this was required because the likely enemy of the British soldier would be equipped with the longer Mauser-type rifle, meaning that Tommy would be at a disadvantage in a lunging bayonet fight.

As the war developed, the hand grenade was to replace the rifle as the primary offensive weapon of trench warfare; it required little training to use and, placed correctly, grenades had a wide kill-radius that was more efficient than the well-placed shot of even the most skilled marksman. The British army went to war in 1914 with an extremely cumbersome 16-inch stick-grenade, replaced in 1915 by temporary solutions – the 'jam tin' of 1915 being typical, literally a tin filled with explosive gun cotton and shrapnel balls; other short-lived types were also produced. But it was with the introduction of the Mills Grenade in May 1915 that the grenade was to become widely used. The secret of the Mills' success lay with its ignition system, using a spring-loaded striker, activated when a pin was removed

Soldier of the Royal Fusiliers on guard at a railway station, armed with SMLE and fixed bayonet. His webbing equipment is of a pattern issued only to territorial battalions.

and a lever released; a four-second fuse was initiated, during which time the bomber had to throw the grenade.

The equipment carried by the British soldier in the First World War has been much maligned by some historians, who suggest that its burden was to impede movement and prevent him from leaving the trenches fast enough. In fact, the 1908 webbing equipment used by the British soldier was innovative and well balanced: a complete 'system'. The set consisted of belt, cross straps, left and right cartridge carriers (designed to carry 150 rounds in ten pouches, each holding three five-round chargers), water bottle, entrenching tool head carrier and bayonet frog. In addition, there was a small haversack, and a large pack (not usually seen in the front line). The equipment could be taken off like a jacket, and, on the march, the 3-inch-wide belt could be unbuckled for comfort. It was to be no more of a burden than that carried by other soldiers throughout the twentieth and twenty-first centuries.

The Webley .455 calibre service revolver. Large and cumbersome, it nevertheless was effective at stopping an enemy.

In 1914, due to supply difficulties with the webbing equipment sets, leather versions were issued. These had distinctive, simple leather ammunition pouches, designed to take fifty cartridges, each in five-round chargers — one hundred rounds in all. The resulting set is most commonly seen being worn by the men of Kitchener's New Army. Mounted troops were

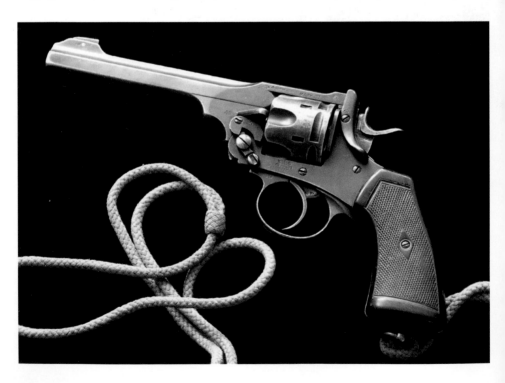

Fully equipped Scottish soldiers of the Highland Light Infantry rest on their way to the front near Ypres in September 1917. [IWM Q.6006]

to carry their ammunition in equally distinctive leather bandoliers, part of an equipment set first issued in 1903. These bandoliers usually distinguish men of the Royal Field Artillery in wartime photographs. Officers would similarly wear their equipment festooned about their person, supported by the leather Sam Browne belt, and armed most commonly with a .455 calibre Webley revolver, carried in a leather holster and with a lanyard. Machine gunners and tank crews would also carry the Webley. Thus equipped, the British soldier would be ready for war.

JOINING THE COLOURS

WHEN Britain went to war in 1914, it had a small but highly trained army. The army had been overhauled in 1881 by the Cardwell Reforms, which had created county regiments each with a distinctly regional feel. After the reforms, there were sixty-one regiments, each allied directly with a county or region, with a home depot and two, locally recruited, regular battalions. Further reforms by Lord Haldane in 1908 granted regiments a special reserve battalion (whose purpose was to gather recruits), and three locally raised territorial battalions. Men serving as territorials did so on the understanding that they would serve as part-timers engaged on home defence, with no overseas commitment. Although part-timers, however, the 'terriers' would still be liable for full-time service on the outbreak of war, the implication being that they would serve at home, while the regulars proceeded overseas.

Opposite:
Recruits giving their particulars. In the early days of the war, the crush of recruits would be overwhelming. [IWM Q.30074]

Above: The Overseas Service Commitment badge, worn by all territorial soldiers who volunteered to serve overseas.

Left: A territorial Royal Field Artilleryman, wearing a leather bandolier and Imperial Service Badge – volunteered for overseas service.

Britain went to war ostensibly to guarantee the neutrality of Belgium; the German Chancellor would remark to the British ambassador in Berlin in August 1914 that 'just for a scrap of paper Great Britain was going to make war on a kindred nation'.

A WEE "SCRAP O' PAPER" IS BRITAIN'S BOND.   No. 7

The pre-war Territorial Army had a long-standing relationship with its local regions, and drill halls were located in communities up and down the country. These provided a means for men to join up and engage in part-time soldiering. With the coming of war, most 'terriers' joined the colours for full-time service overseas, and territorial recruitment was placed on the same level as the regulars. All those who signed accepted liability for service outside the United Kingdom and were entitled to wear a special Imperial Service Badge on the right breast pocket, commonly seen in family photographs.

For the regular soldier, mobilised for war, there was the usual budget of training: six months with the third battalion at the base depot before being deployed into the first or second battalion. The Regular Army was to maintain its cachet throughout the war, and belonging to the first or second battalion of an infantry regiment was seen as a mark of honour. The regular battalions available at home in 1914 were to form six infantry divisions; each division was to have three infantry brigades – with each brigade in turn composed of four infantry battalions. Brigades rarely had more than one battalion from a given regiment. The typical infantry division of 1914 would also have a significant artillery presence, and an attached cavalry squadron, as well as components from all the other arms and services required to keep it operating in the field, a massive undertaking with around 15,000 men in a typical, full-strength British division. The six original divisions were to form the British Expeditionary Force in 1914, the first four of them taking part in the retreat from Mons in 1914, the other two being present in France by September 1914. By the end of the war, the British Army had expanded from its original six to seventy-five infantry divisions.

When Field Marshal Earl Kitchener of Khartoum took over as Secretary of State for War in August 1914, he was quick to understand that this war would be costly in manpower. Not confident that the territorial battalions could be sufficiently flexible to allow rapid expansion, Kitchener made a direct appeal to the public – his sights set on expanding the army by 500,000 men – with separate appeals, in 100,000 tranches, to be numbered successively K1, K2 and so on. The 'First Hundred Thousand', or K1, was recruited within days of the appeal. Kitchener was to issue four further appeals through the late summer and early autumn of 1914, the final 100,000, K5, being sanctioned by government in October of that year. In the days before wireless and mass media, this appeal for manpower was made through newspapers, and, most effectively, through the use of posters seen in every public space.

The Parliamentary Recruiting Committee, an all-party group employing the local infrastructure of political parties, was to approve and distribute such posters. Most famous is the image by Alfred Leete of the head and pointing finger of the Field Marshal first published as a cover of the magazine *London Opinion* in September 1914, and used subsequently in a variety of posters with the slogan 'Your Country Needs You'. Other posters attacked the conscience of the average man: 'Are You in This?', 'Daddy, What Did You Do in the Great War?' In this way men in civilian garb were assaulted on all sides by messages compelling them to join the nation's armed forces. Other forms of compulsion were available: common in the early war was the award

Cap badges of the British Army in the Great War.
From top:
Cheshire Regiment,
Cameron Highlanders,
Norfolk Regiment,
Welsh Regiment,
Royal Dublin Fusiliers,
Manchester Regiment.

One of a series of
recruiting posters
bearing Alfred
Leete's image of
Kitchener: 'Your
Country Needs
You!'

of a white feather by a woman; feared by many men not in uniform, the
device carried an explicit implication of cowardice.

Recruiting offices sprang up across the country, as the demand for men
increased. Existing facilities were unable to cope with the throughput of men;
as such, local municipal buildings were pressed into service, usually bedecked
with banners and posters. Mobile recruiting offices were also used, with
buses and trams carrying the message 'Britain Needs More Men'. Recruiting
sergeants and other military personnel would be on hand to give an
impression of military efficiency, and to provide the necessary persuasion. On
arrival, recruits would be asked their age – nineteen being the minimum. It
is well known that there were to be very many under-age soldiers; the army
would later insist that such boys were taken in good faith, having 'lied about
their age', and would release them only in exceptional circumstances.

Would-be soldiers were given the briefest of medicals, based around their
height (at first, above 5 feet 3 inches) and chest measurements (34-inch
maximum expansion), the condition of their teeth (to bite the almost

unbreakable ration biscuit – in fact, it has been estimated that 70 per cent of all recruits would require treatment), and their eyesight (to be able to sight a rifle effectively). Found fit (categorised A1), recruits would 'attest', swearing an oath of allegiance; signing their forms, they would receive the 'King's Shilling', the symbolic issue of the first day's pay of what was to be a long stint in the army – for three years or 'the duration'. The issue of the Shilling, and the repeat of the oath of allegiance to the Crown, would bind the Great War recruit to service for 'the duration of the war'.

With so many men joining the army as private soldiers, more officers would be required to command them, and there would be a severe shortfall. Regular officers and NCOs would provide the backbone for the new battalions that were raised following Kitchener's call but, with the demands of regular battalions to be met, manpower resources were tight. Other sources were men on the reserve lists – usually just retired from service, but including more senior men 'dug out' of retirement – together with men on leave from the

New recruits from all walks of life with their recruiting sergeant. [IWM Q.30072]

Right: The King's Shilling. The upper sample, issued in November 1915, has been kept as a souvenir of enlistment.

Far right: Recruits to the Royal Engineers pose in their new uniforms, c.1914.

Indian Army. Direct recruitment from public schools and universities was also tried, but as many had joined the ranks as private soldiers it would take some time to persuade them that they might have the skills to command.

The phenomenon most closely associated with the hothouse of recruitment in 1914–15 was the raising of 'pals' battalions' by local dignitaries, 1000 men strong. The phenomenon is most closely associated with Lord Derby, who suggested the raising of battalions of men of the 'commercial classes' in a letter published in the Liverpool press on 27th August 1914. The response would be dramatic; within just over a week, sufficient men would be found for three battalions of 'Liverpool Pals', the fourth being added shortly thereafter. Lord Derby's example was to be emulated in major towns and cities up and down the country. In all 144 pals'

Cap badges from the City Battalions of the King's (Liverpool) Regiment – Lord Derby's 'Liverpool Pals'. Lord Derby would personally issue a silver version of the badge, which was based on his crest, to each recruit who joined in 1914.

battalions would be raised, enough for twelve infantry divisions of the K4 and K5 recruitment tranches.

The first recruits to join Kitchener's New Army were forced to make compromises: little in the way of equipment, no uniforms, no barracks. In the early stages of the war, supply of arms, uniform and equipment to the enthusiastic recruits of Kitchener's army was a difficult task; the Kitchener battalions were to be fed, housed and equipped at the initial expense of the authority that raised them. This meant sourcing uniforms from official and even commercial suppliers at a time when the country was alive with such pleas along its length and breadth. As a consequence, recruits were more often than not clothed in civilian garb, and as training camps had not yet been formed or established, Kitchener's men found themselves still living at home. Kitchener's men went to war training in flat caps and tweed suits with broom handles, before simple uniforms were supplied in what has become known as 'Kitchener Blue' – blue serge in place of khaki, reputedly surplus to requirements from the General Post Office.

Despite the efforts of the Parliamentary Recruiting Committee, the flow of volunteers decreased steadily month on month in 1914–15, and the War Cabinet became increasingly concerned that the British Army would not be

Above: Derby Scheme armbands, worn by attested men – khaki for the army, blue for the navy.

Left: 'Kitchener Blue' – a recruit in blue serge, an emergency solution to a clothing crisis.

able to withstand its losses at the front. The National Registration Act introduced in July 1915 required every citizen between the ages of fifteen and sixty-five to register their name, place of residence, nature of work and other details. By October 1915, registration had identified 5,158,211 men of military age, with at least 3.4 million technically able to join the forces, but who had not yet volunteered. The redoubtable Lord Derby, appointed Director of Recruiting in 1915, drew up a scheme entailing the voluntary registration, or attestation, of all men between eighteen and forty. This legal undertaking to serve only when needed was meant to be a draw, attested men wearing a khaki armband (or blue for Navy men) to repel the attentions of the white-feather vigilantes. The scheme failed: by the closing date on 15th December 1915, two million men available for military service had failed to attest. The Military Service Act of January 1916 would follow, announcing to the world the introduction of conscription for all fit single men between the ages of eighteen and forty-one, the first of five such acts through the war. Conscripts would make up the majority of the army that marched to victory in 1918.

Camps were set up across the country to house the vast influx of new recruits to the armed forces; they would vary considerably from villages of bell-tents to timber-constructed huts. All would form the basis for the transition from civilian to soldier, prior to being named for a draft to the frontline. As the war ground on, camp occupants would vary from volunteer to conscript, and those soldiers unlucky enough to have been wounded, returned home and then, once again, passed fit for frontline duty. In all cases, camp routine was one of early to rise, early to bed. Recruits could expect to engage in a diet of training. For the most part, this included a simple regime of physical training, involving the application of the Swedish drill system of 'physical jerks', long runs and the use of route marches in full equipment. For those unused to such exercise, this was a new, challenging experience. For the average soldier, military instruction included the use of the bayonet and the proper use of a soldier's principal weapon, for the most part, his rifle. Bayonet training involved charging sacks marked with discs denoting head, eyes and heart, yelling like maniacs as they struck home; many found the experience terrifying.

In Kitchener's New Army, valuable weapons such as the SMLE would be in short supply, and trainees would have to make do with wooden stand-ins while learning how to carry out manoeuvres with appropriate military bearing. For later war recruits, weapons use was a significant component of the training, including the correct deployment of the Mills Grenade – a function of the needs of trench warfare. For all, training on the rifle range was the opportunity to fire live rounds. Officers too would be expected to gain proficiency in arms. At late stages of the war, training also involved the acclimatisation to gas warfare – the correct fitting of the respirator, and the

entry into gas chambers intended to check both the nerves of the wearer and the adequacy of the equipment. Specialist training – for the coveted 'sscout's, signaller or expert marksman's badges, for example – would also be offered for those of ability; in return, as well as the badges, extra pay would be forthcoming. The average recruit would receive at least two months of training at home before 'leaving for the front'.

A soldier would then make his way to one of the English Channel ports before being sent overseas as a member of his battalion, or, as time passed in this long war, as a replacement to make up the losses sustained through casualties. In this way, soldiers were commonly transferred from one regiment to another. Drafts were invariably to leave the country through Dover or Folkestone if their destination was France, and Southampton if elsewhere. Leave, all too short, was granted before proceeding overseas, and parting at rail termini was heart-wrenching for many. For most troops, arrival at their destination would involve a further period of training – battle-hardening and acclimatisation to local conditions that saw, in France at least, the use of vast base camps and harsh training in so-called 'bull rings'. The most infamous was that at Étaples: a vast camp with training in the dune fields presided over by 'canaries', physical-training instructors distinguished by their yellow armbands. For some, this period would be uneventful; for others, it would have a dehumanising influence – particularly the bayonet practice. In either case, when the British soldier left in a slow-moving train, housed in a truck marked 'Hommes 40, Chevaux 8', it was at least a relief to know that, finally, he was to go 'up the line'.

Men at a hutted camp somewhere in Britain.

Following page: Soldiers crowded together in a wattle-revetted trench in Ploegsteert Wood, near Ypres, in June 1917. [IWM Q.2314]

IN THE TRENCHES

To those new to the front, the first taste of trench duty would be a defining moment in their military careers, if not their lives. Issued with iron rations of 'bully beef' and biscuits, and a full complement of ammunition, it was an ominous sign that soldiers were also instructed to destroy any personal papers, and to complete the wills provided in their paybooks. Letters would be hurriedly written and the men would move up the line to replace soldiers only too happy to leave the trenches.

In their simplest sense, the trenches of the Great War were linear excavations of variable depth mostly open to the sky. Their purpose was to provide protection to the frontline troops from small arms fire and artillery. For the most part, trenches were between 6 and 8 feet deep. This, of course, was the ideal, for in some cases it was impossible to dig more than a foot or so before reaching water-saturated ground, especially in the Ypres Salient, with its underlying foundation of water-repelling clay. Here, instead, the trenches were built up with sandbags rather than dug down.

Most trenches were 'floored' with wooden duckboards, which were built up to allow drainage beneath. Trench sides, known as slopes, were supported or revetted with whatever was available, sometimes wattle, often corrugated sheeting and expanded metal (XPM), at other times chicken wire. Timber was used universally to hold these materials in place, and layers of bonded sandbags strengthened the whole. Sandbags were to become an important part of trench life, filling gaps in the line, creating a parapet or ultimately being built upwards as breastworks. They would also be used to disguise periscopes and sniper loopholes, as additional leg coverings, as containers to bring up the rations and ammunition, and, as covers for steel helmets.

In the main there were two consistent trench types: fire trenches, which formed the front lines, and communication trenches, which joined them. Fire trenches (or fighting

Private Fergus Mackain joined the 23rd (1st Sportsman's) Battalion of the Royal Fusiliers early in the war, answering Kitchener's call. His illustrations, drawn in France, illustrate with wry humour the conditions of trench life.

From somewhere in France

It gives you a confortable feeling to be under shelter !

27

Barbed wire was an effective barrier; screw pickets like these allowed noiseless insertion of wire supports at night.

trenches) were divided into a regular pattern of fire bays and traverses, which meant that no soldier could walk in a straight line for long without having to switch left or right. This was intended to limit the effects of shellfire, or from the possibility of rifle and machine gun fire along the length of a trench – with inevitable consequences. The spoil removed in digging a trench was used to form a parapet – a mound of earth in front of the trench on the enemy side – and a parados – a slightly higher mound at the rear. Each fire trench was equipped with a fire step, ideally of regulation 2 feet high and 18 inches wide: sufficient to raise an average man's head above the protection of the parapet, when required to do so.

Fire trenches were usually arranged in successive parallel rows, with the frontline, support line and reserve line all connected by communication trenches (CTs), which were the main thoroughfares of trench warfare. The purpose of communication trenches was to link the forward or fire trenches, and to allow men, munitions and supplies to travel up to the line – as well as wounded soldiers to come out of the line. In well-established trench systems the frontline consisted of a fire trench and ancillary support trench

Preserved 'CT' trenches at Hill 62, near Ypres. Although undoubtedly 'improved' over the ninety-plus years of their existence, these trenches still have an authentic voice.

Sketches of Tommy's life Up the line — Nº 10 Sometimes you get so far in the rear, marching in, you are as good as lost when you come to a spot where different trenches branch off.

As trench systems proliferated, so did their trench sign boards, intended to guide the returning soldier.

with deeper dugouts providing accommodation for the troops. Due to the complexities of the growing trench systems, it was possible to get hopelessly lost in the re-entrants, salients and redoubts interconnected by communication trenches, and minor branches intended as latrines, entrances to dugouts, trench mortar batteries and so on. Trench signboards were fixed to allow newcomers to a particular stretch to get orientated, and trenches were named or numbered, a complex system recorded on equally complex trench maps.

Between the frontlines of the opposing trenches was no-man's-land, a strip of contested ground that varied in width from a few feet to tens of yards, with the forward trenches on both sides protected by belts of barbed wire. Wiring parties on both sides would enter no-man's-land under the cover of darkness in patrols of two to three men, to inspect the integrity of the defences or cut paths through their own wire in preparation for a raid; or, in larger fatigue parties, to repair and improve the frontline wire. A great many barbed-wire cutters would be patented during the war.

No-man's-land was generally crossed only when soldiers went 'over the top': when they climbed out over the parapet to face the enemy. Looking over the parapet in daylight was most unwise; putting one's head above the trench was virtually suicidal, and head injuries were common in tall soldiers and the curious. Snipers would have weapons fixed in position, targeted

Day sentry at a box periscope. Putting one's head above the parapet by day was suicidal.

Rum jars – SRD stood for the Supply Ration Depot, based in Woolwich; tradition has it that the initials actually stood for 'Soon Runs Dry'.

at dips in the parapet, at latrines and crossing points, and at loophole plates. For the most part, no-man's-land was observed by day through 'trench periscopes' set up for the purpose.

Life in the trenches was dominated by its routine; the beat of daily existence that commenced with 'stand-to' (from 'stand to arms') at one hour before dawn, when all troops in the frontline would stand upon the fire step armed and ready to confront an attacker in the early light. Stand-to would last at least an hour and a half, but would finish when the enemy parapet could be seen through the periscopes set up along the line of the trenches. Following stand-to, most men were stood down, but leaving sentries on duty, one per platoon, to man the fixed box periscopes. With stand-down, a tot of rum would be issued to each man, a welcome respite from the often freezing conditions.

Service rum was thick and fiery; its positive effects after a night on the fire step are remembered in most soldiers' memoirs. Rum was issued from ceramic jars labelled 'SRD', spawning a host of explanations, from 'Soon Runs Dry' and 'Seldom Reaches Destination' to 'Service Rum Dilute'. The initials actually stand for 'Supply Reserve Depot', a large establishment based

Soldier's mess kit consisted of a mess tin, cotton holdall to contain knife, fork and spoon (among other essentials), a clasp knife, and a simple cotton bag for 'unexpired rations'. All too often rations would rely on 'bully beef' and biscuits; sauces helped break the monotony. A Primus stove would be a luxury from home.

in Woolwich. Famously, rum was also issued to those men about to go 'over the bags', either at dawn with a large-scale attack, or at night prior to a raid. The rum ration was issued by a senior NCO and poured into a mug or mess tin top; it was to be drunk there and then in the presence of an officer.

Breakfast would follow, with the meal comprising rations that had been brought up at night, meant to last a 48-hour period. Tea, bacon, bread — these were the staples, but often it could be simply bully-beef and biscuits. Night fatigue parties would bring up hot food in specially designed carriers where possible; all other goods were brought up in sand bags, often a hopeless jumble of loose and tinned rations. Corned beef — 'bully' to the troops — was a variously received staple. Other tinned-food staples included 'pork and beans' (beans with a small cube of pork fat) and Maconochie ration (a vegetable and meat concoction). Jam was a versatile ration; but the frequency of Tickler's plum and apple variety was unpopular, strawberry largely suspected to have been removed by transport men earlier in the supply chain. Fresh rations — meat, bacon, vegetables — would also be supplied where possible. Water was from petrol tins and would never quite lose its petrol taste — something even the strongest tea could not defeat.

After breakfast, it was time for platoon commanders to make their inspection of rifles — which the men had cleaned during their meal — attention being given to breech and chamber, parts of the gun liable to fouling from mud and dirt. Those men not on 'sentry-go' were detailed for fatigues to repair trenches and engage in similar activities, activities which would go on throughout the day, broken for lunch at midday and an evening meal at around 6 p.m.

Smoking was an essential pastime to most soldiers in the trenches, chain-smoking a consequence of anxiety and boredom. Cigarettes came up with the rations or were sent from home. 'Wills' 'Woodbines' and 'Gold Flake' were favoured. A variety of 'trench lighters' and 'trench matchbox covers' were used — sometimes made by the soldiers themselves.

The night routine would commence with another 'stand-to' before dusk, and another officers' inspection. The trenches then came alive to a routine of repair, supply and patrol, with men engaged on endless trench improvement, and with patrols and wiring parties out in no-man's-land, keeping an eye open for star shells that could catch them starkly silhouetted against the sky, targets for watchful sentries and searching machine guns. Night sentries, with a round in the chamber ready for an alert, were detailed to look over the parapet – dangerous when the enemy had his guns trained at head height for the same reason. Sleep on sentry duty was a capital offence; experienced NCOs made it their business to visit their charges every fifteen minutes, and officers would also be vigilant in their duties. Other men would sleep, if they were lucky, or be detailed to go on endless carrying details, bringing up supplies from the rear along communication trenches.

There was to be a rhythm to trench warfare, with most men spending typically five days in the frontline, five in reserve, five at the front again and finally five days in reserve. In fact, spending anywhere between four to eight days in the front line was common, depending very much on circumstance. While some were in the front fire trenches, others would occupy the support lines behind, ready to provide reinforcement when hard-pressed in an attack or raid. Relief saw a battalion removed from the frontline trenches and taken to the rear areas.

Lice (*Pediculus vestimenti*) were the constant companion of the soldier in the trenches, an inevitable consequence of the crowd of unwashed soldiery. Soldiers would resort to removal of the 'chats' by hand, running the fingernail through seams or playing a candle flame along them, hearing the insects 'pop'. Neither method was effective for long. 'Chatting' was to become a social event. Plagues of flies (particularly abhorrent in the heat of Gallipoli) and rats ('as big as cats') were other vermin frequently endured, an inevitability of the squalid conditions of trench life, and the abundance of unburied bodies in no-man's-land.

For the infantryman, going 'over the top' or 'over the bags' was, relatively speaking, a rare event. Nevertheless, most infantry soldiers would experience at some point the terror of rising out of the trenches – often in broad daylight – to face the enemy of whom they had previously caught only fleeting glimpses through trench periscopes, and the resulting battles have become heated discussion points over the decades since the end of the war. More common were trench raids; everything from single officers exploring no-man's-land, to organised miniature offensives protected by complex box barrages. Trench raids also called for a return to medieval weaponry, with clubs and knives widely used by both sides. In many cases, the stated purpose of trench raids was to provide intelligence on the disposition and activities of the troops in the opposing trenches, encouraged by High Command,

Going 'over the top' on major set-piece battles was a relatively rare occurrence; smaller trench raids were more common. The sounding of officers' whistles, like that illustrated from 1916, signified 'zero hour'.

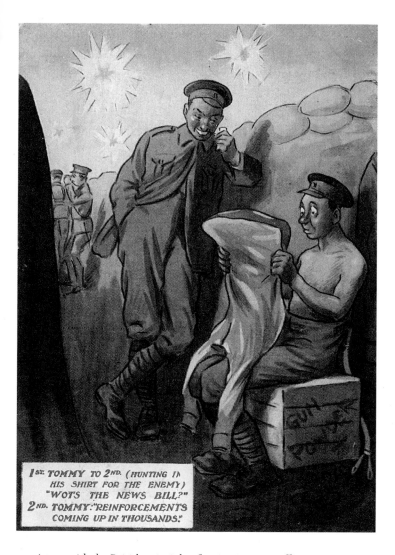

1ST TOMMY TO 2ND. (HUNTING IN HIS SHIRT FOR THE ENEMY) "WOTS THE NEWS BILL?" 2ND. TOMMY:"REINFORCEMENTS COMING UP IN THOUSANDS."

Lice were constant companions in the trenches, widely accepted as an inevitability of war.

consistent with the British principle of maintaining an offensive spirit.

Despite the sharp close-combat of the raid, trench warfare is more often associated with the rise of industrial warfare: killing on a large scale. The power of the British Vickers Mark 1 machine gun (and its German MG08 equivalent) was truly frightening. Fired in short bursts of 200 rounds per minute, both guns had a maximum effective range of 2000 yards, accuracy and hit rate increasing as the range decreased. The British Army went to war with the machine gun as a specialist weapon, with just two heavy Vickers machine guns per infantry battalion. With deeper considerations of machine

Men of the Machine Gun Corps in action with their Vickers, April 1917. [IWM Q.5172]

Below: A young soldier of the newly formed and short-lived elite Machine Gun Corps in October 1918.

gun tactics, came the idea that the Vickers guns should be taken away from infantry battalions and given, in larger numbers, to the newly formed Machine Gun Corps (MGC). Infantry battalions were issued with the lighter Lewis Gun, more suited to an infantry role.

It has been estimated, however, that 60 per cent of all casualties were wounded or killed by artillery fire on the Western Front. Heavy shells would kill by the action of the high explosive that could tear apart fortifications and human flesh alike; wounds from jagged, cruel shell fragments were particularly feared. Quick-firing guns could also deliver high explosives, but were often packed with hundreds of lead-shrapnel balls, each of them with deadly intent. Soldiers soon got used to the sound of incoming fire: the 'whizz bang' of the quick-firing field gun, or the 'crump' of the explosion of the heavy howitzer – explosions which created forceful blast and plenty of black smoke. These would also be given the names 'woolly bear', 'Jack Johnson' (after the hard-hitting heavyweight boxer) and 'coal box'.

The main arm of the Royal Field Artillery (RFA) was the 18-pounder quick-firing field gun, which had a maximum range of over 6500 yards and was capable of firing

Above: British shell fuse caps recovered from the battlefields of Ypres.

Left: British artillery shell fragments: part of the British legacy on the Somme.

shrapnel, high explosive and star shells; 10,000 would be produced during the war. Heavier guns, howitzers, were designed to lob shells with a high trajectory, so that they might drop slap-bang into the enemy's trench systems. Such heavy siege guns would be crewed by gunners of the Royal Garrison Artillery (RGA) situated farther back from the front line. With increasing precision, artillerymen developed new ways of delivering their goods, with creeping and box barrages intended to provide a protective screen around those attacking, isolating those within from the attentions of the defenders outside the curtain of shell fire.

Gas warfare is most commonly associated in the modern mind with the 'horrors' of the trenches. Poison gas was deployed in an active sense in April 1915, when the Germans first used it during the opening phases of the Second Battle of Ypres. Early gases were chlorine and phosgene released from cylinders, causing irreparable damage to the lungs; later on more complex mixes, including the caustic mustard gas (promoting temporary blindness and severe burns) would be deployed in artillery shells as tactical weapons. Primitive respirators were quickly extemporised from field dressings soaked in alkaline bicarbonate of soda, a solution capable of neutralising the chlorine gas. Later in 1915, flannel hoods soaked in sodium hyposulphite ('Hypo Helmets') followed, replaced by more sophisticated versions with eyepieces and exhalant valves, the 'Phenate (P)' and 'Phenate-Hexamine (PH)' helmets. These nightmarish creations, officially known as 'tube helmets' but to the

Above left:
Contemporary coloured *Daily Mail* postcard depicting Vickers machine gunners in P or PH helmets – 'goggle-eyed buggers with the tit'.

Above right:
The British Small Box Respirator effectively countered the gas threat by the end of the war.

soldiers as 'goggle-eyed buggers with the tit', were superseded by the Small Box Respirator (SBR) in 1916, which had a facemask and tube connected to a 'box' that was filled with lime-permanganate granules between two layers of charcoal to counteract poison gases. This mask was to prove highly effective, and gas was to become just another weapon to be endured by the man in the trenches.

In the Great War, the rate and scale of casualties is breathtaking: infamously, the opening hour of the Battle of the Somme on 1st July 1916 saw at least 50,000 men killed, wounded or reported missing. In fact, the term 'casualty' as used officially is misleading, as it refers to anyone effectively taken out of action, with deaths forming a smaller proportion of the whole. It was relatively rare for a soldier to survive the war completely unscathed, and multiple wounding was a common experience. Ensuring that men survived their wounds was the responsibility of the army medical services, and particularly the Royal Army Medical Corps (RAMC).

The role of the RAMC was to care for the wounded and to evacuate them efficiently from the frontline and, and it was hoped by most soldiers, home to Britain. The casualty chain was a long one: first to the Regimental Aid Post (RAP), run by an RAMC doctor close to the frontline. Next was the Advanced Dressing Station (ADS), at the limit of wheeled transport. The wounded would be transported from RAP to ADS through a variety of means: on foot, by cart, on a stretcher. Stretcher-bearers were battalion men who gave up their arms to carry their stretchers, ideally, at least six men would be needed per stretcher; this was not always achievable, and German prisoners were often drafted in to carry wounded soldiers back. Battalion stretcher-bearers' responsibilities ended at the regimental aid post; from here men would be dispatched to the rear areas and would be in the care of RAMC orderlies. Wounded soldiers could then expect to be transported down the line to Main Dressing Stations (MDS), beyond the range of medium artillery fire; then to Casualty Clearing Stations (CCS), set up beyond the artillery zone; and finally, still within the theatre of operations, General and Stationary hospitals. From here, soldiers would hope to receive their 'ticket' – a label that marked them for transportation on hospital ships bound for home, 'Blighty'.

Battalion stretcher-bearers (with 'SB' armband) and RAMC men tend a wounded man at a Regimental Aid Post during the opening of the Battle of the Somme on 1st July 1916. [IWM Q.7390]

AT REST

AFTER a tour of duty on the frontline, on average seven days, a battalion would be relieved. Its destination would be the reserve trenches – less prone to sniping and trench mortars, but still subject to the random vagaries of artillery fire. Men in reserve could be called upon to reinforce the front when under pressure, and would be the main stock of reinforcements when the front was under attack. More welcome was the withdrawal of a battalion out of the line completely, a means of gaining some rest, a chance for officers and NCOs to reassert military fastidiousness, and an opportunity for the average soldier to gain some mental freedom – washing, speaking to locals, buying trinkets. Rest camps were set up in rear areas, though often still within range of the largest guns.

Soldiers out on rest were based in variety of billets. In France and Flanders, this could be a battered village, each showing the scars of long-range shelling or the movement of armies in the early days of the war. Billeted-upon people grimly held on to their existence, their barns, hay-lofts and out-buildings were stuffed with bunks to accommodate the men; in other cases soldiers took up residence in farm houses, sharing the kitchen with the still-resident family. Hutted camps were another option – these at least provided reasonably dry and secure accommodation; tented camps were least favoured.

For the men, being in billets and out on rest meant an escape from the tension of frontline life. On rest, soldiers could once more feel human. In many cases, they could mix with thoe civilians brave or foolish enough to be close to the battle zone, talking in strange, anglicised versions of the prevailing language with their French, Belgian and Middle Eastern hosts. They could also engage women in hopeful conversations, although most who remained close to the frontline were long past an age where this hope would bear fruit. Paid in the local currency, this new wealth could be put to work on the purchase of alcohol – often of lamentable quality – and to indulge in other vices normally frowned upon at home: gambling, fraternisation with women of 'ill repute', visits to brothels. Tommy would also have some

Opposite: Expeditionary Force Canteens, run by the army, provided a means whereby some essentials, such as stationery and cigarettes, could be purchased. These men at Bapaume have just come out of the line, March 1916. [IWM Q.8592]

Billets at rest could vary considerably, from haylofts to tented encampments; the opportunity to buy *œufs-frites* and hot coffee was greatly appreciated.

*Sketches
of Tommy's life
Out on rest − N° 5*

A regular carouse of coffee and fried eggs is one of the things we always have when we get to one of these villages.

freedom to make simple purchases, souvenirs, postcards and the ubiquitous *œufs-frites* from those civilians brave enough to remain.

Out on rest meant the opportunity for the army to re-impose military standards of cleanliness and 'bull' – the polishing, cleaning and delousing of uniforms, and visits to bathhouses and showers. Work in the frontline was also typical, with soldiers detailed to deliver food and essential supplies, and to take part in reconstruction of trench lines and barbed-wire fences. Despite these military intrusions, there was also the possibility of engaging in harmless pursuits, of 'escaping' with some form of entertainment; the value of such activities to morale was not lost on the High Command. Concert parties, cinemas, canteens, all were seen as a means of keeping up morale, and helping the men to keep reasonably clear of temptation.

The YMCA provided an excellent service for the men of His Majesty's army – providing home comforts and the opportunity for a get-together in their huts. Under the sign of 'Tommy's triangle', the YMCA was to operate in quite advanced areas, providing some comforts to the troops. Away from the immediate front, the YMCA and other charitable organisations, such as the Church Army, provided huts that allowed soldiers to gather to drink tea, eat sandwiches, write letters home on the paper provided, to kill time before their return to the trenches. Devoid of alcohol, these huts were not always as welcome as they could be.

While on rest, Tommy was paid in local currency and used his money to obtain whatever was available – food and cigarettes from army-run Expeditionary Force Canteens, weak beer and *vin blanc* from the local estaminets, egg, chips and coffee from the kitchens of local people. Gambling too was a draw, especially when Tommy had money in his pocket. Illegal gambling schools would spring up – engaged in the traditional soldiers' games of 'crown and anchor', or 'two-up'. The banker – the likely winner of these 'mug's games' – would usually be an old soldier with the gift of banter. Such activities were strictly frowned upon by the army, with 'Housey-Housey' (bingo) being the only officially sanctioned gambling game.

Women were largely absent from Tommy's life in the battle zone. He might encounter them at the base, and in the rear areas, where a few hardy souls scratched out a living as best they could. Some soldiers harboured romantic ideals about foreign women, all too soon to be dashed. Farther back in the lines, nurses and, later in the war, members of the Women's Auxiliary Army Corps (WAAC), provided 'decent' women who could be admired. More often than not, however, men found solace in locally run and

British soldiers chat to a local French girl in May 1917; not all such advances would be welcomed. [IWM Q.5297]

While on rest, soldiers had the opportunity to buy some souvenirs for loved ones; postcards were popular, especially those hand-worked in silk.

YMCA Pierrot troupe; troupes like these proliferated and did a valuable job in entertaining the troops while out on rest.

officially tolerated brothels (denoted by a red lamp for men, a blue lamp for officers). Risqué postcards and racy 'pin-ups' of lingerie-clad ladies published in *La Vie parisienne* also provided some mild diversion. Fearing that these would be sent home with their personal effects if they were killed, the men usually discarded them on return to the front.

In order to keep Tommy's mind off gambling, drinking and other vices, and to maintain morale in general, it was understood at a very early stage that

providing suitable entertainments would be a benefit to morale. As early as 1914, concert parties were being created from those servicemen who had a theatrical bent, and the concept was to spread so that every theatre of war, and almost every major unit of the British Army, was to have its own brand of concert party, most often associated with the divisions. Others were laid on by charitable organisations such as the ubiquitous YMCA, all with soldier 'Pierrot' troupes to entertain the troops at rest. Female roles would be convincingly played by young slim men, and soldiers could forget they were fellow combatants; in some rare cases, French girls could be drafted in to provide a feminine flavour – as with the celebrated pair from Armentières, 'Glycerine and Vaseline', who were to see 'action' in many a concert party in the area.

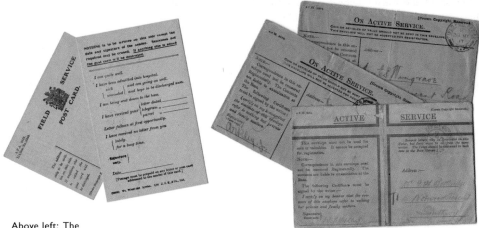

Above left: The Field-Service Postcard allowed only the barest of information – but provided a means of getting messages home in moments of haste.

Above right: 'Green envelopes' provided the opportunity for some intimacy – soldiers had to sign a declaration that their contents would not divulge secrets.

Right: The postcard was the favoured medium of communication; adding 'On Active Service' would ensure it got home. This collection, from 'Victor', serving in the Oxfordshire and Buckinghamshire Light Infantry (61st Division), was to his best girl 'Alice'.

Letters to and from the front were of great importance in maintaining the morale of the troops. For the soldiers themselves, it was sufficient to write 'On Active Service' on the card or envelope, and the letter would be posted, carrying the postmark or cachet of the army field post-office. Messages were

often short and usually upbeat, a reflection of the relief felt at being out of the line. Each letter would be opened by a relevant officer, who would append his signature to say that he had read its contents, and who would strike through offending passages with a blue pencil. 'Green envelopes' were provided as a special concession to the troops, as their contents would not be routinely read and censored by officers. They were an opportunity for the soldier to share his intimate feelings with his loved ones, or to deal with family matters, and were issued to troops at the rate of one or two a week.

The humble Field-Service Postcard was a means of getting a simple message home without having to go to the trouble of writing a long letter. Supplied by the military authorities, all that was required was that the sender cross out a few lines in order to get his message across, usually expressing the view that all was fine, and that 'letter follows at earliest opportunity'. Millions were sent.

For the average soldier on the Western Front, leave would come only rarely – once a year if he was lucky, more frequently for officers. Leave could be a frustrating experience for those who lived at the remote corners of the

I was fairly taken off my feet when he came home!

Leave was a rare occasion for most soldiers – the best they could hope to receive being one leave period a year, slightly more for officers.

Leave was often a disorienting experience for soldiers fresh from the front, and there was precious little time to make the most of it. 'The Better 'Ole', written by Captain Bruce Bairnsfather of the Royal Warwickshire Regiment, and featuring his creation born of the trenches, 'Old Bill', was a hit when it opened in 1917.

45

British Isles, as the journey would be long and arduous, and it was common for the soldier to return home in full kit, with the mud of Flanders on his boots. Getting home required considerable skill and determination, as well as the required paperwork. Detailed direct from the front line, getting to the port of embarkation was bad enough: the men would have to find their way back on the long, laborious trail home. Leave from more remote fronts was an even more difficult proposition. And there would be no guarantee that the returning soldier would rejoin his own battalion.

If leave was a barely hoped-for luxury in the First World War, it is not surprising that the average soldier wished for a simple wound or debilitating

LUCKY DEVIL!

Above: Getting a 'Blighty wound' – a wound serious enough to be sent home, innocuous enough not to be dangerous – was the hope of many.

Right: Two men in 'hospital blues' at a British hospital.

Regimental brooches were purchased widely by soldiers on leave for their sweethearts – there were many available.

Charity 'Flag Days' provided funding for war hospitals; images of men in 'hospital blues' were commonly used.

illness that would take him out of the frontline, into the green fields of Britain. Such wounds became known as 'Blighty' or 'cushy' wounds, sufficiently serious for him to be sent home on a hospital ship, sufficiently slight not to be life threatening or incapacitating. Getting a 'Blighty wound' was dreamed of by most soldiers, and some took it into their own hands – self-inflicted wounding was a serious offence carried out only by the desperate.

There was a general feeling of good will to wounded heroes that was to persist throughout the war; crowds would often gather to greet the wounded heroes at main railway termini. War hospitals up and down the country received soldiers 'from the Front'. Set up in large private houses and municipal buildings in order to satisfy the demand for suitable accommodation, they were often staffed by 'VADs', volunteer nurses belonging to the Voluntary Aid Detachments. Soldiers sent to hospital were ordered out of their familiar khaki and into hospital blue, a simple suit of blue clothes worn with a bright red tie. Although a poor fit, 'hospital blues' provided a distinctive sign of a wounded soldier's status, a badge of honour that distinguished him as a man from the front.

47

DEMOBILISED

A T home, enthusiasm for the war was to dim as the years rolled on. The
breathless excitement of 1914 was quickly to give way to a dull
realisation of the truth of modern warfare; and by 1917–18, with
the reality of conscription, the daily news of casualties and the bite
of shortages, air raids and rationing, the 'new adventure' of the
Great War was to become mired in the mud of Flanders.

When the war ended, the British Empire had seen over 947,000
men killed, and 2,121,906 men wounded. For Tommy, returning
home was often an alienating experience, and to those who survived
and were discharged to a 'Brave New World' life could be hard and
unrewarding. The cost had been high, and in many cases soldiers
who had served their country well were left without work or a
stable home, forced to see out their days selling matchboxes or
scraping a living. Medals were issued, all of low intrinsic value – in
some cases only the silver war medal could be pawned for coppers
to keep body and soul together.

The war officially ended with the Armistice of 11th November
1918, after a succession of hammer blows that had fallen on the
German Army since the opening of the Battle of Amiens on 8th August 1918
– the beginning of one hundred days of continuous advance. During this
advance, the Allied armies pushed the Germans back to a line that was
broadly similar to the one where it had first met the British 'Old
Contemptibles' four years before. With the Armistice agreed, the war on
the Western Front was to end abruptly, and the British Fourth and Second
Armies commenced their advance into Germany as an occupying power on
17th November. The news of the end of the war was received in many ways
– for the soldiers, its occurrence was almost 'matter of fact'. The terms of
the Armistice with Germany required the cessation of hostilities at 11 a.m.
on 11th November 1918, the evacuation of occupied territory, the surrender
of large quantities of arms and equipment, and the disarming and internment
of the High Seas Fleet. German soil was to be occupied west of the Rhine.

Above: 'Armistice
signed with
Germany'; an entry
in the diary of
Private Frederick
Walker of the
King's Own
Yorkshire Light
Infantry, 11th
November 1918.

Opposite:
Demobilised
soldiers at a camp
in Italy, January
1919. [IWM
Q.26209]

49

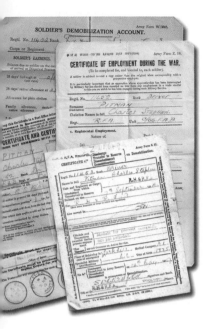

Above left: 'Demob' papers for Driver Charles Pitman of the Royal Field Artillery.

Above right: The Silver War Badge awarded to all those who were invalided out of the army. This example was awarded to Gunner Alfred Shelis of the Royal Field Artillery, invalided out due to injuries sustained during the crossing of the St Quentin canal in 1918.

For those troops not instructed to take on occupation duties, demobilisation could not come soon enough.

Demobilisation was available for some men from the end of November 1918, but many more would have to wait some time for their 'ticket'. Tradesmen deemed vital for the rebuilding of Britain's peacetime industry were released first, the rest following, with around 2,750,000 men processed by August 1919, although the process would not be complete until 1922. Men leaving the army overseas were sent to one of the many dispersal centres, where their paperwork would be processed. Allowed to keep their greatcoat and boots, and often their uniform as well, soldiers were also issued with either an allowance for new clothes, or a 'demob' suit. The issue of several official forms completed the process. Any arrears owed were paid (itemised on the 'Soldiers Demobilisation Account' form), a travel pass was issued, as was a guarantee of unemployment benefit of up to 24 shillings a week, the allowance to last twelve months (as indicated on the 'Protection Certificate'). The 'Certificate of Employment' was intended to act as a bald statement of what the soldiers had been doing in the army; whether it was of any value to potential employers remained to be seen. Finally, despite demobilisation, the army was at pains to point out that each soldier was transferred to a reserve – the nation could still call upon them again in times of need.

Serious wounding or disability would lead to soldiers being discharged from the service, receiving a war pension (the scale of which varied according

Souvenirs of war: the uniform buttons, badges, medal ribbons and trench art carried by Corporal Gethren Davies of the Royal Welsh Fusiliers.

to the severity of the injury) and a Silver War Badge intended to distinguish the ex-soldier from the civilian. Some 2,414,000 men were to be entitled to a war pension, the maximum they could hope to receive being 25 shillings a week. The Silver War Badge was the visible evidence that a serviceman had served his country honourably and, through sickness or wounding, had been discharged from service. It was first initiated in September 1916, awarded to all who had been honourably discharged from the start of the war. In addition to the badge, discharged soldiers also received a handsome scroll, and a wallet that would also contain their discharge papers and pension certificate.

The 'Dead Man's Penny' – awarded to all next of kin of dead servicemen (and women). Robert William Wheatley died in Gallipoli.

At the end of the Great War, old soldiers had little to show for their efforts. The medals of the Great War, mean in comparison with the galaxy of campaign stars issued for the Second World War, fall into just two possibilities: stars for early participants – the 'Old Contemptibles' of 1914, and the men who followed in 1914–15 – and from then on, for the men who served from 1916 onwards, just two simple awards, the War Medal and the Victory Medal. The silver War Medal has been described by some experts as 'uninspiring', and the Victory Medal 'like some of the cheap coronation medals handed out to children'. Nevertheless, old soldiers would wear these with pride – though others would never take them out of their boxes of issue. In the hard times of the 1920s and 1930s, old soldiers down on their luck would find that these hard-won items would have little intrinsic value and were difficult to pawn. Gallantry

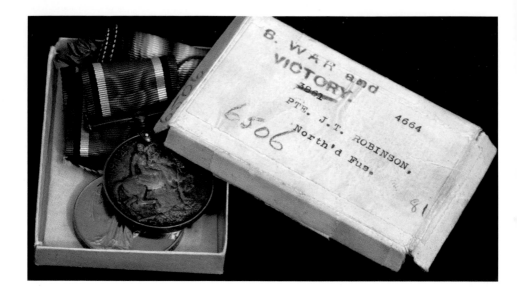

War and Victory Medals, unworn, and still in their original box of issue, belonging to Private J.T. Robinson of the Northumberland Fusiliers.

medals would have greater value, and two new ones, the Military Cross and the Military Medal, would be awarded for acts of bravery not warranting the award of the existing Victoria Cross (VC), Distinguished Service Order (DSO) or Distinguished Conduct Medal (DCM). Great War campaign medals are individually named and so have become the starting point for many family historians in tracing the actions of their forebears.

Captain Bruce Bairnsfather's 'Old Bill' deployed on a collecting tin for St Dunstan's, the charity for blinded servicemen.

The next of kin of those who had given their lives as servicemen (and women) in the First World War would receive not only their medals, but also a plaque that resembled an oversized penny – earning it the nicknames of the 'death' or 'dead-man's' penny. The idea of the plaque, given by the Government in honour of the fallen, was first mooted in 1916, and by November a committee had been formed to consider making the idea a reality. A competition was announced to find the best and most appropriate design to adorn the plaque. The winner, announced in March 1918, was Edward Carter Preston of Liverpool, whose design depicted a figure of Britannia, holding a laurel wreath crown over a space intended for the name of the individual commemorated. The name of the soldier was worked in relief on the tablet left for the purpose. Mass production of the plaques commenced in December 1918, and a total number of around 1,150,000 plaques were produced for all those who had died during the war or from war-related causes between 4th August 1914 and 30th April 1920.

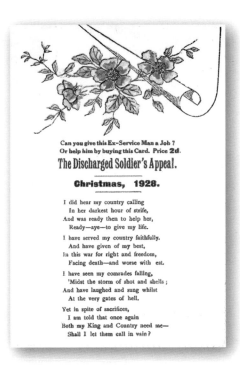

Can you give this Ex-Service Man a Job ?
Or help him by buying this Card. Price 2d.

The Discharged Soldier's Appeal.

Christmas, 1928.

I did hear my country calling
  In her darkest hour of strife,
And was ready then to help her,
  Ready—aye—to give my life.

I have served my country faithfully,
  And have given of my best,
In this war for right and freedom,
  Facing death—and worse with est.

I have seen my comrades falling,
  'Midst the storm of shot and shells ;
And have laughed and sung whilst
  At the very gates of hell.

Yet in spite of sacrifices,
  I am told that once again
Both my King and Country need me—
  Shall I let them call in vain ?

A land fit for heroes; 'will you buy this card from an old soldier?'

It is a cliché that soldiers returned from the war expecting a 'land fit for heroes'. In fact, with so many men demobilised, and in the depth of a post-war slump following the gearing of a nation for 'total war', finding employment was a nightmare task. For those disabled, there were few choices, although for those blinded St Dunstan's provided a lifeline. Arthur Pearson, proprietor of the *Evening Standard*, set up St Dunstan's in 1915. Pearson was himself blind and believed that, given training, servicemen who had lost their sight during the war could have their lives transformed and lead independent lives. His organisation, based firstly in Regent's Park in London, helped give hope to those who had been disabled, funded by charity, through donations or the sale of cards. For many others, charity, and the sale of small goods like matches or cards, would be the only way of scratching a living in the 'land fit for heroes'. The long struggle of many ex-servicemen to find employment in the post-war era was to become a national disgrace, one from which many would never recover.

SUGGESTED READING

Ashworth, T. *Trench Warfare 1914–1918: The Live and Let Live System*. Macmillan, 1980.

Brown, M. *Tommy Goes to War*. J. M. Dent, 1978.

Brown, M. *The Imperial War Museum Book of the Western Front*. Sidgwick & Jackson, 1993.

Bull, S. *World War One British Army*. Brassey's, 1998.

Bull, S. *World War I Trench Warfare, I: 1914–1916*. Osprey, 2002.

Bull, S. *World War I Trench Warfare, II: 1916–1918*. Osprey, 2002.

Chambers, S. J. *Uniforms and Equipment of the British Army in World War 1: A Study in Period Photographs*. Schiffer, 2006.

Chappell, M. *The British Army in World War 1 (1) The Western Front 1914–16*. Osprey, 2003.

Chappell, M. *The British Army in World War 1 (2) The Western Front 1916–18*. Osprey, 2005.

Chappell, M. *The British Army in World War 1 (3) The Eastern Fronts*. Osprey, 2005.

Coppard, G. *With a Machine Gun to Cambrai*. Imperial War Museum, 1980.

Corrigan, G. *Mud, Blood and Poppycock*. Cassell, 2003.

Doyle, P. *Tommy's War 1914–1918 British Military Memorabilia*. Crowood, 2008.

Dunn, J. C. *The War the Infantry Knew, 1914–1919*. Abacus, 1994.

Ellis, J. *Eye-deep in Hell: The Western Front 1914–18*. Croom Helm, 1976.

Groom, W. H. A. *Poor Bloody Infantry*. William Kimber, 1976.

Haselgrove, M. J. and Radovic, B. *Helmets of the First World War, Germany, Britain and Their Allies*. Schiffer, 2000.

Haythornwaite, P. J. *The World War One Source Book*. Arms & Armour Press, 1992.

Hitchcock, Captain F. C. *'Stand To': A Diary of the Trenches*. Naval and Military Press, n.d.; original edition, 1936.

Holmes, R. *Tommy. The British Soldier on the Western Front 1914–1918*. Harper Collins, 2004.

Jones, S. *World War I Gas Warfare Tactics and Equipment*. Osprey, 2007.

Liddle, P. *Soldiers' War, 1914–18*. Blandford, 1988.

Lloyd, A. *The War in the Trenches*. Granada, 1976.

Martin, B. *Poor Bloody Infantry*. John Murray, 1986.

Messenger, C. *Call to Arms: The British Army 1914–18*. Weidenfeld & Nicolson, 2005).

Middlebrook, M. *Your Country Needs You: Expansion of the British Army Divisions 1914–1918*. Leo Cooper, 2000.

Pegler, M. *British Tommy 1914–18*. Osprey, 1996.

Rawson, A. *British Army Handbook 1914–1918*. Sutton, 2006.

Saunders, A. *Weapons of the Trench War 1914–18*. Sutton, 1999.

Saunders, A. *Dominating the Enemy, War in the Trenches 1914–1918*. Sutton, 2000.

Saunders, N. J. *Trench Art: A Brief History and Guide 1914–1939*. Pen & Sword, 2001).

Simkins, P. *Kitchener's Army: The Raising of the New Armies, 1914–1916*. University of Manchester Press, 1988.

Westlake, R. *Kitchener's Army*. Spellmount, 2004.

Wilkinson, R. *Pals on the Somme 1916*. Pen & Sword Military, 2006.

Winter, D. *Death's Men: Soldiers of the Great War*. Penguin, 1978.

Men of the Royal Garrison Artillery parade in full equipment, *c*.1915.

INDEX